Praise for *Keith Urban*

"Keith Urban has done just about everything in country music that anyone could ever imagine. This biography by Jeff Apter reveals the highlights and struggles in getting there. I loved looking at the pictures, not just the celebrations that he's had, but the pictures of his youth really caught my attention. The look in his eyes had the look of destiny. To use one of Keith's quotes, 'Nashville's not my dream. It's my destiny.'"

—Ricky Skaggs, 15-time Grammy Award-winning musician

"Jeff Apter's Keith Urban had dreamed of Nashville stardom ever since he was a young, guitar-pickin' boy from a working class home in Australia. It didn't happen easily or quickly, but came through hard work and tenaciousness. In lively prose, Apter takes us on every happy twist and frustrating turn that Urban faced on his way to the top."

—Elizabeth J. Rosenthal, author of *His Song: The Musical Journey of Elton John* and *The Master of Drums: Gene Krupa and the Music He Gave the World*

"He ain't just that Aussie cowboy with the golden locks and godly good looks who seemingly came out of nowhere in the early 2000s, set the country and pop charts ablaze with his honey-sweet songs, and married a movie star. No, ma'am. There's more than that to Keith Urban— much more. From his humble beginnings in blue-collar Brisbane to crooning for swooning swarms in rhinestone-studded Nashville, over-coming addiction, and filling stadiums and tabloid covers around the world, Urban has ridden a long, rocky road to the top, a road full of breathtaking highs, heartbreaking lows, and everything in between. Jeff Apter's long-awaited biography of this beloved modern troubadour is a riveting read that no music fan will want to miss."

—Peter Aaron, author of *The Band FAQ* and coauthor of Richie Ramone's autobiography, *I Know Better Now: My Life Before, During and After the Ramones*

KEITH URBAN

JEFF APTER

CITADEL PRESS
Kensington Publishing Corp.
www.kensingtonbooks.com

CITADEL PRESS BOOKS are published by

Kensington Publishing Corp.
119 West 40th Street
New York, NY 10018

Copyright © 2022 Jeff Apter

Originally published by Allen & Unwin, Australia

All Kensington titles, imprints, and distributed lines are available at special quantity discounts for bulk purchases for sales promotions, premiums, fund-raising, educational, or institutional use. Special book excerpts or customized printings can also be created to fit specific needs. For details, write or phone the office of the Kensington sales manager: Kensington Publishing Corp., 119 West 40th Street, New York, NY 10018, attn: Sales Department; phone 1-800-221-2647.

CITADEL PRESS and the Citadel logo are Reg. U.S. Pat. & TM Off.

ISBN: 978-0-8065-4273-7

First Citadel hardcover printing: October 2023

10 9 8 7 6 5 4 3 2 1

Printed in the United States of America

Library of Congress Control Number: 2023938844

ISBN: 978-0-8065-4275-1 (ebook)

This one's also for me

Contents

Prologue   ix

1 The Caboolture kid   1
2 'The guitar was my security blanket'   14
3 How to become an extraordinary alien   30
4 'I hope you come back to Nashville and find a home here'   39
5 Down and out at the Lucky Snapper   53
6 'I'm probably not going to make it until tomorrow'   68
7 'Garth Brooks called me mate!'   80
8 Shake-ups and breakthroughs   94
9 Cleaning house and topping the charts   106
10 'You fucking hypocrite! You're not the guy in the song'   116
11 Walking the *Golden Road*   127
12 'Keith Urban is the Australian heartthrob of American country'   139
13 'I swear that she floated across the room. It was out of this world'   151
14 'I make out with my husband and pretend it's Keith Urban'   166
15 'Abstinence is the ticket into the movie. It's not the movie'   182
16 'A little ray of sunshine in the shape of a girl'   200
17 'The most autobiographical song I never wrote'   216

18 'It was an experiment that went terribly wrong.
    I'm glad Randy was there'   228
19 'Ever since we've been married . . . people make
    up the most insane crap'   246
20 A farewell, a guy named Pitbull and a bold new
    beginning   255

Keith Urban: selected awards   283
Ten essential Keith Urban performances   286
Acknowledgements   287
Selected bibliography   288

Prologue

Fan Fair, Nashville Fairgrounds, Tennessee, June 1998

I'm standing in the guest area at the Nashville Fairgrounds, the site of the annual country music Fan Fair, chatting with some Australians who've flown over for the event. One of them, a country music insider, has nudged me, nodding in the direction of Keith Urban, who's just joined the Oz contingent. There are some people here that Keith hasn't seen since shifting to the USA in 1992, and he's catching up.

'Keith's done it tough, you know,' I'm told.

It's mid-afternoon and a trio of hopefuls—Troy Cassar-Daley, Gina Jeffreys and Shanley Del—are about to take the stage. Part of an Australian showcase, they hope to catch the eye, and ideally the ear, of Nashville tastemakers. But the truth is that no one of note plays Fan Fair before the evening show. It's a scorching hot summer's day, and the fairground is barely half full. Many of the 20,000 or so fans are still in their campervans and RVs, which are parked next to the grounds. Their vehicles will be their base for the duration of

Fan Fair, which only adds to the strangeness. It feels more like a grey nomad convention than a music festival.

Fan Fair draws a certain type of fanatic. It's a Stetson-wearing, big-belt-buckled, trailer-park free-for-all, a week-long celebration of all things country, where Music City's newest and shiniest stars gather to play infotainment-length sets to their gushing devotees. (Sometimes old-stagers play Fan Fair, too; the 1998 event is kicked off by the Bellamy Brothers, the siblings who told us to 'Let Your Love Flow' back in 1976.) As the music flows, thousands of fans, cameras in hand, shuffle along in front of the stage, where they stop briefly and take their prized snaps before the steady arm of security swiftly guides them back in the direction of their seats. After playing, each act then retires to one of the fairground's huge, un-airconditioned farm sheds to sign everything that's flung their way—CDs, hats, photos, you name it—all the while pushing their latest product.

Two years earlier, country king Garth Brooks, who'd play his part in the Keith Urban story, had spent 23 hours in a Fan Fair shed, signing, signing, signing, leaving only when his arms went numb and the crowd finally thinned out. No wonder he sold so many records: the guy truly knew how to connect with regular folk. In 2010—by which time the event had been renamed the CMA Music Festival and moved to downtown Nashville—Taylor Swift signed for thirteen hours straight. Remarkable things happen here, things unlike any I've witnessed before. During this Fan Fair, country band The Mavericks take the stage just as the sun sets with a full mariachi band in tow, turning the gig into a full-blown Tex-Mex party. In the process they even blow away Brooks himself, who'd made a surprise appearance earlier in the afternoon. Few rock-and-roll bands I've encountered would pop up and play unannounced, yet Garth Brooks, who was a genuine superstar, did. Fan Fair is like that.

Keith Urban, however, isn't here to sign autographs or play. He's just a face in the crowd—a good-looking face, but not one that a lot of American country music fans recognise, at least not yet. As the Aussie contingent performs their brief set on the main stage, he looks on, shakes some hands, exchanges a few pleasantries and pretty much keeps his own company. We speak briefly and then he says he has to leave.

I have more to say to Keith—I'd been hoping he'd agree to speak for a story I was writing about the event—but don't get the chance. A month earlier, his record company, Capitol Nashville, had issued a press release stating 'Urban Under Doctor's Orders', which sounded very much like music industry-speak for a drug problem. I was more than curious. There'd been another recent press release announcing that time was up for his band The Ranch, who'd been with him since the start of Keith's Nashville odyssey.

And, as I soon learned, Keith was 'doing it tough'—in fact he was about to go into rehab. He knew what was required to truly succeed in the USA: you had to stick around, for one thing, and not just fly in for a week's schmoozing, like the Fan Fair hopefuls. He'd been in the USA for six tough years and was still learning how to play the game, despite the toll it was taking on his mental and physical health. But he genuinely believed that Nashville was where he was meant to be. This wasn't simply some career move; this was his calling.

As Keith once explained, 'I always wanted to go to Nashville . . . I'd read about it in all of my liner notes and all the records I had. It was a fictitious place to me and I wanted to see what it was like because to me it was the long-term view. It was the goal that I was working toward.'

'It must feel great to be living your dream,' a friend once said to him.

'[Nashville's] not my dream,' Urban replied. *'It's my destiny.'*

But Keith Urban would soon achieve more than simply fulfilling his destiny. Much more. The journey to reach his personal nirvana, however, was one wild ride.

1

The Caboolture kid

With a face that belonged on Mount Rushmore, a bottom-less voice and enough presence to raise the dead, 41-year-old Johnny Cash sure knew how to leave an impression. He certainly left his mark on five-and-a-half-year-old Keith Urbahn when he attended his first concert, at Brisbane's Festival Hall, in late March 1973.

Keith, who'd heard Cash's music at home—his father Bob was a serious country music devotee—sat with his parents, way up the back of the room, in the cheap seats. He and his brother Shane were decked out in matching Western outfits, bolo ties, the works; they looked like little cowboys. Despite the distance from the stage, the impact of the concert was huge, life changing, so much so that Keith was still overwhelmed almost 50 years later when he described the experience to US TV host Stephen Colbert in 2020. The audience, as Keith remembered it, was drunk, 'so noisy and intense and rowdy . . . The lights went out and it got even louder. This guy walked out on stage with a guitar and a spotlight and then he talked and then the whole crowd just went into this quiet hush . . . It was amazing.'

Keith would insist that at that moment he made a promise to himself. 'I want to be that guy in the spotlight.' (He'd sing about the experience of seeing Cash in his 2021 song 'Wild Hearts'.)

It had been just a few years since the Urbahns relocated to Brisbane from Whangārei, a small city on New Zealand's North Island, probably better known at the time of Keith's birth for its crime and unemployment problems than for being a hub of musical creativity. Whangārei's temperate yet soggy climate inspired locals to christen the area 'the winter-less north'.

Yet it was there that Keith Lionel Urbahn entered the world, kicking and screaming, on 26 October 1967. He was the second and last child of Bob and Marienne Urbahn; their first boy, Shane, had been born two years earlier. Keith was named after iconic Kiwi race caller Keith 'Haubie' Haub, a larger-than-life man of the track. Haub became Keith's godfather. (His middle name, Lionel, was the name of one of his mother's brothers.) Once, when asked about Haub, Keith said: 'My godfather is New Zealand's best race caller—and he'd kill you if he heard you say that.' They remain close to this day.

During the 1950s, while still in their teens, Haub and Keith's father, Bob, who was a drummer, played in a covers band, pounding out the songs of the day, including the best of Buddy Holly, Elvis Presley and Bill Haley & His Comets. But then Bob's tastes shifted. 'As the 1960s rolled around,' Keith recalled, 'my dad went more the country route than the rock-and-roll route and has remained a fan ever since.'

2

Keith would joke that his father played the drums until 'he had to get a real job', but Bob's love of music lingered, seeping into his son's very being—as did his drummer's sense of rhythm, which Keith would incorporate into his guitar playing. He'd sometimes beat on his guitar as if it was a drum, tapping out a rhythm.

Like his pal and former bandmate Keith Haub, Bob Urbahn was a colourful local identity, sporting a large moustache and even larger cowboy hats. Sometimes he'd wear a Greek fisherman's cap. His car of choice was anything American, ideally a Pontiac, although for a time he did own a 1960 Chevy Bel Air, a massive tank of a car with huge rear fins and a hefty V8 under the hood. This was one badass, gas-guzzling ride. You couldn't miss Bob. And he loved country music with a passion.

Bob, however, was a man with a problem: he liked a drink, although it wouldn't be until 2016 that his famous son came totally clean about the problem, finally admitting in a US *Rolling Stone* interview that his father was an alcoholic. Keith also described his father as a 'physical disciplinarian', although he said that Bob denied it, saying: 'Hitting you? I never did that!'

Keith alluded to something more when he spoke with Scott Evans from Access Hollywood in 2020, although he didn't go into great detail. 'I grew up in a house where we didn't really speak about intimate things . . . and there were times when we should have said things but we didn't.' (Keith had recorded a song that made him reflect on his childhood. It was called 'Say Something'.)

This complicated father–son relationship—and there was no question that Keith loved his father deeply—was one of the reasons he devoted himself to country music. '[My dad] was into it, and I wanted his approval. I feel very sure if he'd been into African music, I'd be living in Zimbabwe.' Interestingly, those from the family who stayed behind in the Shaky Isles, such as Bob's brothers Brian and Paul, hung on to the original spelling of the Urbahn name, but Keith shed that bothersome 'h' on the road somewhere between Australia and Nashville.

When the family settled in Brisbane, they opened a corner store in the city, living in a tiny house at the back of the shop. Keith and his brother slept on mattresses on the floor; they couldn't afford beds. 'We were very working class,' Keith recalled. 'We didn't have any money.' As successful as he would become, Keith never quite outgrew his roots.

When asked about his adopted hometown, Keith said this: 'It still feels like a country town and I love that about Brisbane.' What Brisbane also had going for it when Keith was a kid was its radio stations, including 4BC, 4BH and 4IP, that pumped out the hits of the day, many of which caught the ear of Bob and, in turn, Keith. 'Top 40 radio was so diverse,' Keith said in 2000. 'You could hear Jethro Tull next to The Doobie Brothers, Led Zeppelin then The Beatles.' It was a golden era.

Bob was mad for Dolly Parton, Charley Pride, Buck Owens (who, in 2001, would team with Keith on an episode of TV's *Family Feud*) and Glen Campbell, who Keith came to idolise. Marienne, the 'rock' of the Urban household, who had met Bob when she was a teenager, favoured the smoother sounds of Neil Diamond and The Everly Brothers.

'My folks' record collection has been the main influence

on what I've done musically,' Keith admitted in 2000. 'You can't help being influenced by your surroundings.'

But equally important to their second son was Bob's passion for Americana. 'I inherited this kind of love for the American dream,' Keith admitted. 'I fell in love with the music, the cars'—and crucially—'the whole idea of America.' Marienne also fell hard for all things American.

Keith's older brother Shane began school at Toowong, while Keith was enrolled at the now heritage-listed East Brisbane State School. (Keith had been nicknamed 'Sub-Urban' by a local kid because he was the younger sibling.) Some nights, after school, Bob and Marienne would bring their barely school-aged sons along to concerts. They'd sometimes leave Keith to snooze beneath the table while they took in the gig, and this musical baptism remains one of Keith's most vivid early memories. 'I would curl up under a table and go to sleep,' he said in 2004, 'with the bass drum and the bass guitar pulsing through the carpet. In hindsight, it was terrific training for me—great rhythmic influences.'

★

Even before having his young mind blown by Johnny Cash, Keith had started to play—or at least tried to play, clumsily wrapping his fingers around the strings of a ukulele for the first time when he was four years old. But he strummed along to the songs on the radio enthusiastically enough for Bob and Marienne to agree that when the boy turned six, he was ready for his first guitar, a three-quarter-sized Suzuki acoustic. 'He was short for his age,' remembered Marienne, 'and it was huge on him.' Keith duly placed a Pizza Hut sticker on the top of it, which faded into a sticky mess pretty quickly. But still he loved it.

Learning wasn't easy; Keith would complain to his parents that his fingers ached. Their reply was simple: 'Don't play, then.' This wasn't what Keith had expected to hear, but it only encouraged him to keep trying, even though, as he admitted, his fingers 'hurt for a long time' as he struggled with the basics.

Keith's big breakthrough came when he bought the sheet music to The Stylistics' 1974 soul-pop hit 'You Make Me Feel Brand New'. He was thrilled when he worked out the first chord. 'Yay,' he said to himself, 'I can play guitar.' Keith likened it to the experience of riding a bike without training wheels for the first time.

One day, a woman named Sue McCarthy (now Sue Crealey, and to this day a family friend) walked up to the counter of the Urban corner store and asked if she could place a handwritten ad in the shop window.

'What's the ad for?' Marienne asked.

When Sue replied that it was for guitar lessons, the Urbans couldn't believe their luck. They agreed to let her place the ad for free, on one condition: 'Can you teach our son?' Although she was hesitant at first—Keith was just a kid, after all—she agreed to at least sit with him and see what the boy knew. When Keith played for her, she could see that he had a solid grasp of the basics and agreed to teach him everything she knew.

When asked about him, in 2005, Sue said that Keith was a natural. 'He just had it in him,' she said. 'It was like a focus, even back then. [Playing music] was all Keith ever wanted to do.' The first song that he learned to play in its entirety was the spooky old blues 'The House of the Rising Sun'. It was a pretty grim choice for a kid still in primary school, but was in keeping with his eclectic tastes. Country, rock and roll, 'You Make Me Feel Brand New', the blues—there was a big world of music out there.

Keith made his public debut, such as it was, while under Sue's tutelage, when he and some other students played at a nursing home. The gig provided Keith with a ready-made punchline, which he'd roll out often later in life. 'It was a captive audience,' he'd recall with a smile.

Within months, Sue pulled Marienne aside. 'I just can't teach him any more,' she admitted. 'I just know the basics.' Keith had outgrown his first guitar teacher.

*

Making music was all about rites of passage—your first guitar, your first big show, stepping out in public for the first time, your first bash at recording. There were also rituals specific to the world of country music. In Australia, that meant a trip to Tamworth, in northern New South Wales. To country fans, it was Mecca.

Keith made his initial pilgrimage in 1973, the first year that the Golden Guitar Awards for country music were staged in the rural centre. This was nothing like the money-spinning annual event that the Tamworth Country Music Festival grew to become—only a last-minute $45 donation from Tamworth business Insulwool Insulations enabled the awards to be broadcast on local stations 2TM and 2MO in that first year. It was that humble.

This didn't matter to starry-eyed Keith, who made the

600-kilometre road trip with his parents. He drank it in as they walked the length and breadth of Peel Street, Tamworth's main drag. Over at the Golden Guitars, Slim Dusty won the first Golden Guitar for the immortal 'Lights on the Hill', a song written by Joy McKean, Dusty's wife, after a particularly hairy late-night long-distance drive. It was the first of an amazing 38 Golden Guitars for Dusty. The paths of this Aussie country legend and Keith Urban would intersect in due course.

Soon enough, Keith was meeting an even bigger name in country music. Glen Campbell, whose songs (especially those so brilliantly crafted by Jimmy Webb) provided a roadmap, quite literally, for those who'd never been near such places as Galveston and Wichita, toured Australia in late 1974. Somehow Keith managed to meet Campbell when the Arkansas native played in Brisbane.

The movie-star-handsome Campbell didn't quite know what to make of the eager seven-year-old, but Keith managed to break the ice.

'I play guitar, too, Mr Campbell,' Keith told him, setting new standards for cockiness. Campbell raised his eyebrows and handed the kid a guitar, who duly impressed him with his chops.

'He could play the guitar better than I could when I was his age,' Campbell admitted afterwards.

*

Every aspiring guitar-slinger needs a band, and Keith came about his in the strangest way possible. Not long after he'd appeared in public, singing and strumming Tanya Tucker's

'San Antonio Stroll' in a talent quest, where he won $50 (and duly lost it), his parents began taking him to see a covers act named Country Fever that played regularly at the local country music club. Country Fever registered strongly with Keith—he really liked the band, but he really *loved* their name.

Keith thought to himself, 'Man, I wish *I* had a band.'

The Urbans' house in Brisbane had a detached garage. Keith had pieced together a rudimentary stage, which he'd set up alongside the outside wall of the garage. It was there that he 'played' concerts with his imaginary band, which he dubbed Rock Fever. One day he asked his father if he could spray-paint the band's name on the side of the garage.

'No,' Bob replied. 'Absolutely not.'

Of course, as soon as Bob left for work and Keith was alone in the house, he went ahead and did exactly what he was told not to. Rock Fever felt much more real to him if its name was tagged on the garage. When his parents returned home, they were less than impressed. But how to punish the amateur graffitist? Right where it hurt the most.

'No guitar for you for four weeks,' they told him, locking away his beloved six-string.

Keith actually felt relieved. Four weeks—that was all? While he did complain about it at the time, he considered himself pretty fortunate to get away with such a lenient sentence. After a week, however, the urge to play kicked in so strongly that he hopped on a bus to a music store in the city, just so he could strum a guitar—any guitar.

'When I got my guitar back, I never let it go,' he said. 'And I never spray-painted any band name on the side of a building ever again.'

It would be another twenty years before Keith was again deprived of his guitar. And then it was because he was in rehab.

*

The Westfield Super Juniors was a showcase of local Brisbane talent, sponsored by the shopping centre giant, which had thrown open its doors at suburban Toombul in 1967. At the age of seven, Keith auditioned and was accepted by the Juniors. As one shopping-centre employee recalled, he was the first performer picked for the Super Juniors, and was 'a natural entertainer', even though 'the guitar was taller than he was'.

In an interview with *Vintage Guitar*, Keith likened the Super Juniors to the Mouseketeers. 'We did musicals and I had to learn a bit of dialogue and do a bit of dancing.' Keith also played guitar and sang. The troupe would perform on weekends and school holidays, at such glamorous spots as Indooroopilly Shoppingtown in suburban Brisbane. Their family-friendly repertoire included a take on the then-not-frowned-upon *Black and White Minstrel Show*. Keith wore the costume of the Juniors: the striped shirt, vest and an oversized bow tie, but grew his hair longer than the other boys in the troupe, all the way to his shoulders.

Kids Country was another young talent team that Keith joined. Like the Super Juniors, they'd entertain shoppers and anyone else who'd host them. It was there that Keith met guitarist Reg Grant, who introduced him to the music of Dire Straits, a band all over the airwaves and charts during 1978 with their hit 'Sultans of Swing' and their critical and commercial smash of a self-titled debut album. Keith was hooked; he'd play the record repeatedly and decipher

Knopfler's solos note by note. But Keith held Reg Grant in the same esteem as he held Straits' Mark Knopfler; likewise Barry Cluff, another local guitar-slinger. As Keith explained during a sitdown at the South by Southwest (SXSW) music seminar in 2018, 'The guy who lived up the street, the guy in the local band . . . [they were] unknowns, [but] for me it was like, "I wish I could play as good as that guy."'

The Urbans had recently shifted base to Caboolture, about 50 kilometres north of Brisbane, at the time a smallish dairy town, where they settled into a property big enough for Bob to grow vegies, and for Keith and his brother Shane to ride horses. One of Keith's chores was to 'clean out the pigsties and shovel shit out of the chicken coops'. But most of the time he and Shane roared around the neighbourhood, on BMX bikes and, later on, motorcycles.

These days Caboolture is a middle-sized Brisbane suburb, but in the late 1970s it was an outpost, home to just a few thousand; the place didn't even have traffic lights. That was one of the first things that struck Keith when they moved there. 'No traffic lights anywhere,' he laughed. It seemed very strange to him.

Bob got a job at the local tip, while Marienne opened a takeaway in what passed for the main street. Bob would drive around town in a black 1959 Pontiac, his cowboy hat perched on his head, windows down, country music blaring. He was soon known, not surprisingly, as something of a colourful local identity.

Keith got his kicks in a far simpler manner. He would wander down to the local race track and collect used betting stubs, which he'd then hand out to his family, pretending they were concert tickets. Imagining their lounge room was

Festival Hall, he would only sing for them when they had surrendered their 'tickets'.

It was around this time that Keith and his parents joined the Northern Suburbs Country Music Club (NSCMC), a group of amateur pickers and singers based at Bald Hills in Brisbane's north, who'd get together once a month. Anyone keen for a sing could get up and play with the house band. 'There were a lot of these clubs around Australia,' said Keith. 'I spent my whole youth immersed in that kind of culture.'

'There was a real down-home, friendly, small-town kind of vibe,' said Jewel Blanch, who, along with her father, renowned country singer Arthur Blanch, would sometimes be asked to judge music club events. Keith's parents became friends with the Blanches at these get-togethers, and when Keith was nine, Arthur taught him some guitar chords. Jewel would come to play a key role in Keith's future, and one day she'd be his late-night confidante when he was at his lowest ebb, not even sure if he wanted to live, let alone play.

It was through the Northern Suburbs club that Keith met Angie Marquis, a curly-haired, straight-talking Queenslander, who was also born in 1967. They'd eventually join forces in a duo called California Suite, in 1981, playing covers, and would remain an on- and off-stage couple for several years. 'She was the Stevie Nicks of the group,' Keith laughed, when he reminisced with *Vintage Guitar*. When Keith took his first serious bash at Tamworth, it would be alongside Marquis.

Not surprisingly, throughout their history, the NSCMC would enthusiastically talk up Keith's youthful membership. Who wouldn't? Keith won some of his first trophies there— and he wouldn't forget them, either, duly thanking the club in the liner notes of his debut album in 1991.

But the club was just another starting point, like the Westfield Juniors and Kids Country. One day, while waiting for the school bus with his brother, Keith asked Shane what he hoped to do with his life. Shane was by then an accomplished sportsman—a competitive tennis player, swimmer and footballer—but Keith's question surprised him: after all, the kid hadn't even started high school. After a pause, Shane replied: 'I want to get married, have children, own my house, get a good job. You know, the normal things.'

Keith chewed this over for a while and then tried again. 'Yeah, *but what do you want to do?*' *His* dream life was somewhere way off, far from Caboolture and domestic bliss.

Keith dreamed about Nashville. He didn't quite know where it was, but it was a name that he'd noticed in the liner notes of all of his dad's records. 'Made in Nashville'. 'Recorded in Nashville'. 'Produced in Nashville'. Given how much he loved those records, he figured that it had to be the place for him. Keith later admitted that 'Nashville was this fictitious place to me'. It was mythical, his very own Holy Grail. Getting there, of course, was a long way in the future. There were bands to be joined, then discarded, likewise bogan haircuts and other crimes against fashion.

Keith's first paying gig was organised by Keith Chisholm, who ran the local music store in Caboolture, doing a lively trade in Slim Dusty cassettes. Keith's parents had been in Chisholm's ear, talking up their son, and when Chisholm had heard enough, he gave the kid a 'between acts' set at a local festival, paying him the princely sum of $50. Many years along, Chisholm had a wry chuckle about the gig. 'You probably wouldn't get Urban these days for $50.'

2

'The guitar was my security blanket'

Having your house burn down is the stuff of country songs, surely not of real life. But that's exactly what happened to the Urbans not long after moving to Caboolture. Keith was still in primary school when he received the biggest shock of his short life.

'It's a crazy thing,' he said during an episode of SBS's *The Feed*, 'to leave home in the morning and there's your house, and then come back about three o'clock in the afternoon . . . everything, everything [gone]. It's just a strange, surreal feeling.'

Bob had been baking a cake when he went outside to tend to their orchard of lemon trees. While in the yard he heard a siren but at first didn't think too much of it. When the sound appeared to be getting louder, and closer, he looked up and was stunned to realise that the house was on fire—the combustion stove had caught alight. There was nothing that he, or the local fire crew, could do. The house was gone;

the blaze was so intense that when they sifted through the wreckage, they discovered Keith's melted music trophies.

Keith's strongest memory was that almost everything inside the house was burned to cinders and crunched beneath his feet when he walked through the debris. Fortunately, the fire hadn't spread to the garage, which was where his father's drum kit, and Keith's guitar, were stored. They were the only two things to survive the blaze.

The fallout was a huge shock for the Urbans—they had to depend on the local Red Cross for clothes and were forced to stay with friends while they looked for a new home. They spent some time living in a tin tractor shed. Shane and Keith shared a single bed, as did Bob and Marienne, and the family ate off the workbench in the middle of the shed. As Keith recalled, it 'looked like a squatter's residence'.

It would be three years before they finally settled into a place they'd call home, at 17 Douglas Drive, which was where Keith would spend the rest of his ten years in Caboolture.

If there was an upside to this unstable period of his life, it was the generosity of the Northern Suburbs Country Music Club, which staged a fundraiser for the Urbans. Their benevolence left a deep impression on Keith—years down the line, when he could finally afford to give back, he did in a very practical way, becoming an advocate for any number of different charities. 'That spirit in action stuck with me,' he said.

Despite this drama—or perhaps to escape it—the Urbans continued their annual pilgrimages to the Tamworth Country Music Festival. In 1977, Keith won a CCMA Special Encouragement Award for under-tens. A starstruck Keith was presented the award by none other than country music great Smoky Dawson, Australia's very own singing cowboy. A photo was taken of Keith as he accepted the award—a pint-sized kid with shiny hair and an even shinier silk shirt, a huge smile on his face. Unusually for Dawson, his loyal horse Charlie was nowhere to be seen.

*

Reg Lindsay was another Australian country star to connect with a very young Keith Urban. Lindsay had worked as a jackeroo in Broken Hill immediately after World War II, but his musical career really took off after he was injured in a rodeo accident. By the time his path first intersected with Keith's, Lindsay had scored a mainstream Top 10 hit with 'Armstrong', had hosted his own national TV show, and had been the first Australian to sing at the Grand Ole Opry in Nashville—where he went over so well he was invited back for a second performance.

From 1977, Lindsay hosted a Logie-winning TV show called *Country Homestead*, filmed at the QTQ 9 studio in Brisbane, and it was here that Keith made his small-screen debut in 1978. Keith performed Dolly Parton's 'Apple Jack'—with Lindsay's house band just out of shot, playing along—wearing a shimmering green-and-silver outfit, with a shirt collar so wide and sharp it could take out an eye, on a stage setting meant to resemble a barn.

'I was prepubescent there,' he laughed in 2020, 'so I couldn't even sing in [Dolly's] key.'

In his next *Country Homestead* appearance, sometime in 1979, Keith was part of an eight-piece ensemble, all decked out in matching sky-blue Kids Country T-shirts and nervous smiles (though Keith seemed more at ease than the others). Keith played rhythm guitar and sang harmonies as they performed a frightfully earnest take on the Linda Ronstadt hit 'It's So Easy'.

Keith's third appearance on the show, also during 1979, was as part of a duet. He and Jenny Wilson—who towered over twelve-year-old Keith—sang the sombre 'An Angel Rejoiced Last Night', which had been recorded by country greats Gram Parsons and Emmylou Harris. It was a curiously solemn song to cover at a time when the charts were awash with Kiss, Blondie and Racey. But this was country, and country was a serious business, even when you were a small kid with a big guitar. Fortunately, their matching brown waistcoats—and Keith's broad smile—brought just a little levity to their performance.

Keith, by his own admission, was a shy kid, a bit withdrawn, but grew in confidence when he performed. 'The guitar was my security blanket,' he admitted. 'I did definitely find that playing guitar was a good calming mechanism.' He'd even carry it with him when he went to school, strumming it on the bus.

During another trip to Tamworth, in 1981, Keith reconnected with Glen Innes native Jewel Blanch, a singer who'd just claimed her first Golden Guitar. The pretty, golden-haired Blanch was not your typical Tamworth hopeful: she'd recently returned to Australia after several years in Los Angeles, where she had acted on TV, appearing in such shows as *Fantasy Island* and *The Mod Squad*—and knocked back the lead role for torrid horror flick *The Exorcist*, which duly went to Linda Blair. (The obscenities and projectile vomiting were a touch too much for Blanch.) She'd also recorded for RCA in the States after being 'scouted' by country music legend Chet Atkins, with some chart success. Blanch seemed poised to become the first local artist since Olivia Newton-John to make a legitimate breakthrough in Nashville, but soon after she returned to Australia.

Blanch's father Arthur was Oz country-music royalty. Not only was he a regular winner of Golden Guitars but way back in 1952 he'd cut the first Australian country music recordings—and he went on to record for Capitol Records in the US, the future home of one Keith Urban. The Blanches carried some weight; they were good people to know.

'I remember watching Keith,' Jewel said. 'He was a very talented kid. He was polite, very respectful.' Reconnecting with Jewel gave Keith's nascent career a boost because the Blanches duly hired him to back them at various shows throughout Queensland and at the Wandong Country Music Festival in Victoria. Although barely in his teens, Keith 'was a professional already', according to Jewel. He was on his way.

*

Unlike a lot of rootsy artists who devote themselves to just the two types of music—country and western—Keith was no music snob, even as a kid. He may have known the song-books of Charley Pride and Glen Campbell inside out, but he also binged on commercial radio. The late 1970s and early 1980s were a ripe time for rock and pop, and Keith, along with his brother Shane, imbibed heavily. They bonded over the Eagles, the Electric Light Orchestra and Fleetwood Mac, acts big on melodies and harmonies. Keith loved Queen, especially their way-over-the-top frontman Freddie Mercury. In the future, whenever he was short of inspiration, Keith would reach for a DVD of Mercury 'conducting' a packed Wembley Arena in London during 1986; it was a masterclass in stagecraft. It never failed to give him a lift.

At the other end of the scale was the completely unpretentious Malcolm Young, the driving force behind AC/DC, the man with the best right hand in the business. Keith admired Young's ability to build a riff that could rattle windows; he was a human powerhouse. That ability to bash an audience over the head with his guitar—metaphorically, of course— helped when Keith started playing the beer barns of rural Queensland. And the music of Dire Straits, which Keith had discovered via guitarist Reg Grant, remained a constant. Keith could play 'Sultans of Swing', the British band's signature song, in his sleep. He also loved Mark Knopfler's outros on such songs as 'Romeo and Juliet' and 'Tunnel of Love', which he felt were songs in themselves.

Keith's early performances weren't exclusively playing country songs. For a heartbeat, in his mid teens, he played in a heavy metal act called Fractured Mirror, named after a track on Ace Frehley's 1978 solo LP. They dabbled in the rock-and-roll dark arts, covering the songs of Judas Priest, Saxon and the Scorpions—with a little AC/DC thrown in for local colour. Keith had only been asked to join the band because the original guitarist fancied himself as a vocalist and stopped playing, but this meant Keith had use of the guy's imposing Marshall stack. 'It was great,' he'd recall.

Keith had recently discovered the chicken pickin' style of American guitarist Ricky Skaggs and, about three gigs in, decided to experiment with this mid-song. 'It sounded awesome to me,' said Keith—but not so much to his band-mates, who, as he recalled, 'freaked out' and fired him. So much for metal.

Musicals, however, were fair game for Keith. While at Caboolture State High School, he snagged the lead role in a production of *Oliver*—he could still recite the lines in 2021, when probed by TV host James Corden—and also played in the band when the school staged *Bye Bye Birdie*. Keith grew close to the school's music teacher, Megan Grimmer, who was a big inspiration. She wrote a musical called *Music Is, Music Was* that gave students like Keith free rein to show off their chops.

'She knew she had a class full of some truly gifted musicians who couldn't read music,' Keith wrote for the school's 40th anniversary magazine. 'It was radical think-ing for a teacher . . . I have a music career that I couldn't have dreamt of, thanks in a large part to a passionate teacher who only wanted her pupils to succeed.'

For the first time in his life, girls started paying atten-tion to Keith, although he noticed it only lasted as long as the production he was involved with. Still, he twigged pretty quickly that this was a handy by-product of music, especially given that he was so shy away from the stage.

It was during his time at Caboolture High that Keith befriended Sherry Rich, another budding musician. Rich and her brother Rusty, who'd appeared with Keith in *Bye Bye Birdie*, were mad for the new wave and post-punk sounds coming out of the UK. It was none other than Megan Grimmer, who was still in her early twenties, who had opened their eyes and ears to this new music.

'The town Caboolture was fairly conservative and had a

healthy dose of the rural, redneck element,' recalled Sherry. 'There was, however, one good record store that would order in our hotly anticipated imports from the UK new wave scene.'

The Richs were impossible to miss in Caboolture—they were the only kids to sport the skinny ties, angular hairstyles and garishly coloured outfits of new wave. Not so Keith. According to Rich, Keith 'looked pretty much the same as he does now except with a more pronounced mullet, tight jeans and a fierce love of Dire Straits and Iron Maiden. Even so, we had a lot of common ground musically. My mother was a guitar teacher and country-folk performer, so we grew up around that music.' Rich saw Keith play with his country music club and sensed straightaway that he was far and away the best musician there.

Keith started spending a lot of time jamming with the Rich family; he'd sometimes stay with them on Bribie Island, just off the coast near Caboolture. 'He didn't do a skerrick of schoolwork,' remembered Rusty, who'd go on to a successful career—as Rusty Berther—in the comedy duo Scared Weird Little Guys. '[Instead] he used to come and stay over at our place and we used to rehearse and muck around recording.'

Sherry and Rusty decided to form a band with Keith. They named themselves Obscure Alternatives, which could easily have been mistaken for some edgy act straight out of London or LA. (They'd actually lifted the name from a 1978 album by UK outfit Japan, key players in the new wave world.)

Keith, according to the Richs' mother, was a 'well-mannered house guest'. He was such a perfect guest, in fact, that she decided to make stage outfits for Keith and her kids: matching red bomber jackets with sequinned initials. Keith and the Richs—aka Obscure Alternatives—were quite a sight, and quite the hit, when they plugged in to play at a Caboolture High social around 1982, the year that fourteen-year-old Keith moved into Year 10. They covered everything from The Vapors' 'Turning Japanese' to songs from Mental As Anything and The Monkees, sweeping from the 1960s to the latest chart hits.

As Sherry recalled, the band 'gave us a taste of the performing high—as well as briefly lifting us out of nerd status'.

Obscure Alternatives, however, were short lived. They performed another gig at the Bribie Festival, but after that they folded pretty quickly. Sherry and Rusty knew that Keith was a skilled player who genuinely loved playing, even if they were heading in different directions musically. One day, Sherry looked on as Keith arrived at school with a guitar case, which he opened in class with due ceremony. Inside was a shiny red Fender Stratocaster, his first serious axe. *His baby.*

'It seemed to me that performing and playing guitar was his great singular passion and path in life,' said Sherry. 'Luckily he realised it early on.'

There was a noticeable change in Keith's mood as Year 10 dragged on. By his own admission, he 'hated' high school; all he wanted to do was play music. Megan Grimmer, his music teacher, sensed that something had changed in Keith. 'Kids like that who have those sorts of abilities are often emotionally fragile,' she said, looking back. 'I'm not a doctor, but you see it.'

At the age of fifteen, Keith dropped out of school. His parents, who'd been driving him to gigs on the weekends and supporting his musical dreams, accepted that it might be for the best. Maybe Keith could make some kind of living playing music—and there was only one way to find out.

*

Long before *Australian Idol* or *The Voice* offered potential shortcuts to a career in entertainment, the big dream was to be spotted on TV by competing in talent quests—*New Faces*, *Pot of Gold*, *Pot Luck*, take your pick. But there was a very big downside: you might come up before Bernard King, an acid-tongued judge with severe sideburns and an even more severe line in career killing. When Keith was 9, he was torn to shreds by King after performing a Dolly Parton song on *Pot of Gold*. King gave Keith a score of eight—out of a possible 25.

The judges on *New Faces*, where Keith appeared in 1983, were a little kinder. Bert Newton was the host and he introduced Keith with his trademark flourish. 'Keith Urban is a vocalist and guitarist, sixteen years of age, and Keith's ambition is to be a radio announcer. He's done nightclubs and school dances; he appeared on Reg Lindsay's *Country Homestead*; and tonight he's got "All Out of Love". Act Four—Keith Urban from Queensland!'

Keith didn't look much like your usual *New Faces* hopeful: his hair was a golden mullet, his outfit was a shiny maroon and silver, while the gap between his front teeth was so big you could squeeze a 50-cent coin through it. It was a bold move on his part, taking on the syrupy Air Supply ballad, but he did a more than reasonable job, despite straining for the high notes. Keith also knew exactly where to look when the camera moved in for a close-up; his appearances on *Country Homestead* were coming in handy.

Local entertainment legend Bobby Limb passed judgement on the teenager. 'Keith, you're only sixteen, so you've got plenty of time. What actually is showing up in your voice is just immaturity, that's all. You love singing . . .' Limb went on to analyse Keith's breathing and some other technical issues, recommending vocal exercises, perhaps coaching.

'Sixteen, my goodness, you've got the world in front of you,' Limb said in conclusion. 'Good luck to you, Keith. I gave you 39.'

Keith's final score was 79 out of a possible 100, a far better result than when he had fronted the ruthless Bernard King. Before Keith left the set, Bert Newton had a question for him: why did he want to become an announcer and not a singer?

'I think radio announcing would be good publicity for a singer,' replied Keith. It was a savvy response for such a young kid. Keith had just finished a week of work experience at 4KQ, he told Newton, but he neglected to mention that he didn't actually impress the management during his stint there. Keith had convinced the station manager to let him use an empty studio to produce his own show, and quickly started gathering records to play. Keith had decided to use Waylon Jennings' theme song from *The Dukes of Hazzard*, which he'd splice in between news clips. But Keith hadn't yet mastered the desk, because as he worked on his show, he randomly flipped a switch and looked up to see a sudden commotion in the corridor outside. He'd accidentally interrupted a news broadcast from the next studio with a snippet of the Dukes' theme. ('It wasn't my calling after all,' Keith admitted.)

At the time, Keith was playing in a duo with Angie Marquis, his sometimes girlfriend. They called themselves California Suite. Keith and Angie were human jukeboxes, singing crowd-pleasers from Fleetwood Mac, Linda Ronstadt, Creedence Clearwater Revival, Nicolette Larson, the Eagles, The Beatles, James Taylor, even UB40. Sometimes they'd slip in country tracks like George Strait's 'You Look So Good in Love' and 'Dixieland Delight' by Alabama. 'Jack & Diane' by John Mellencamp (then known as John Cougar) was a stayer in their set; Keith was a huge fan. These gigs were long hauls—sometimes four hours, occasionally even longer—for which they were usually paid $250. It was money hard earned because the venues they played were frequented by loud drunks and disinterested locals.

'They were all different clubs,' Keith said. 'Rowdy pubs. A lot of people didn't want to listen. You had to *make* them listen.'

Keith and Angie had a gig booked in Sydney, and on the flight from Brisbane Keith was astonished to find himself seated alongside legendary guitarist Tommy Emmanuel, a native of Muswellbrook in the NSW Hunter Valley. Keith was a huge fan and quickly struck up a conversation. As Emmanuel recalled, 'He had pink hair; he looked like a little punk.'

Keith told Emmanuel that he had big plans—much bigger than anything Australia could accommodate. Emmanuel understood completely; he, too, was coming to the same realisation about his career after spells in such acclaimed local outfits as Goldrush and The Southern Star Band. And, like Keith, he'd also done the rounds of talent quests as a teenager, having first played professionally at the ripe old age of six, hitting the road with his brother Phil, another fine picker, as part of a family band, living out of two station wagons as they crisscrossed Australia. While not yet 30, Emmanuel was already a veteran, and a rare talent.

'What you should do,' Emmanuel told Keith, 'is get the hell out of here and do what it is that you know you want to do.' But, as Emmanuel advised him, it wasn't as simple as booking a one-way ticket to Nashville. 'I've gathered the right people around me. You need to be surrounded by people you trust and you have to give it everything you have every time you go out to play.'

Keith knew this was great advice—and from a guitar master and one of his heroes, no less. But he still had a musical apprenticeship to undertake.

★

In the mid-1980s, the tagline 'Brisbane's best party band' belonged to an act named Rusty and the Ayers Rockettes. Rusty Hammerstrom led the band. An American by birth, a chef by trade and a bandleader by nature, he named the group as a nod to the several months he and his wife Lisbet had spent camping near Uluru. They were at the Rock when Azaria Chamberlain went missing in 1980 and even helped in the fruitless search for the missing baby.

Apart from playing originals with such authentic names as 'Kakadu' and 'Gondwanaland', the Rockettes' stock in trade was covers of Oz-rock standards. The Rockettes had a very fluid line-up; its members had included guitarists Brad 'Hoola' Hooper and Daryll Mitchell, and Brisbane-born drummer Peter Clarke.

Rusty Hammerstrom checked out Keith's moves at a California Suite gig at Caboolture. There weren't many people in the room, but that didn't matter to Hammerstrom, who'd just lost a guitarist. Keith was his guy. 'Even back then, Keith was an awesome guitar player,' Hammerstrom said in 2005. 'His music was superlative. And he always had that country edge to his playing.' He referred to Keith, even then, as a 'shining star'.

Hammerstrom first hired Keith to play guitar in the Rockettes during 1987. Keith would stay in the band for two years, juggling it with California Suite bookings. Keith and drummer Peter Clarke grew close; when on the road, they'd typically share a room. That relationship would last way beyond the Rockettes.

One night, James Blundell—another country music hopeful and fellow Queenslander—caught the Rockettes at a pub in Mossman, not far from Port Douglas in Far North Queensland. Keith impressed him hugely. 'It was one of those things—I'm watching the band and thinking, "Fuck, that guy can play guitar."'

In many ways, Keith's gigs as a Rockette were every bit as challenging as those with California Suite, even though he was now part of what Ayers described as 'a Vegas act where everyone gets to show off'. This didn't mean, however, that the audiences were easier to please or any less raucous. 'Australian pub audiences are not a forgiving crowd,' Keith later observed. 'You've gotta work for it.'

It was during a California Suite gig, however, that Keith met one of the biggest figures in his early career, his first real 'booster'. Greg Shaw was a Brisbane entrepreneur who ran several venues, including General Jacksons beneath the

Crest Hotel in the city. With his conservative dress sense and sensible haircut, Shaw looked more like an accountant, but he'd had a colourful past—he'd once been the star waterskier at Brisbane's Sea World resort. He had an ear for quality country music, too, having worked with James Blundell when James was a teenager.

Shaw was in need of some talent for his Thursday night gig at General Jacksons, but after watching Keith for a few minutes, he sensed something much bigger. He turned to his girlfriend and said, 'I'm going to manage that guy and take him to number 1 in the US'. After the gig, Shaw spoke with Keith and offered to be his manager. Keith agreed in a heartbeat. He'd just met his first true believer.

Tommy Emmanuel had advised Keith to surround himself with the 'right people'. It seemed to Keith that Greg Shaw fitted that bill perfectly—and Shaw was gobsmacked by Keith. 'The guy's a superstar,' Shaw said to his friends and colleagues, and duly set about turning Keith into one.

But there was one problem. Breaking out in the US was a massive undertaking for any Australian artist, let alone a young hopeful from Caboolture. There were massive hurdles: simple geography, for starters. To 'make it' in the States you needed to be based there. Presence was crucial. And cracking Nashville was even harder; a non-American playing country made very little sense to the denizens of Music City USA. While the Bee Gees, Little River Band, Men at Work and Olivia Newton-John had proved that it was possible, though difficult, to make a dent in the US rock and pop markets, no Aussie had made a lasting impression in Nashville. Newton-John had scored a couple of country hits in the 1970s, including 'Have You Never Been Mellow', while

Keith's friend Jewel Blanch, plus artists Diana Trask, Helen Reddy and the LeGarde Twins (a 1950s singing cowboys act from Mackay, Queensland), had achieved minor US country chart success. But an Australian with a long-lasting, significant career in Nashville? It just didn't happen. *Impossible.*

3

How to become an extraordinary alien

With Greg Shaw at the helm, Keith was never short of work. In 1987, he landed the opening slot for Scottish comic Billy Connolly when he toured Australia. He was required to play the standard 30-minute set, strumming covers and (hopefully) warming up the audience. Keith owned just the one guitar and, predictably, he snapped a string mid-song early in his set. He struggled to the end of the song but by then his guitar had drifted way out of tune. His only option was to take time to restring his guitar, which would have given hecklers free rein to rip him to shreds. But just as he started sweating, Keith looked towards the wings and noticed Connolly's tour manager holding the acoustic guitar that Connolly sometimes used during his act. The tour manager ran on stage, guitars were exchanged, and the show went on.

'Thank you for doing that,' Keith said to the tour manager afterwards, relieved that he hadn't been booed off stage, or worse.

'Thank Billy,' came the reply. '*He* did it.'

Apparently, when Connolly learned that his support act was in trouble, he despatched his own guitar—and had personally restrung Keith's by the time his set concluded. Keith couldn't believe his luck. He'd been rescued by the Big Yin.

★

The fanboy in Keith was on full alert when John Cougar Mellencamp—as he was known in the mid-1980s—brought his Lonesome Jubilee tour to Australia in April 1988. Mellencamp was on a hot streak: his two most recent albums, 1985's *Scarecrow* and 1987's *The Lonesome Jubilee*, had both been huge commercial hits and also won over critics, who until now had written him off as a poor man's Bruce Springsteen. US *Rolling Stone* gave *Scarecrow* a four-star review, with writer J.D. Considine admiring how it moved 'from heartland rock to an Appalachian-influenced sound that owed more to *Desire*-era Dylan than any Stones album'.

Keith was a huge fan of *The Lonesome Jubilee*, too. He loved the way that Mellencamp, while a rocker at heart, brought in fiddles and mandolin, dobro and banjo, best heard in such standouts as 'Paper in Fire' and 'Check It Out'. These were songs that bridged the divide between roots music and rock and roll; it was Americana even before the term had been coined. When Keith saw Mellencamp play at the Brisbane Entertainment Centre, his mind was duly blown.

'He had such a fusion of sounds and styles that I'd never heard before,' Keith said in 2018, at SXSW in Austin, Texas—a year when Keith himself was crossing genres and mixing styles. 'His band was phenomenal . . . I didn't leave that concert thinking, "I'm going to be John Mellencamp"—I went away thinking, "Okay, just take all the things you love and put them together in your own way. Make your own thing."'

At the time, Keith was still playing covers, doing his human jukebox act, trying to write songs in his downtime. Now, after seeing Mellencamp in action, he started thinking seriously about learning the craft of songwriting.

★

Fully aware of Keith's intention to get to Nashville as soon as possible, and dreaming pretty large himself, Greg Shaw learned about what was known as the Extraordinary Alien visa. Having one of these in his passport would enable Keith to move more freely within the US, rather than having to cope with the stop-start nature and work restrictions of short-term visas. But in order to apply for this special visa, the domain of artists and sportspeople, Shaw knew that Keith needed a CV that featured more than a few appearances at Tamworth and a roasting by Bernard King.

This is where Joanne Petersen entered Keith's story. She worked at the Australian branch of MCA Music Publishing—music publishing, of course, had the potential to provide a steady course of income for someone like Keith, even though he was hardly the most prolific writer. He'd taken his first stab at songwriting while still in school—'really crap poetry', as he recalled, 'probably about my girlfriend'—and had been chipping away at it ever since, most recently inspired by that Mellencamp gig. (He wrote 'Love We Got Goin'' around that time, and 'Future Plans' a while after; both would later appear on his solo debut.) Keith knew that in order to be a complete musician he needed to be involved in writing his own material.

Petersen had an interesting past—she'd been PA to Beatles manager Brian Epstein, and was married to Colin Petersen, who'd played drums in the Bee Gees, as an official band member, back in the mid-1960s. More recently, Joanne had signed INXS to a publishing deal with MCA; they were her first signing, a stellar beginning to her career. She was tipped off about Keith and went to see him play at a half-empty club. She spotted him even before he took the stage; with his wild hair and piercings, Keith was hard to miss.

Impressed by his performance, and keen to introduce herself, Petersen headed backstage but was stopped by Angie Marquis, who was with Keith at the time. This didn't deter Petersen, who intended to offer Keith a publishing deal that would enable him to go to Nashville and get in a room with some serious songwriters, to really learn the craft. Petersen duly called Greg Shaw. 'It must be fate,' he told her, because MCA was the one publisher Keith had dreamed of signing with, due to their impressive American line-up. The King himself, Elvis Presley, had been signed to MCA Music Publishing (not that he did a hell of a lot of songwriting), as were Alabama, Hank Williams Jr, Linda Ronstadt, Randy Travis, Tanya Tucker, The Judds, Crystal Gayle and Reba McEntire—it was a veritable country music all-stars.

With this publishing deal in place—a huge coup in itself, given that Keith didn't yet have a recording contract—he was one step closer to becoming an 'Extraordinary Alien'. He was also booked to take his first trip to Nashville for some co-songwriting sessions. It was 1989, Keith had just turned 21, and anything seemed possible.

★

Keith's first trip to Nashville, however, was both a huge eye-opener and one almighty reality check. The arrangement was that he'd sit down in an MCA office with a total stranger and try to write a song. This was the Nashville method that had been in place for decades, and it was rarely questioned, but it felt awkward and uncomfortable to Keith.

'It was really hard at first,' he admitted. 'A windowless room, a couple of legal pads, a stranger. I'd never written that way before.'

Keith was teamed with three rock-solid Nashville writers. Gary Burr had written Juice Newton's hit 'Love's Been a Little Bit Hard on Me', and also had his songs recorded by George Jones and Randy Travis. Trey Bruce, meanwhile, had just started out, but over time his songs were 'cut' by Trisha Yearwood, Faith Hill and Reba McEntire. As for Dave Loggins, he'd briefly been a pop star himself, nominated for the 1975 Male Pop Vocal Performance Grammy for his hit 'Please Come to Boston'.

In strictly creative terms, not much came from this first visit, apart from a co-write with Burr named 'What Love Is That Way', which would turn up on Keith's solo debut in a few years' time. Dave Loggins, meanwhile, impressed Keith with his tales of hanging out with Beatle John Lennon at the Grammys and writing with Kenny Rogers at the legend's ranch. But Keith learned some key lessons: to succeed in Music City he needed to adapt. He mightn't have felt comfortable writing with a stranger, but that's how it was done in Nashville.

Despite his nonconformist appearance, Keith was willing to play the game—and he couldn't wait to get back to Nashville, despite a lack of encouragement from some quarters. Not too long after returning to Australia, Keith was playing a festival when he bumped into a musician who'd also tried his luck in the US. He spoke backstage with Keith about the experience, dismissing it all with a wave of his hand.

'Yeah, you've got to get it out of your system, don't you?'

Keith was incensed. Fortunately, he was a lover not a fighter because, as he admitted, 'I could have punched him. I felt so infuriated. It was the antithesis of what I felt.'

It only made Keith more determined to succeed in the States. But there was still a lot of business to attend to in Australia.

*

On the Australia Day long weekend in 1990, Keith made his annual pilgrimage to Tamworth, this time taking the trip in a cheap campervan that he was paying off. He planned to compete in the Star Maker competition, a talent quest that was one of Tamworth's key events. He arrived late at night and, while driving in the town's back streets, spotted a power outlet at the rear of a shop. Keith pulled over, plugged in and settled in for a night's sleep, trying to keep cool in the summer heat. He was soon awakened, however, by a loud banging on the door of his van.

'I'm unplugging you, you bastard!' a voice yelled. 'Get off my property!'

Duly busted, Keith drove straight to the site of Star Maker at the Tamworth Town Hall and spent the night in the car park. As he would recall, 'I figured if it started out this bad, it's got to get better. And it got a lot better.'

Tamworth's Country Music Festival was rapidly expanding. By 1990, it featured something like 1000 hours of live music, with more than 600 programmed events. About 30,000 country music lovers descended on the city of 35,000 during the week of the festival, generating a whopping $20 million for the local economy. It was big business.

Star Maker was an oddity in the world of talent quests. The winner received nothing in the way of cash or tangible prizes but instead received the gift of 'image and opportunity', as its organisers attested. And it was beginning to live up to its promise: one former winner was making some waves outside of the insular confines of country music. Farmer's son and Stanthorpe native James Blundell had won the event in 1987; a year later he claimed his first Golden Guitar for Best New Talent. Blundell then signed a record deal with EMI Australia, recorded a successful debut LP and would go on to win three consecutive Male Vocalist of the Year Golden Guitars. In 1990, Blundell was in the process of 'crossing over' into the mainstream, a feat that had last been achieved by Slim Dusty's 'Duncan', a number 1 hit in the pop charts way back in 1980.

At the 1990 Star Maker, Smoky Dawson had the task of introducing the 'stars of tomorrow' (his words). Keith was the third act on the bill and, not surprisingly, didn't look one bit like his fellow contestants. He was wearing his hair in a sort of brush-cut mullet, which added an extra inch or two to his height; at a glance he could have passed for James

Reyne's kid brother. He played an original song, 'I Never Work on a Sunday', and the flashy guitar licks he unleashed were as uncommon on the Star Maker stage that year as his dangerously tight blue jeans. Keith Urban was not your typical country hopeful—far from it.

His rivals were an odd mix of big-haired female belters and earnest male vocalists, among them Troy Cassar-Daley, straight out of Grafton, a twenty-year-old with a Maltese/Aboriginal background and a strong, twangy voice. Another contender, Sam West, wore a fierce moustache and displayed an even fiercer determination to come on like an Aussie Johnny Cash. Sporting an equally fearsome mo was 1989 Star Maker winner Craig Robertson, who stepped up to entertain the full house while the five judges retired to compare their notes.

Keith's parents were in the hall awaiting the announcement. It was all too much for Marienne, who rested her head on Bob's shoulder and covered her eyes. 'I can't look,' she whispered, as Westpac exec Dennis Price stepped up to the podium, envelope in hand. When Price read out Keith's name, proclaiming him the winner, Keith was mobbed by his fellow contestants and was covered in lipstick by the time he reached the microphone, grinning broadly. At the back of the room, Marienne burst into tears.

'Man, oh man,' Keith said, genuinely thrilled. 'What can I say? First of all, there wasn't five or so judges here, there was a thousand and five, as you all know,' he began, acknowledging the crowd inside the Town Hall. 'Actually Westpac, I'd like to say thank you, too—they gave me my first car loan about three years ago . . . and I've nearly paid it off, too!' Keith laughed; the crowd laughed. It was a love-in.

Keith went on to thank Greg Shaw, Angie Marquis, his parents 'and a lot of people who have helped me. You don't know them, but they know who they are . . . This is the end to a lot of hard work and the start of a hell of a lot more . . . so hopefully you will hear from me very soon.'

The next morning, Keith posed by the Peel River for photographer June Underwood, proudly cradling his Star Maker certificate.

The win gained Keith coverage in the mainstream city press. 'Australian country music found itself a new sex symbol this week,' gushed Sydney's *Sun-Herald*, 'when a smouldering young singer from Brisbane took out the 1990 Westpac Star Maker Quest.'

A 'sex symbol'? Things really were looking up.

4

'I hope you come back to Nashville and find a home here'

Keith's next big break took place at a near-empty Bayview Tavern, a pub in the northern Sydney suburb of Gladesville, during 1990. He was now fronting his own group called Three Magic Words, which included two ex-Rockettes: Peter Clarke playing drums, and Marlon Holden, a burly, straight-shooting Queenslander, on bass. Looking after live sound was Steve 'Flo' Law, a friend of Keith's from Caboolture (who still works with him). Keith was starting to assemble his team.

In an effort to book live work, the band had come up with a flyer talking up their peroxided frontman. 'He is a top MUSICIAN and a great ENTERTAINER,' it screamed. 'Keith is an amalgam of all that is positive in music combining strong influences from the past together with playing styles that are very much part of today.'

Looking on at the Gladesville pub that night was Brian Harris, the head of EMI Australia, which was the home of recent ARIA Hall of Fame inductee Slim Dusty and breakout star James Blundell. 'There were maybe two people there,' Harris recalled, 'but Keith was up there playing his heart out. When I first saw him play, I knew he had a great deal of talent but was very raw and needed a lot of guidance,' said the now retired label head. 'I always considered Keith more rock and roll. I felt sure that one day he'd "cross over" into the mainstream. He was a brilliant young talent who could have gone in any direction.'

Harris spoke with Keith and soon enough offered him a record deal.

Another big supporter of Keith's at EMI was Rob Walker, a wiry, good-natured Kiwi with a thing for the books of Cormac McCarthy and petrol-hungry American cars. Walker was head of A&R and had been with the company since 1970. He'd caught Keith playing in Tamworth back when he was still part of California Suite.

EMI's biggest act at the time of Keith's signing was Crowded House, who'd blitzed international charts a few years earlier with the classic 'Don't Dream It's Over'.

James Blundell, Keith's new labelmate at EMI, readily admitted that 'a healthy mutual regard bordering on competitiveness' existed between him and Keith, even though Blundell was a few steps further along with his career, having by then released two (charting) albums.

One of Greg Shaw's first moves was to ensure that those in charge at EMI knew about Keith's Nashville plans. 'Greg used to drive me nuts about it,' said Brian Harris. 'But he played a massive role. Keith was quiet, understated, not a good schmoozer. Greg did that hard work. He also loaned Keith a lot of money, financing him all the way along.'

Keith's first appearance as an EMI artist was on the compilation *Breaking Ground: New Directions in Australian Country Music*, which appeared in late 1990, singing 'There's a Light On'. Also on the record were James Blundell, Anne Kirkpatrick (daughter of Slim Dusty), The Happening Thang and Mary-Jo Starr (aka Kaarin Fairfax, who'd later marry singer-songwriter Paul Kelly). The twelve-track LP was nominated for the Album of the Year Golden Guitar, and even though it didn't win it was a big rap for the up-and-comers who contributed. It was the first small step for Keith Urban, recording artist.

Keith also appeared in a low-budget video for 'I Never Work on a Sunday', a super simple clip, blending live perfor-mance shots with footage of Keith at the wheel of a Ford ute, shades on, fanging down some outback track. It was intercut with images of Keith mixing it up with female fans at sound-check, who enthusiastically clapped along as the band played. Casting was easy—there were always women in the audience at Keith Urban shows.

Keith and Shaw had put together a demo tape—which Keith naively thought was 'pretty good'—which they took with them on their next trip to Nashville. In between more co-writing sessions, the pair covered the length and breadth of Music Row, playing the demo to every record company who'd take a meeting with them. (Keith's deal with EMI was for Australia only.) Despite Keith's enthusiasm about the demo, the response was a resounding 'no' from everyone they met.

However, when Keith was back in Australia, he received

a letter that held the key to his future. It was from a woman named Mary Martin, a renowned talent scout from RCA, who worked with such highly rated acts as Rodney Crowell and Emmylou Harris. But Martin's biggest claim to fame was that in the 1960s she had advised Bob Dylan's manager, Albert Grossman, about four Canadians and an Oklahoman who called themselves The Band, who went on to record two remarkable albums that formed the cornerstones of the style now known as Americana. Martin was a great person to know.

Martin's frank letter to Keith displayed the type of pragmatism only gained after three decades in the industry. Timing, she assured Keith, was crucial. 'I listened to your music and really enjoyed it,' Martin wrote. 'Unfortunately, country is enjoying a traditional time at the moment'—the so-called New Traditionalists, led by stony-faced crooner Randy Travis, were all over Nashville and country radio, while Garth Brooks had just signed to Capitol Nashville— '[and although] I feel your music doesn't fit . . . I hope you come back to Nashville and find a home here.'

Keith didn't feel rejected; in fact, he felt encouraged by her comments. 'What I read from her letter was "Come here and when the pendulum swings, you'll be in the right place,"' he said. 'To me it meant: stick to your guns and be patient.'

*

Keith had recently played one of his stranger shows in Tamworth. The deal for the one-off gig, arranged by an airline, was attractive enough—he and the band would get a free ticket in exchange for playing a few songs. It all seemed reasonable enough, a standard contra gig. When they reached Tamworth airport, which was essentially a small terminal (or a big shed) with one baggage carousel and a snack bar, they were met by a rep from the airline.

'Where's the gig?' Keith asked.

'Right here,' he was told. 'In the terminal.' In fact, the 'stage' was on top of the baggage carousel.

'Okay,' replied Keith, now a little uneasy. 'When do we start?'

'Well, now,' replied the rep. 'If you could.'

Keith, drummer Clarke and bassist Holden reluctantly set up on top of the baggage carousel—not an easy task—after being reassured that a few people would eventually show up. The gig seemed to be going far better than Keith could have expected—a small crowd had gathered—when suddenly the baggage carousel stirred into life, accompanied by a loud beeping noise, which almost drowned out the band. Screw it, Keith figured, so he jumped on the carousel and played a solo while travellers collected their luggage.

His next trip to the land of the Golden Guitars was far more productive. It was the Australia Day long weekend of 1991 and Keith was in the running for the Best New Talent gong, also known as the Horizon Award, for his song 'I Never Work on a Sunday', which had been released as his first single by EMI a few months prior. Keith, typically, dressed for the event: tonight he was wearing a tailored, candy-apple-red jacket, with black brocade on the front and back. His blue jeans were sprayed on, while his bleached mullet was sculpted into a quiff so high it threatened to get tangled in the ceiling fans of the Tamworth Town Hall. When Anne Kirkpatrick read out his name, the look on Keith's face was of pure bliss.

It was his first Golden Guitar—and another step in the direction of that Extraordinary Alien visa he so craved.

Keith wasn't afraid to speak his mind when asked about his success at Tamworth: 'I think's it a good sign that the conservatism of Tamworth is starting to shut down now.'

*

Keith was ready to record his debut album. He was part-nered with producer Peter Blyton (known to his friends as Huggy, an especially apt nickname after he'd had a few drinks). On paper it appeared an unlikely alliance, because Blyton had recently worked with pub rockers the Radiators and the Choirboys (Blyton co-produced their 1987 hit 'Run to Paradise'), as well as Max Q, the avant-garde side project of INXS's Michael Hutchence. But there was a connection: Blyton was a Brisbane native and a good friend of Greg Shaw. And the 32-year-old was hungry for the work.

'I was very young and kind of thrown into that produc-tion,' he said, 'but I wanted to get more work with the majors . . . even though I'd never done country before.'

Blyton had seen Keith play at Shaw's venue General Jacksons, and like so many Urban first-timers he had been blown away. 'The guy had the voice of an angel and he could play guitar like Tommy Emmanuel. He had spiky blonde hair, a pimply face and was skinny as a rake . . . He was playing rock covers, but he had this country yearning.'

Blyton negotiated for the album to be recorded at Starsound Studios at Channel 9 in Brisbane, even though the studio typically didn't take in 'outside work'. There were stipulations: Blyton was told there'd be no drinking or smoking in the facility—quite a challenge given that most albums are created on a diet of booze, tobacco and caffeine. But just as the players and the crew set up, Blyton got a call—the original album budget of $64,000 had been cut in half, in the wake of the departure of Rob Walker, Keith's main man in A&R. And the album would now be recorded at EMI's Studios 301 in Sydney.

Most of the original musicians were let go. In the end, Blyton played a lot of parts on the record because, as he explained, 'There was no one else but Keith and I there, with the drummer and two old mongrel dogs. Everything was hurried and rushed, and we were ushered from the big studio in 301 to the little studio they used for overdubs. We had to make silk purses out of sows' ears.' Blyton was paid just $2500 for his work on the album.

Keith may have been a studio newbie, but he flexed a little muscle during the production, according to his keyboardist Glen Muirhead, who played on most of the album. 'He rode Peter pretty hard; he pushed to get his way. I never saw any conflict, but Keith wasn't sitting back while Peter ran the show. He was right alongside him, pushing buttons and sending directions back into the studio, almost as much as Peter did.' As the sessions continued, those working on the record came up with a tag for Keith's blend of melodic, twangy country and rock and roll—they called it 'saddlepop'.

'He's always had this thing where he was never hardcore country; he's been able to skip across genres,' said Dragon co-founder Todd Hunter, who played on the album's opening track, 'Only You', which he co-wrote with his wife Johanna Pigott. Hunter admitted that the nearest he'd come to country music was singing Glen Campbell songs on the school bus with his brother Marc, but he liked the music Keith was creating. They'd work together again in the future.

Guitarist Kirk Lorange also appeared on the album. He played in a band called Chasin the Train, which held down a residency at the Bayview Tavern, where Keith had been scouted by Brian Harris. Keith was a Chasin the Train fan and was in the audience at a lot of their shows, making himself known to Lorange. 'He was very outgoing, very charming and always smiling, full of energy,' said Lorange.

Soon after the album sessions, Lorange bumped into Keith on the main street of Crows Nest, his face smeared with pancake make-up. Lorange wondered whether Keith had some dark secret that he'd just let out of the bag. Not quite. It turned out that he'd come straight from a recording of *Midday* at nearby Willoughby and had forgotten the face wipes. Not that Keith minded the attention from passers-by, Lorange admitted. 'I'm sure the people wondered,' he said, 'but I think Keith would have been okay with them staring.'

In fact, TV was kind to Keith Urban; he was becoming a familiar face to fans of the small screen. In 1991 alone, he appeared twice on Steve Vizard's *Tonight Live* and twice on the Ray Martin–hosted *Midday* program, singing 'Love We Got Goin'', and a cover of Charlie Daniels' 'The Devil Went Down to Georgia', looking every inch the rocker with his unbuttoned vest and shoulder-length hair. Keith played 'Got It Bad' on *Hey Hey It's Saturday*, dressed in an over-sized red, black and gold shirt, backed by the show's house band: brass section, Red Symons, the works. It seemed to be a conscious effort to set Keith apart from the usual Tamworth crowd, something he touched on when he spoke with a reporter from *The Sun-Herald*. 'You could hardly categorise me as a country and western plucker,' he stated, which was fair enough.

But while he may have been making inroads into the lounge rooms of Australia, the same couldn't be said for his self-titled debut album. When he was interviewed by Channel 9's Richard Carleton at the time of its release, Keith was introduced 'as one of the fastest moving stars around at the moment', but *Keith Urban*, which was released in October 1991, barely made a dent in the Australian mainstream album chart, scraping into the Top 100 and selling just a few thousand copies.

Four singles were lifted from the album; each did well in the local country charts but went nowhere in the Top 40. 'It seemed to us that EMI did everything in their power to knock this on the head,' said Peter Blyton. 'Even the fucking artwork is bad.' The overriding impression was that Keith wasn't EMI's highest priority.

Still, there were some funny moments during the making of the album. Blyton had persuaded Keith to cover the Sutherland Brothers' 1976 hit 'Arms of Mary', one of the producer's favourite songs, as a last-minute addition to the LP. One night, Keith, Blyton and Shaw headed out on a boozy night; when they returned to Blyton's home they discovered that his wife, Kirsty Meares, had locked him out.

Blyton retrieved a guitar from his car and spoke with Keith.

'Play the song,' he slurred.

'What song?' asked Keith.

'Arms of Mary.'

Keith duly did as directed, a spell was cast, Blyton was

welcomed back inside with open arms, and Keith and Shaw laughed all the way back to their hotel.

When Keith turned 24 on 26 October, he celebrated by getting a tattoo of an eagle. 'My freedom at the time was America,' he explained, 'so I felt the eagle was appropriate.' The symbolism couldn't be ignored: Keith was ready to fly.

★

When Keith won his next Golden Guitar, for Best Male Vocalist, in January 1992, his friendly rival and EMI label-mate James Blundell had already struck out for the States. Blundell's second album, *Hand It Down*, had gained a US release in 1991, a first for a contemporary Australian country musician. He'd settle in Music City for a year, and it would be the strangest twelve months of his career. Perhaps his life.

Just like Keith, James Blundell went through the rite of passage that was co-writing Nashville style. He had some productive sessions but hit a brick wall by the name of Skip Ewing (who'd later write hits with Keith). As they chipped away at a song that Blundell thought had real potential, Ewing cut him off.

'No, that won't fly,' he said bluntly. 'They won't play that on radio.'

'How about we just write the song,' Blundell suggested, 'and worry about that afterwards?'

That didn't work for Ewing, who instead suggested that Blundell write another 'Way Out West', which had been a hit for Blundell and James Reyne that reached number 2 in Australia in April that year. That was enough for Blundell, because he didn't actually write the song. 'I realised that there are two very different schools in Nashville,' he said. 'One is the artist and the other is the songwriter. That was tough.'

During one particularly unproductive recording session, Blundell was bluntly advised about his 'shortcomings'. 'I was in the studio with an engineer one day and he told me that I was getting criticism, because I didn't sound like I came from there,' said Blundell. 'I said, "No, mate, I come from a completely different part of the world."' Blundell agreed to an experiment: he'd take a crack at singing in an American accent. That didn't play out well, as Blundell recalled: 'He stopped me quickly and said, "I take your point."'

Keith, however, was a different character to Blundell. He knew and loved the Nashville songbook, the songs of Glen Campbell and Charley Pride and Charlie Daniels, and was far more willing to play the Nashville game than Blundell. Whereas Blundell genuinely thought he could succeed with a style that drew a lot more from the Australian character.

While in Nashville, Blundell made a discovery that would almost be the undoing of Keith Urban. 'There is more sex, drugs and rock and roll in Nashville than in any other city I've been to,' Blundell admitted. Crack cocaine use and abuse were widespread. Keith was about to learn this first-hand, because during 1992 his Extraordinary Alien visa was finally granted.

★

Before leaving Australia for good, Keith gained one more ally, a man with such a following that he was considered an icon of the bush—and he had an MBE to prove it. Keith had first met Slim Dusty at Tamworth during a visit in 1977 for the 2TM Roll of Renown. Keith worked up the courage to ask Dusty to autograph his copy of the sheet music for 'Lights on the Hill', a song that, in Keith's words, was so good it was 'bulletproof'. Now Dusty invited Keith and Peter Clarke to go on tour with him as his opening act, partly on the strength of Keith's electrified cover of 'Lights on the Hill', which Dusty had heard and admired (as did Joy McKean, who wrote the song). Keith and Dusty had just re-recorded the song as a duet, after a request from Greg Shaw. As McKean recalled, 'It was a big ask but Slim had no real hesitation in agreeing to do it. Not long after we took Keith on a short tour with us.'

Despite Slim's blessing, it seemed a highly unlikely pairing: the everyman in the slouch hat who sang about downing beers with a bloke named Duncan, who was the go-to fella for truckers and farmers, mixing it up with a bleached-blond country rocker with multiple earrings, shoulder-length hair and a thing for John Mellencamp. Yet Dusty had a history of helping out artists he felt had something special, who he could offer a leg up. He knew it was a tough road to the top, having done thousands of gigs himself in rural dust-specks over the previous 50-odd years. And he liked Keith.

'It just so happened that Slim and Keith hit it off,' said Nick Erby, an influential figure in Tamworth and host of the syndicated weekly radio program *Country Music Jamboree* for twenty years. 'Slim had immeasurable respect for the young- sters like Keith who were taking the music forward . . . Slim had been in that position.' And, as Erby pointed out, what started out as a business relationship eventually grew into something more personal: 'Their mutual admiration developed into friendship.' Both enjoyed a beer, which didn't hurt, either.

'I know Slim was amused at Keith's "way out" attitude and appearance,' wrote Joy McKean in an email. 'And coupled as it was with his obvious talent and drive, it made us notice him. The whole establishment "noticed" Keith when he made his appearance on the [Tamworth] awards one year wearing cut-off jeans as shorts during his act. We were not quite as shocked as most others, actually.'

But the shows with Dusty presented a problem. Keith just wasn't sure that Slim Dusty audiences were ready for his high-voltage performances, so he cut down on the screaming solos and rockier moves. After a few gigs Keith spoke candidly with the headliner. This was a six-week run, and Keith was concerned.

'Slim, I don't think I can stay on the tour,' Keith admitted. 'It's a bit, I don't know, *boring*.'

Dusty looked surprised and asked Keith if he was doing his regular set. Keith admitted that, no, he was toning things down for Slim's audience.

Dusty told Keith to go on stage and be himself. 'Don't hold back,' he told him in parting. He knew his audiences—if Dusty had hired an up-and-comer to open his shows, they would at least give Keith a listen.

The very next night, as Keith admitted in an interview with *A Current Affair* in 2001, he cut loose and won over the audience. 'We went nuts and the crowd loved it,' he remembered—and the crowd loved it even more so when Keith and Peter Clarke joined Dusty on stage and rocked 'Lights on the Hill'.

Afterwards, Keith caught up with Dusty, who couldn't hide his delight.

'Slim,' he recalled, 'was grinning from ear to ear.'

5

Down and out at the
Lucky Snapper

Keith's odyssey to the States, which began in earnest in April 1992, came with a caveat: money was tight. Very tight. EMI's Brian Harris advanced Keith $50,000 from his record deal to help establish himself. ('And we didn't get the money back for a long time,' laughed Harris.) In Australia, Keith had been part of a five-piece band, but Team Urban simply couldn't afford to bring them all to the States, so Keith agreed to strip things back to the essentials: guitar, bass and drums. Marlon Holden and Peter Clarke, plus manager Greg Shaw, would travel with Keith. That was it.

One of Keith's first American gigs as a fully fledged 'Extraordinary Alien' was at the Exit/In, a Nashville venue famous for being, among many things, the site where country great George 'Possum' Jones allegedly crashed through the front doors astride his ride-on lawnmower. A big boozer, Jones had his car keys taken away from him, so he opted for the next best mode of transport. (Another version of the story had Jones driving his ride-on some fifteen kilometres, from Vidor to Beaumont in southern Texas, in search of a bottle shop.)

Keith's gig was part of a showcase put on for Jimmy Bowen, the heavy-hitting industry exec (and former teen rockabilly star) who was head of MCA Records. Sitting alongside Bowen was none other than James Blundell, fast approaching the end of his failed Nashville adventure. As Keith played, Bowen turned to Blundell.

'So what do you think?' he asked.

'The guy is monstrously talented,' Blundell told him without hesitation, 'but I don't know how he's going to go. He's a strong character and has a unique style of music.'

He had a point: Keith was more way rock and roll than the leading lights of the so-called 'hat acts' dominating country music, stars like Garth Brooks, Alan Jackson and Clint Black. Bowen nodded and turned back to watch him play. As the gig rolled on, Blundell came to a realisation. 'That's where I really clocked the fact that Keith had committed to staying in Nashville and was going to succeed, come hell or high water,' Blundell said, 'and it very near did fucking kill him.'

Also at that Exit/In gig was the former Jewel Blanch, now Jewel Coburn, who'd shared a stage with Keith way back in 1981 at Tamworth, when she won her first Golden Guitar. Jewel, along with her Kiwi husband Barry Coburn, now ran Ten Ten, a leading Nashville-based management and publishing company. Barry had once managed Split Enz, and one of Ten Ten's star clients was lanky, laconic Georgia native Alan Jackson, whose 1992 album, the tongue-twisting *A Lot About Livin' (And a Little 'Bout Love)*, would shift six million units. The Coburns were players, even though they preferred to think of their business as a sort of musical 'mom and pop store'—relaxed and very client friendly.

'I guess because we're a husband-and-wife team it's always had a family vibe,' said Jewel. 'It's a little like a corner shop, I guess.'

Jewel hadn't seen Keith much for the past decade and was blown away by his Exit/In performance. 'It was amazing,' she recalled. But she wondered, as James Blundell had, how Keith would fit in the country scene. 'There was no Rascal Flatts or Shania Twain; he was ahead of his time,' said Coburn. 'Barry was going, "Oh, this guy is going to be a superstar." I thought, "You're probably right, but I think he's just too pop for Nashville; I don't think they'll accept him, being Australian yet almost English in his pop sensibilities." I just couldn't see Nashville going for it.'

Keith and the Coburns would reconnect in time. Also working at Ten Ten was another expat Aussie, record producer Mark Moffatt, who was the company's director of A&R. He, too, would one day work with Keith.

★

Keith may have been a very square peg in the well-rounded country mainstream, but he couldn't have picked a better time to relocate to Nashville. In strictly commercial terms, it was boom time in Music City. Garth Brooks, a 30-year-old advertising grad from Oklahoma State with a thing for the music of Billy Joel and undeniable marketing savvy, was in the midst of a staggeringly successful run. *Ropin' the Wind*, his third LP, which had been released in September 1991, was the first country album to debut at number 1 on the *Billboard* 200.

Ropin' the Wind would eventually sell fourteen million copies in the US alone and became a hit worldwide, everywhere from Ireland to Spain, Zimbabwe to Norway. It also reached the mainstream Top 20 in Australia. Brooks' next album, *The Chase*, which dropped in September 1992, did almost as well, selling a handy ten million copies. Brooks' two albums spent a total of 31 weeks atop the country chart during 1992 alone. Brooks also brought a little rock-and-roll flash to his now arena-sized shows. The nightly smashing of a guitar was straight out of the Pete Townshend playbook, while the on-stage pyrotechnics were more commonly seen at rock-and-roll gigs.

Brooks' heady success was known as Garth Mania, a term that harked back to the heyday of The Beatles. And Brooks would play a role in Keith's gradual rise to the top.

But Brooks wasn't working in isolation. Billy Ray Cyrus was a handsome hunk from Flatwood, Kentucky; he was the voice, the mullet and the bulging pecs behind 'Achy Breaky Heart', a smash hit that revitalised linedancing. Cyrus's 1992 album *Some Gave All* was number 1 in the country chart for four months, from June to October, and would go on to sell nine million copies. Wynonna Judd and Trisha Yearwood also had banner years, releasing their own platinum-plus LPs. Country Music Television, Nashville's answer to MTV, proved so popular that a CMT Europe was launched in 1992.

By 1993, country had also become the prominent radio format in the USA, with more than 2500 stations reaching twenty million more listeners than its nearest rival, 'adult contemporary'. And country wasn't a Nashville-only phenomenon; it was the top-rated format in cities such as Seattle, Baltimore, San Diego and Buffalo. (By 1995, country album sales had surpassed US$2 billion annually in the USA.)

While country music may have been the music of the moment, Keith still had to start at the very bottom—more specifically, at the Lucky Snapper, a recently opened water-front bar and grill in Destin, Florida, where Keith, Holden and Clarke secured their first residency. The venue was run by none other than Rusty Hammerstrom, the trio's former bandleader when they were the Rockettes. Hammerstrom had left Australia in 1991 and, as a musician, host and racon-teur, had become a cult figure among the Destin locals, many of whom referred to themselves as 'Hammerheads'.

As the house band, Keith, Clarke and Holden played the Lucky Snapper five nights a week, then drove the 700 kilo-metres back to Nashville for showcase gigs on the weekend. 'Like every band,' said Keith, 'we'd blow our money on a showcase, we wouldn't get a bite, and then we'd go back to Destin and go back to work again.'

The grind proved too much for Marlon Holden, who handed in his notice during the month that he and the others spent in Destin. The Lucky Snapper hadn't lived up to its name, at least as far as Holden was concerned. An American player named Richie Compton was brought in as a replace-ment, but he didn't last long.

Enter Jerry Flowers.

Flowers was a recent transplant to Nashville, hailing from Pinch, West Virginia. He was a towering twenty-something with a sharp crew cut who rolled up to audition with Keith and Peter Clarke after a tip from a mutual friend. While he admitted that he was more a rock and roller than a country guy—his first-ever gig was Van Halen, in 1984, when they were at their hard-rocking peak—Flowers liked what Keith was doing, what he described as 'country but really aggressive'. 'He looks like he'd kill you in a heartbeat, but he's such a gentle soul,' said James Blundell, who got to know Flowers well. 'And he's one of the best bass players on the planet.'

Flowers was the first to audition for the bass player's spot—and Keith and Peter Clarke were sold straightaway.

'Do you have a passport?' Keith asked him.

'Passport?' Flowers asked. 'Why? Where am I going?'

'Australia,' said Keith. 'Next week.'

Keith wasn't kidding around. In order to top up their bank balance, Greg Shaw had organised a month of dates back in Australia. As it turned out, that one month stretched into four, and the tour was the making of the power trio that became The Ranch. They played anywhere they could land a gig, hit-and-run style, living out of a van, getting to know each other personally and musically. One booking took them to, of all places, Australia's Wonderland, a pseudo-American theme park on the suburban fringe of Sydney.

Glen Muirhead, who'd played keyboards with Keith before he left for Nashville, checked out the new line-up. 'It was rainy, and there was bugger-all people there,' Muirhead remembered, 'but I watched them and thought, "Why isn't this guy big?" I thought that a lot during the gig: *Why isn't he huge?*" I was gobsmacked by them.'

*

Jerry Flowers was a perfect fit, that was beyond doubt, but when they returned to Nashville in 1993, Keith and the band were back to where they started: nowhere in particular. When Keith's Aussie friends called and asked about his progress, he'd reply, 'We're cutting this week,' which gave the impression they were in the studio. Then he'd add, a little reluctantly: 'Cutting *lawns*.' (They also painted houses.)

Admittedly, Keith didn't do a lot of the mowing work— that was for the other guys in the band and Greg Shaw. But it was hard going. The band came up with a term for it, as Keith reported in a letter he wrote to Slim Dusty: when things were tough, they were 'doing a starve'.

In 1994, Keith played Jewel Coburn some very rough demos of his new band, and she came to Keith's rescue, offering him a publishing deal with Ten Ten. (His old MCA deal had long expired.) As Jewel recalled, 'When he came to us about a publishing deal, we said yes straightaway. We totally believed in him and his ability, but we also knew it may take a while. I still had my doubts about him being too pop for Nashville. But we signed him as a writer and he developed really well.'

But Jewel harboured a suspicion that Keith might be a solo act in waiting. 'Even though [The Ranch] was great, I sometimes wondered why he decided to be with them rather than be a solo act. Obviously, he was very loyal to those guys. I think in a way he felt more comfortable in the band because he didn't have to be out front as much; he was part of a band.'

The Coburns teamed Keith with some solid Nashville writers, more than a dozen over time, including Harley Allen, who'd written for Garth Brooks, Alan Jackson and George Jones. They also provided a place—the Ten Ten offices, located at Music Square West—where Keith could hang out, unwind and try to plot his next move. But just as importantly, the Coburns put Keith on a weekly wage. He desperately needed the cash because he was slowly succumbing to his darker urges.

'I was just lost and confused,' Keith admitted in a 2002 interview with Australian *60 Minutes*. 'I had no idea what I was doing, just kind of wandered around aimlessly for a while. I found a deviation in [drugs].' Keith was angered by his lack of momentum, so much so that booze and cocaine became his 'deviations' of choice. 'I thought [Nashville would] be like a small little town, easy to get around in . . . I was expecting a little quicker acceptance. That didn't happen. It was frustrating, and I kept thinking, "Boy, I didn't think it would be *this* hard."

'I think, in hindsight, I have a tendency to get depressed to the point where I find solace in less-than-healthy things.'

Keith was house sharing in a dodgy part of town, living with a roommate who liked to freebase coke. 'And then one day he offered me this massive pipe,' Keith recalled. 'I'd never had it, it looked good, so I took it. Things didn't immediately go pear-shaped, but that was the beginning of it.'

Keith's love life was equally torturous. One day he was on the phone with a woman he'd been seeing, who was trying to break up with him.

'What the hell?' Keith asked, genuinely confused. 'What's happened?'

'For fuck's sake,' she told him, 'can't you see that the novelty of you has worn off?'

As he would tell US *Rolling Stone* in 2016, 'I was feeling insecure, and the fact that me and my accent would be a novelty to somebody cut me to the core. Oh, my God. Really bad. It devastated me. It was a turning point. After that, shit started to really go awry.'

★

There was one escape from Keith's various crises, and that was to hit the road, which The Ranch did frequently, as 1994 bled into 1995. They'd hire a fifteen-seater van, remove the back seat and load all their gear in. The driving would be shared between the band and a tour manager, who travelled with them. Often they'd clock up as many as 16,000 kilometres in a month. Drummer Clarke had acquired a US working visa, which allowed them to stay on the road.

Touring took them to some strange places, such as the Dingo Bar in Albuquerque, New Mexico, an alt-rock dive that was not suited to a band being touted as 'the country Police'. As the band set up to play, they counted six people in the room. After a few songs, the only people who remained were the barman and the manager, who were shooting pool. Keith looked at the others, they shrugged, stopped playing, packed up their gear and drove off into the night. It was a long way from Nashville, too—almost 2000 kilometres.

There was a Ranch gig at the Boston venue Mama Kin that drew a similar-sized audience—about ten people this time. 'But it was a rowdy crowd,' Keith insisted. Wilbert's in Cleveland was another eminently forgettable and very empty gig. Things improved, at least for Keith, when The Ranch played the Mercury Lounge in New York. After their set, Keith got to chatting with a member of the opening act.

'We talked for ages,' Keith recalled, 'and he just loved the band.'

Keith mentioned Glen Campbell, and how much he admired those classic songs like 'Galveston' and 'By the Time I Get to Phoenix'.

'That's funny,' came the reply. 'That's my godfather.'

It turned out that Keith was speaking with Christiaan Webb, the son of master songwriter Jimmy Webb, who'd composed some of Campbell's biggest hits. Keith was flabbergasted.

Back in Nashville, The Ranch found regular gigs at such venues as 12th & Porter and Jack's Guitar Bar. They weren't making much money, and they seemed to be treading water career-wise, but there was simply no way Keith was giving in, and the others bought into his determination. 'I was just full of that blind faith,' Keith said of the time. 'I was just absolutely committed; I had no intentions of failing. [But] I didn't realise it would take so long, and I'm glad that I didn't.'

To their credit, The Ranch began pulling crowds to the small rooms they were playing—mostly fellow musos, although there was no shortage of female fans, either. ('The place was full of young girls,' remembered Tommy Emmanuel.) Word had spread about this power-rock country trio fronted by a flashy guitarist who looked nothing like the current crop of country stars. Keith described their sound as 'funktry': 'Country music with a rhythm and blues beat to it.' They'd also begun hosting Sunday afternoon jam sessions at a house on the outskirts of town, where, as one picker recalled, 'The locals would rock up in their pick-ups and Keith and the band would set up on the porch and play for hours.'

Yet when Keith spoke with his new fans afterwards, he found their reaction a bit strange. 'Musicians used to come out and see us,' Keith recalled, 'and everyone seemed to like what we were doing. But when they heard me talk, it just raised eyebrows. They thought I was a novelty.' (Not unlike the girlfriend who rejected him.)

Keith's 'Australianness' was playing against him. And it could be a real problem in a city like Nashville, which wasn't the most welcoming of places to outsiders. Why would a major label bother signing some country act from Caboolture when they had hundreds, possibly thousands, of homegrown contenders? And Keith didn't even wear a hat, let alone learned singing in the church choir, as most Nashville stars had done.

One local who had no problem with Keith's assumed short-comings, however, was 40-year-old Kix Brooks, one-half of the hugely popular combo Brooks & Dunn. Brooks was the moustachioed, hat-wearing member of the duo, who were in the midst of a major hot streak. Their 1994 album *Waitin' on Sundown* had just produced three country number 1 hits, and they'd graduated to playing 20,000-seat arenas.

One night, Brooks appeared unannounced at Jack's, dressed immaculately—Keith couldn't miss him when he took a seat near the front of the stage and watched The Ranch play. Afterwards he came backstage and offered the band a Brooks & Dunn support slot. Keith smiled and laughed it off, figuring it was never going to happen. Not in a million years.

But the call did come through, and the gig provided Keith with an eye-opening introduction to life at the top. Keith and the band, plus one sound guy, squeezed into their rented van and rolled up to the arena, parking backstage alongside the two huge, fully customised coaches in which

Brooks & Dunn travelled, their smiling faces painted on the side. Keith felt way out of his league, even more so when he witnessed the big-budget spectacle that was a Brooks & Dunn show—for starters, they entered the arena in racing cars. Yet Brooks was, as Keith recalled in a 2013 interview with Bobby Bones, 'such a class act'. Playing to a huge audience was a giant leap forward from Jack's, but it proved to be just the first step up the ladder for Keith and The Ranch.

*

Keith was still without a US record deal, but in 1995 that was about to change. Brian Harris, the former head of EMI Australia who'd first given Keith a recording contract (and loaned him some serious cash to set up in Nashville), had been reaching out to his American connections, urging them to sign Keith.

Another key player now entered the frame. Bob Saporiti was the senior VP of international marketing at Warner Bros, having joined the company in 1984. Saporiti was also a musician and a big fan of Keith's playing, which he described as 'a cross between Albert Lee and Alvin Lee, with a bit of Mark Knopfler thrown in'. Saporiti was aware of the hard luck Keith had endured in recent times and knew he could fully utilise it as a marketing angle. 'The whole painting houses, mowing lawns thing—as a marketing guy, well, you couldn't write a better script. It was like a country song, a wonderful story.'

Saporiti had seen Keith play back in Australia, at the invitation of Brian Harris; he had spent quite a bit of time drinking with Keith, Clarke and Flowers, and jamming in various hotel rooms. While in Tamworth, Saporiti got into what he called a 'knockdown, drag-out' shouting match with broadcaster Nick Erby, who'd told Saporiti that if Keith signed with an American label, he'd no longer be eligible for Golden Guitars.

As Saporiti recalled, 'I told him that it was so provincial—an American can come down here and do well, but an Australian can't go to Nashville? I told him that he had to keep rooting for this guy. I said, "You should stop this; you push these guys to get on the world stage and then you penalise them?" To his credit, that never happened. He backed down.'

Back in the States, Saporiti met with Warner's boss Eddie Reeves and discussed signing Keith. Saporiti thought Keith should be signed as a solo act, as much as he loved The Ranch, and managed to convince Reeves that was the best option. Although he'd continue working with The Ranch, Keith signed to Warner Bros as a solo artist in 1995.

But there was another complication: who, exactly, was Keith Urban? A country-pop star in the making, or a Fender-wielding rocker? Where did he fit? Reeves and Saporiti had totally different views on what path their new signing should pursue. 'I loved The Ranch, I loved the whole thing,' said Saporiti. 'My whole plan was to let it develop, just let it happen and let Keith find his own way, do his thing. [But] Eddie Reeves . . . had what turned out to be the correct vision, I have to admit. He wanted to take him more pop and was seeking outside material. It was frustrating Keith because he wanted to rock out more.'

This was the starting point of two years of abject frustration for Keith, as he set about the seemingly never-ending task of recording his debut album for Warner's. His off-stage problems—coke and booze were still part of his regime—didn't help his state of mind. Keith spent quite a bit of time at Saporiti's home, discussing what path—if any—his career should take.

'What am I doing here? What's my direction?' he'd ask Saporiti.

Due to the conflict that Saporiti had with his boss, he had no firm answers for him: 'Eddie [Reeves] and I were at such philosophical loggerheads about which way to go with Keith.'

There was also the issue of management. Despite Greg Shaw's best efforts—Saporiti referred to him as the 'world's strongest man'—he was way out of his depth in the US. Breaking an artist in Nashville was a very different thing to booking bands to play at a bar in Brisbane. Shaw also had a family back in Australia, whom he rarely saw. When he accepted that he needed help managing Keith's career, the plan was to hire Ten Ten's Barry Coburn. Keith had discussed it with Coburn, and the deal was as good as done when Keith did a U-turn and decided to sign with Miles Copeland's Firstars Management. (Copeland knew Jim Ed Norman, who was president of Warner's Nashville, Keith's label.)

Copeland had form: he'd turned power trio The Police—which featured his younger brother Stewart on drums—into a global phenomenon that sold more 75 million records and filled stadiums from Melbourne to Mumbai during a hot streak that ran from the late 1970s to their split in 1986. He saw The Ranch as a country-rock version of The Police (for a time, Keith was nicknamed 'Stang', a nod to The Police's single-named singer). But there were downsides: for one thing, Copeland was based in LA, not Nashville, and he had no track record with country acts.

One night, Keith walked into the Ten Ten office, sat down with Barry and duly dropped his bombshell.

'I've signed a management deal,' Keith announced.

Coburn was confused, given their recent conversation about representing him: 'With who?'

'Miles Copeland,' Keith replied.

Coburn had one key question: 'Does he know anything about the town?'

'Clearly,' Coburn later observed, 'the unspoken answer was "not much".'

6

'I'm probably not going to make it until tomorrow'

As 1995 rolled into 1996, and then dragged into 1997, Keith juggled his time between playing here, there and everywhere with The Ranch, and recording his never-ending album for Warner Bros. And while the business side of his career may have been complicated, it was nothing in comparison to the record Keith was trying to make.

He felt as though he was powerless, as he recalled in his 2016 interview with *Rolling Stone*. 'It was mind-blowing. We recorded some of those songs twelve times, the same song in different studios, different producers, always trying to get the right combination of radio-ready stuff.'

Stuck in what must have felt like the musical version of *Groundhog Day*, Keith, Clarke and Flowers (plus an assortment of studio players) would re-record songs endlessly, trying to fit in with what was being played on the radio, only to be informed by label execs 'that doesn't sound like you'. And this being his first Nashville album, Keith was hardly in a position to question the decisions being made.

Keith's problems were best summed up by an encounter with someone he referred to simply as a 'famous producer'. One night, after finishing a track, Keith and the band were asked: 'All right, boys, what do you want? Fiddle or steel?'

'I don't want either,' he replied.

'Look, kid,' came the reply, 'I don't make the fucking rules. You choose, fiddle or steel. I don't give a shit.'

As Keith told *Rolling Stone*, 'Those two years were full of moments like that.'

The Warner's execs would listen to works in progress, talk among themselves and then advise Keith to keep trying. 'It doesn't sound like anything on country radio,' they'd say. But at the time, Keith wondered: was that *really* a problem?

'They rejected everything we did,' Keith later admitted. He was clearly frustrated.

The actual recording of the album was equally messy—it seemed as though Keith spent time in every single studio in Nashville, and even now it's a challenge to document what was cut where and with whom. The variety of studios employed was staggering: 16th Avenue Sound, MCA Studios, Scruggs Studio, Sound Emporium, The Castle and Woodland Digital were all used, along with at least half a dozen other Nashville studios, as well as Brooklyn Studios in LA. One of Keith's best songs, 'Walkin' the Country', was cut in five different studios 'with three different producers', as Keith remembered it. There were enough players and crew on the finished album to fill out two, possibly three, soccer teams.

At least eighteen months was spent on the record; when Keith was asked how much it cost to make, he shook his head forlornly and said, simply, 'Way, way too much.' At their absolute wits' end, at one point Keith and the band decided to choose their favourite takes of individual songs, prep them as the finished album and present the package to Warner's.

'Nope,' they were advised. 'No good. Do it again.'

Vernon Rust, who co-wrote several songs on the album, was one of Keith's crew, a songwriter and fellow partier who was also a client of Miles Copeland (he had a deal with I.R.S. Songs, Copeland's music-publishing arm). Barry Coburn knew Rust pretty well, describing him as a 'wild character, almost impossible to find for long periods of time. He could be living on a farm or in his car.' (In later years, Rust lived on the street.) Bob Saporiti knew him, too. 'He was a pretty wacky guy, very right-brained, not a lot of common sense. Definitely smoked the old "herbage" too much, and that wasn't necessarily a good thing, but he was a pretty damned good writer.' Promoter Rob Potts, who worked closely with Keith, met Rust when he travelled to Australia with Keith. 'He's a wild, wild boy,' Potts said.

For a time, Rust was living in the attic of The Ranch's shared house. He'd sometimes come racing down the stairs, dressed in nothing but socks and jocks, waving lyrics and excitedly talking about a new song.

Without doubt, Keith's US debut was a chaotic record, and that chaos extended into who was actually recording the album. Keith wanted The Ranch to be properly credited because Clarke and Flowers played on the record, and they were his guys. 'We're a band,' Keith told execs from Warner's. But he got blowback on this. 'We got pushed and pulled around so much during that time,' Keith recalled. 'Everyone advised me against it: don't drop my name in favour of the band. Call it "Keith Urban *and* The Ranch". Even the band wanted to just call it that; they didn't seem overly concerned. [But] it caused me so much grief. People didn't understand that I needed my own band.' Keith fought back and insisted that the album simply be credited to The Ranch, with no mention of his name. (It was later re-released in 2004 as *Keith Urban in The Ranch*.)

Then there was more background drama. The conflict between Warner Bros' Bob Saporiti and Jim Ed Norman regarding Keith's musical direction had reached boiling point. Norman told Saporiti, 'Look, we're going to ruin this kid's career. Let's call Capitol and see if we can get some money back and let him go.' Keith was duly on-sold to Capitol Records, whose boss, Scott Hendricks, was a big fan.

★

On 15 April 1997, a week before the album was finally released, Keith and The Ranch made their Nashville TV debut on a show hosted by Shannon McCombs, who was a fan of the band. ('You guys are great live,' she told them during their chat.) After tearing into 'Walkin' the Country', Keith and the band were individually introduced by McCombs.

'This has been a long time in the coming, hasn't it?' she asked, holding up a CD of the album.

'Yes it has,' Keith said, suppressing a sigh.

McCombs spoke with Keith about how the album wasn't going to be plugged to a strictly country audience. Keith explained that they'd be playing 'a lot of different places . . . people that like Tom Petty are as likely to like this as people who like Don Williams'.

That night, The Ranch played an in-store at Tower Records in Nashville, and a week later they set out on a day trip that provided the comic relief that Keith desperately needed after the drama of making the record. They were shooting a video (two, actually) in Adams, Tennessee, a locale so small and empty it could have passed for a ghost town. The plan was simple: set up on one side of the street and shoot a clip for 'Walkin' the Country', then change their clothes and set up on the other side of the street and shoot a video for the instrumental 'Clutterbilly'. Easy, quick and cheap.

It was about nine in the morning when the camera started rolling and almost immediately a local staggered up to the crew, slugging from a jug of moonshine, 'tanked to the gills', as Keith remembered it. A few other locals gathered.

'Mind if I dance?' the man with the moonshine asked, and duly performed a lively jig for the camera. The band and crew were in stitches and they figured, what the heck, they'd make it part of the video. It turned out that the man was a retired baseball player, a local identity, and he provided the clip with more colour and quirkiness than anyone had anticipated.

*

The Ranch was not a hit record—far from it. In fact, the album gained very little attention until its 2004 re-release, by which time Keith was a star. On the week of its original release in 1997, the number 1 song on the *Billboard* country chart was George Strait's 'One Night at a Time'. Strait's LP *Carrying Your Love with Me* topped the charts for six weeks straight. As much as Keith respected big names like Strait, a man whose western shirts and blue jeans never ever seemed to crease, the two of them were nothing alike. The charts for the rest of the year were dominated by acts such as Tim McGraw and Faith Hill, country's golden couple, as well as LeAnn Rimes, Lonestar, Alan Jackson, Kenny Chesney and Garth Brooks. Shania Twain was set to explode with her huge crossover hit *Come On Over*, essentially a big splashy pop record with a twangy undercurrent. The Ranch, however, sounded like they came from another planet altogether— and their record simply didn't click for radio. And it was radio that made songs into hits.

'I'm not sure that the label knew what to do [with the record],' figured Jewel Coburn, 'and Keith was having some personal stuff . . . and that was slowing down the process.'

The chance arose for Keith and the band to play some Australian dates in September 1997. It was a respite from what wasn't happening in the US—the album wasn't selling, and the first single, 'Walkin' the Country', despite the entertaining video, made it to just number 50 in the country singles chart (although it did reach number 1 in the Australian country chart).

Perhaps Keith's frustration explained what happened when he and the band played the album track 'Desiree' on *Midday with Kerri-Anne* during their Australian visit. 'Desiree' was more a slow-burning ballad than a rocker, but Keith, his hair now a little shorter, his shirt a shimmery maroon, ripped into the type of guitar solo rarely witnessed by the grey-rinse set that dominated the show's audience. They didn't seem to mind the volume. (It was also ample proof of how musically tight The Ranch had become.)

When he spoke with the show's always effervescent host

Kerri-Anne Kennerley, Keith didn't deny that it had been a tough graft in Nashville. 'It's been hard. Initially it was a lot harder than all of us were prepared for,' he replied. 'Nashville's a place where you have to stay. You've got to go and stay there, and really show them that you're committed.'

Talk turned to a recent, rare breakthrough for Keith and the band. Country trailblazer Garth Brooks had just achieved the unimaginable: not only had he staged a concert in New York's Central Park on 7 August—hardly the epicentre of all things country—but he had managed to fill the joint. Depending on who you asked, the audience for 'Garthstock' ranged from 300,000 (mayor Rudy Giuliani's estimate) to up to a million, according to Team Garth. Either way, it was tangible proof that country had crossed over into the mainstream in a way not seen since the days of the hit movie *Urban Cowboy*.

As part of the celebration of Garth, huge screens were set up to broadcast the concert in several arenas outside of New York. The Ranch was the warm-up band for one of these satellite gigs, hosted in Birmingham, Alabama. Keith summed it up this way: 'We came out and played half an hour, 45 minutes, got the crowd all warmed up . . . It was a very indirect support but it was still lot of fun.'

This wouldn't be the last time Keith was linked with the king of country. Brooks was in the process of piecing together the performances for his first concert album, *Double Live*, which would emerge in November 1998. Even though Keith wasn't part of Brooks' live band, he was asked to overdub some guitar and was given an album credit. It was only a bit part, but you couldn't buy a better credit in country music at the time. It was another small step up the ladder for Keith.

Keith's more immediate future, however, was a little more homely, quite literally. He was about to play Caboolture, for the very first time with The Ranch. Two weeks later, Keith was back on the *Midday* set, with a huge grin on his face. How did it feel to play the Caboolture RSL, he was asked, especially given that his parents were in the audience looking on?

'It was awesome,' Keith replied. 'They turned people away at the door. It was amazing.'

The same couldn't be said when he flew back to Nashville soon after. Keith's world was about to fall apart.

*

It was early 1998. Keith was living in Franklin, about 30 kilometres south of Nashville, and found himself staring at a hefty pile of coke, set to begin another binge. 'There was no stopping this time,' Keith admitted when he summed up his meltdown in very gruesome terms in 2016.

He'd do some lines, crash, wake up a couple of hours later and start all over again, drinking to take the edge off even more. At one point, as Keith recalled, he thought to himself: 'I'm probably not going to make it until tomorrow.' And he genuinely didn't care. 'I remember thinking, "Oh, good, this is the end of it, yahoo." I was quite happy about it.'

Keith couldn't sink any lower—his record had stiffed, his personal life was in chaos and there was a comet-sized dent in his self-confidence. What was left?

Somehow, he made it through to the next day—and was surprised he was still alive. 'Guess I'm not going to get to go this way,' he said to himself, and proceeded to snort up the rest of the drugs.

Keith took to driving around Nashville with a large metal garden scythe under the seat of his car for protection. He described it as a 'psychopath's fucking tool'.

Ged Malone was Miles Copeland's right-hand man, and he witnessed Keith's issues at close range when he and the band flew to New York for a Ranch showcase, where they were supporting R&B legend Bo Diddley. In what was essentially their first conversation, Keith asked if Malone could score some coke for him. Malone said no. After the showcase, Keith was clearly agitated by something—possibly his reluctance to score. The very proactive Malone did what he felt was right. 'I grabbed him around the neck and told him that if he didn't stop, I'd punch his face in. After that,' Malone added, 'he was fine and we got on great.'

It was clear that Keith couldn't continue this way. His label, Capitol Nashville, issued a press release on 8 May 1998 stating 'Urban Under Doctor's Orders'. The statement revealed that he was suffering 'a severe throat problem' and had been advised by his doctor to 'take an immediate break from singing'. It stated that Keith's vocal cords had 'haemorrhaged' and he'd be out of action for an unspecified period. It went on to report that Keith was on a strict diet, with 'instructions to speak as infrequently as possible to assist the healing process'. There was also speculation that if his vocal cords didn't respond to treatment, 'laser surgery will be required'. Another planned Australian tour for The Ranch was put on hold; the band was now on an 'enforced break', according to the press release.

The euphemisms were being laid on thick and fast, although Keith certainly did have problems with his voice. But most seasoned reporters knew that this was a roundabout way of saying that Keith had a big problem, possibly drug-related, and would be out of commission for some time—that is, in rehab. Which proved to be the case, soon enough.

Those close to Keith, such as the Coburns and Mark Moffatt at Ten Ten, were well aware of his problems. 'Anyone fighting disappointment and self-esteem issues [could get] in trouble,' said Moffatt. He noted that Ten Ten was 'a special little family that cared very much for their own', but there were times when even they felt they'd lost Keith to the pipe.

A new Capitol press release followed three weeks after the first, in the last week of May, announcing the end of The Ranch. 'After careful consideration', it read, the band had opted 'to part ways in what is a completely amicable decision'. As for Keith, the press release revealed that he was already moving forward, 'using the time to write new material for a solo album for Capitol Records'. (Peter Clarke eventually moved back to Australia, while Jerry Flowers joined the Dixie Chicks' touring band.)

Finally, Keith took the advice of those around him and checked into a rehab facility named Cumberland Heights. It was a non-profit facility, opened in 1960, set amid 170 isolated, woody acres on the banks of the Cumberland River to the west of Nashville. Among Cumberland Heights' rules was a no-guitars policy; it was the first time Keith had been without his beloved axe since he went all Banksy and spray-painted 'Rock Fever' on the side of the family garage back in Caboolture. This time he was guitar-less for three months.

Part of Keith's Cumberland Heights treatment was coming to grips with the philosophy of the 'Twelve Steps', familiar to members of Alcoholics Anonymous, with whom Keith was later involved. The Twelve Steps became guiding lights for Keith. They included admitting to being powerless with regards to your drug of choice; believing a higher power could restore you to sanity; and making a 'searching and fearless moral inventory' of all your foibles.

While at Cumberland Heights, Keith would often call Jewel Coburn, sometimes at two or three in the morning. He'd come to rely on her a lot. Fortunately for Keith, Coburn was a good listener, because he had a lot to get off his chest. 'We'd talk about whatever he wanted to talk about,' she recalled. 'He'd ask my opinion a lot about what he should do, but I never had the answers, so I'd just listen and try to be supportive and make a suggestion if I had one. Even though he wanted help, he sort of knew inside what he wanted to do.'

When Keith discussed his musical future, Coburn did have clear and specific advice for him. She told him he needed to think about what he wanted to say as a solo artist, not as the guy out front of The Ranch. That was in the past. 'He had to develop that confidence,' said Coburn. 'I think he also went through some spiritual stuff, searching, and relationships—all sorts of things that helped him get to a point where he knew what he wanted to write about.'

If there was one key piece of advice that came out of these conversations, it was pretty simple. 'Just keep writing,' Coburn told Keith. '*Just keep writing.*'

Keith had also reached out by letter to Slim Dusty at the time The Ranch was coming undone, expressing his mixed emotions about 'going solo'.

'It was a terribly difficult decision for him to make, but in the end, it has turned out to be the correct one,' noted Dusty's wife Joy McKean. 'Slim was keeping in touch with what Keith was doing, and how he was going. In his usual way, he approved of Keith's doing what he had his heart set on no matter whether it was something Slim would do himself.

'An artist can have all the talent in the world,' continued McKean, 'but without that burning, single-channelled drive and stickability, that artist may never realise his or her full potential. Keith had all that.'

7

'Garth Brooks called
me mate!'

Keith emerged from Cumberland Heights towards the end of the northern summer in 1998. But it wasn't as though his life was somehow 'fixed'—far from it. He had problems in his romantic life. Keith's girlfriend throughout a lot of the craziness was 28-year-old Laura Sigler, who worked at a Nashville veterinary surgery. She'd been by Keith's side in Australia in January 1998 when he accepted his Golden Guitar for 'Clutterbilly' and he thanked her effusively from the stage. Keith had let it slip in an interview that he and Sigler had joined the Mile High Club. 'We wanted to see if it could be done,' he admitted. 'And it can. But boy, you need to be supple.' He'd written a song named 'I Thought You Knew' that was inspired by Sigler and a flashpoint in their relationship when she fled with a friend to Canada when things turned particularly toxic. (Keith tracked her down and called her, convincing her to return.)

Keith had even proposed to Sigler, but not in the

conventional manner. Instead, he invited her to lunch and had a friend stand outside the window of their restaurant booth, holding a handwritten sign that asked, 'Laura, will you marry me?' She accepted his offer, but then the madness intervened and it was never mentioned again. By the time Keith left Cumberland Heights they were over, at least for the time being.

Sigler only spoke about her relationship with Keith long after they'd finally, irrevocably split and had ceased speaking to each other. 'There were lots of lows with the drugs,' she said. 'I don't have any dark past—he was probably the darkest part.'

James Blundell happened to be in Nashville soon after Sigler and Keith split and spoke with her at a party. According to Blundell, Sigler admitted that 'she adored him, but they'd broken up a couple of times [and that was enough]. She was very upset. She was a very smart woman and knew that it was an inevitable outcome.'

Keith was now going solo, both on stage and off. There'd been whispers that he might return to Australia for good, but that was never going to happen. Why, he figured, would he rebuild his life only to run away from what he considered to be his destiny? That made no sense. As his mother Marienne said in a rare interview, 'I'm sure people thought, "Well, he'll go back home," but Keith was determined to prove them wrong.'

Keith's spirits lifted considerably when he bumped into Garth Brooks in a parking lot, which could easily happen in a small town like Nashville. Brooks recognised Keith, and they chatted; as Brooks left, he called back, 'See ya, mate.' Keith jumped into his car and raced over to the Ten Ten office; he just had to share the news. 'Garth Brooks called me mate!' he told Mark Moffatt.

Keith's rep around the traps in Nashville, which had developed during his time with The Ranch, continued to spread. He was soon tapped for studio work with the Charlie Daniels Band—whose classic 'The Devil Went Down to Georgia' was a favourite of Keith's. But perhaps Keith's biggest break was being asked to play guitar on the Dixie Chicks' album *Fly* (which would sell a whopping ten million copies in the US alone).

The Dixie Chicks were the real deal—they were fine players, multi-instrumentalists, who could sing the birds from the trees. And singer Natalie Maines, who joined sisters Martie Seidel (now Maguire) and Emily Robison (now Strayer) in the band during 1995, is the daughter of pedal steel great Lloyd Maines. (Lloyd also played on *Fly*.)

When Keith got the call to work with the Dixies, in the spring of 1999, he was told that they wanted to cut a Ranch song. That would be huge for Keith, who was deep in debt to Brian Harris, among his many other backers. But then Keith was told he was being brought in to work on 'Some Days You Gotta Dance', a song which, while it may have been recorded by The Ranch, Keith had not written.

Still, Keith agreed to the cameo. He would have been mad not to; the Dixies were on a roll. But he was a bit concerned when he learned they were recording 'Some Days' in a different key to The Ranch version. 'Oh, great,' Keith mumbled under his breath and made the necessary adjustments.

The Dixies were big fans of Keith, as Martie Maguire admitted: 'There's always something sexy about a man who plays the crap out of the guitar—and a great Australian accent can never hurt.' It was probably the first time that Keith had been praised by a Nashville star for his 'Australianness'.

Despite being busy with studio work, Keith didn't aspire to becoming a session player. 'I was very careful not to pursue that,' he said. The work was great, and helped reboot his career, but there were also a lot of seasoned players in the city who didn't want him cutting into their territory. And Keith really wanted to get cracking on his own record. It was time.

Keith made a crucial connection during his time in the studio with the Dixie Chicks. He got to know keyboardist Matt Rollings, a Berklee College of Music grad who'd been Nashville based since the mid-1980s. Rollings' résumé as a player was impressive, having worked on albums for Lyle Lovett, Johnny Cash, Kenny Rogers, Glen Campbell, Vince Gill and Trisha Yearwood, among many others. He was also a budding record producer.

When Rollings and Keith started talking music, they realised they were simpatico; they bonded over early Elton John albums in particular. 'There are some producers who are very good golf players,' Keith said when asked about Rollings, 'and some who are good musicians. I wanted to work with the musicians.'

Rollings only had a few production credits to date but, like Keith, he was ambitious. And it wasn't as though producers were knocking down Keith's door begging to work on his next record. They agreed to collaborate—and their partnership would be a career maker for both of them.

★

The late 1990s was a time when hip-hop exploded into the mainstream. *The Miseducation of Lauryn Hill*, the breakout album from the former Fugee, was released in August 1998 and had sold almost three million copies by the end of the year (and some fourteen million now). Hill went on to win five Grammys, while the album charted for 91 weeks, a record that stayed in place for twenty years.

Hill wasn't the only hip-hop act making serious waves. Jay Z's *Vol 2 . . . Hard Knock Life* was a big hit, as were records by Gang Starr (*Moment of Truth*), Jurassic 5, Black Eyed Peas and numerous others. R&B acts like Destiny's Child and Usher were also having major mainstream success. 'Bling' was the fashion accessory du jour, as white kids from the suburbs began dressing like rappers rather than rock stars.

Keith wasn't immune to this exciting new music; in fact, he embraced it. He was working on a song that he thought could cross over from country into the mainstream, possibly even to the R&B charts. He said it 'sounded like a back porch stomp but with a drum machine', adding that he wanted to 'infuse more rhythmic stuff into country'.

Around the same time, Pat Quigley had become Keith's new label boss at Capitol. Like Miles Copeland, Quigley was viewed with great suspicion by much of Music City—he was a New Yorker, for a start, and came from a sales rather than a musical background. He'd told *The New York Times* that 'country for me . . . was the Hamptons', which didn't particularly endear him to anyone on the Tennessee side of the Mason-Dixon Line. Nor did his comment 'America is so much better educated than a lot of the music this town makes'. But Quigley saw massive potential in Keith.

'Keith has all the elements of a superstar, but he doesn't know it,' Quigley said in an episode of *Music Country: True Stories*.

Quigley, to his credit, had an open mind. When Garth Brooks decided to record *The Life of Chris Gaines*, for which he adopted a new whole new identity and style—swapping his Stetson for a soul patch and trading twangy country for melodic pop—Quigley teamed him up with a producer named Stevie J (real name Steven Jordan), who'd produced Puff Daddy's massive 'I'll Be Missing You', featuring Faith Evans and R&B foursome 112. Quigley sat down with Keith and floated the idea of Keith, too, working with Stevie J on his Nashville solo debut record. Keith was surprised by the idea but agreed.

You could witness many things in the car park of Nashville's Ocean Way studios, but a hip-hop posse was not a common sighting, as Stevie J and his crew rolled up to work with Keith—in a flotilla of limos, no less—in the summer of 1999. But when he and Keith got to chatting, Keith found him to be 'this well-mannered, really charming guy'. Keith asked Stevie about working with legendary diva Mariah Carey. What was she really like?

'He had nothing but praise for her,' Keith revealed. 'He just didn't tell any gritty stuff.' (Keith would work with Carey a few years later when they were judges on *American Idol*.)

Ten Ten's Mark Moffatt was at Ocean Way, and at Keith's request he brought in a couple of more traditional players: one on fiddle, the other playing pedal steel. Stevie J pulled Moffatt aside. 'Can you stick around?' he asked. 'My engineer has no idea how to work with instruments like those.'

Ultimately, the song they were working on didn't make

the final cut—Keith felt it was a bit too 'beat driven and not enough country'—but his eyes, and ears, were opened. And it wasn't by any means the last time he dabbled with hip-hop and beats. Clearly, there were many ways to make music, not just via the Nashville method.

*

Keith wrote with a variety of people for his solo record, some unlikely, some very much part of the Music City landscape. One of the latter was Skip Ewing, the same writer that James Blundell had clashed with during his frustrating Nashville tilt. Ewing sat down to work on a sketch of a song that Keith brought in, with the clunky working title 'The Man Who Assumed'. It was inspired by Keith's failed relationship with Laura Sigler.

'It's about a guy who assumes that his girl knows how he feels about her,' Keith said, 'although he's not very good at telling her.'

Ewing chewed this over for a few minutes.

'In what context did *you* not tell her?' Ewing asked him, point blank.

'Well,' Keith replied, fully aware his cover was blown, 'I always thought she knew.'

'Why don't we just call it "I Thought You Knew"?' Ewing suggested.

'So, I told Skip my story and cried like a baby,' Keith later revealed. 'Skip was like the psychologist, jotting down all my thoughts. It was like a therapy session.'

Keith admitted that this wasn't his preferred method of songwriting. He'd had enough therapy while staying at

Cumberland Heights. 'It was strange,' he said. 'Something I wouldn't want to do again.'

Another collaboration was brought about by Ged Malone, whom Keith had tussled with in New York a couple of years before. Malone was married to Jane Wiedlin, a former member of trailblazing female rockers The Go-Go's, best known for the timeless hit 'Our Lips Are Sealed'. Wiedlin was now a song-writer for hire, working with fellow Go-Go Charlotte Caffey out of Los Angeles. On Malone's suggestion, Keith flew out to meet them, hoping some creative sparks would fly.

But it was an uncomfortable session. Caffey and Wiedlin had spent some time in Nashville, where they'd tried their hand at co-writing Music City style, and they weren't taken by the place. 'They came to Nashville thinking of country a certain way,' said Keith. 'It was stereotypical clichéd stuff like rhinestones and cowboy hats.' This frustrated Keith, who, during their day together, tried his best to convince them that Nashville was evolving.

As Keith later admitted, he simply wasn't 'feeling it' as the hours ticked by; the music wasn't flowing. Just as Keith was about to leave, Caffey threw out an idea.

'Does anyone like the name "But for the Grace of God?"'

Keith certainly did. He stopped at the door, unpacked his guitar and started playing, humming a melody, as Wiedlin chipped away at a lyric. Ged Malone came home just after they'd finished the rough draft of the song.

'How'd it go?' he asked Keith.

'Okay,' Keith shrugged. 'We wrote a song, but it's not for me.'

Malone insisted he play the song. 'I think it's a hit,' he said.

Keith didn't realise it, of course, but he'd just co-written his first country number 1.

'But for the Grace of God' fit with something label boss Pat Quigley had said about Keith. He'd said that in order to succeed he needed to 'get the female agenda and apply it to a sensitive new man'. 'Grace of God' was perfect, as were other songs in the works that had 'sensitive New-Age man' written all over them—including the big ballad 'Your Everything'.

Of all the tracks Keith was recording, only the ass-kicker 'Where the Blacktop Ends' nodded towards his rockier past. One of the song's two co-writers was Music City journeyman Steve Wariner, who Keith had first met when he was about to play a set at an outdoor show. Keith was stringing a borrowed guitar, his gear lost in transit, and not in the best of moods. Wariner walked past and cheekily asked Keith if he knew what he was doing. 'Fuck off,' Keith shot back, before he real-ised it was Wariner, a guitar player who he really respected. Keith quickly apologised, and a bond formed.

As Keith's solo debut neared completion in the late summer of 1999, the Capitol marketing department kicked into overdrive, producing a slick press kit, featuring soft-focus portraits of Keith (taken by Russ Harrington) and a press release with an irresistible pitch—at least to a good chunk of Keith's audience. It read: 'Keith Urban, Music For All Audiences—What Every Woman Wants To Hear And Every Man Wants To Say.' Keith had been transformed from a country rocker into a fully blown metrosexual.

Mind you, label boss Quigley thought the cover image Keith chose for the album could have been a little edgier. 'Damn, son,' Quigley told him, 'it looks like the picture that came with the frame!' (Keith would later joke that the album 'has no stubble—and I have the picture on the front to prove it'.)

In a pre-release interview with trade magazine *Billboard*, Keith hinted at what he'd just been through, mentioning a 'black period'. 'Life just came barreling down on me all in one year,' Keith admitted. 'Everything went wrong.' But media-wise, the spin was upbeat, forward looking. 'Keith Urban's music appeals to all women looking for wide open spaces,' read another Capitol press release, cheekily 'borrowing' the title of the Dixie Chicks' hit album of the previous year.

Keith, meanwhile, slipped back to Australia in July for some low-key gigs and a tell-all interview with Sydney's *Sunday Telegraph*, in which he spoke about the demise of his relationship with Laura Sigler. 'It was hell,' he told writer Kathy McCabe. 'If you have a partner on your side, you need to acknowledge them and bring them closer, but I was focussing too much on my career and my problems.' However, his upcoming record, Keith insisted, was life affirming. 'There is definitely a thread running through the album and it is very optimistic. You need people, you really do.'

During his visit, Keith was playing to a very full house at Sydney venue The Basement, backed by a 'pick-up' band that included Buzz Bidstrup of The Angels and Paul Christie from Mondo Rock, when Keith invited a surprise guest up on stage. It was none other than pint-sized belter Angry Anderson, the heavily inked frontman of Rose Tattoo. Together, they furiously jammed Rose Tattoo's 'Bad Boy For Love', and as the song reached its barnstorming finale Keith was dripping sweat and smiling broadly.

'Angry fuckin' Anderson,' Keith gasped as the pint-sized screamer disappeared stage right. 'How do you top that?'

★

For those introduced to Keith Urban via The Ranch, his self-titled debut (well, actually, his second self-titled debut) came as a bit of a shock when it appeared in October 1999, a little more than a year after he checked out of Cumberland Heights. And it wasn't just the fact that Keith had taken a liking to spelling his name using all lowercase letters. There was no raw 'funktry' to be heard here, despite the presence of Jerry Flowers, who was back playing bass; nor was there anything that resembled 'the country Police', as Miles Copeland had described Keith's former band. And it was only during the instrumental 'Rollercoaster' that Keith really cut loose on his Fender. No, this was a very mainstream country-pop record, with a sprinkling of twang and a hefty dollop of sugar, all polished to perfection.

Keith had compromised creatively with his new record, no doubt about it, but he had done it to save his career. In the letter that Keith prized so highly, from Mary Martin, she'd hinted that Keith needed to wait until he somehow 'fitted' in Nashville. What he'd done instead was change his approach to fit more comfortably in Music City—but he did it with his eyes wide open. Bob Saporiti, who'd worked with Keith in the early days of The Ranch, could see that. 'He's not a stupid guy. That's part of his desire to make it, the willingness to compromise the edge for the success. I think he did realise that there's no success in failure.'

And Keith, at least publicly, had no major issues with his change in direction. 'It's a big margarita mix,' he said, when asked to describe the album on the show *Sudzin Country*. 'I was able to cover more styles than I could with The Ranch. I think solo you're a little more freer to try different things.'

Keith was asked if he really was the sensitive guy depicted in the songs.

'You'd have to ask my ex-girlfriend, probably,' Keith laughed. 'Maybe not . . .'

The album garnered more reviews in Australia than it did stateside, where its coverage increased when Keith's career exploded. Australian *Rolling Stone* praised 'Urban's top-shelf picking, singing and a heart so big it'd put Phar Lap to shame'. *The West Australian*, meanwhile, said this: 'What's best is his confessional and very human songwriting.'

Capitol in the US, however, did manage to get some handy plugs from influential country radio DJs. This was helped, no doubt, by an appearance Keith put in at Nashville's annual Country Radio Seminar, as part of their New Faces Show, playing a twenty-minute set to 2000 radio taste-makers. John Marks from KWNR stated that 'his music is sensitive enough to appeal to women and gutsy enough for men'. 'Keith is bright, talented and very unique,' said KSKS's Ken Boesen. 'He's just what we need.' And then the clincher, from Dave Ervin at KZLA, who predicted that Keith could be 'the Bruce Springsteen of country'.

The first sample of the newer, freer Keith Urban had actually emerged back in May, when the album's lead track, 'It's a Love Thing', was released as its first single. This was country with an R&B undercurrent; clearly, his sessions with Stevie J had left their mark. And it sounded nothing like the big hits of the moment, such as Tim McGraw's treacly 'Please Remember Me', which came on like the sonic equivalent of a Hallmark card. The track was new and fresh, as was Keith's current look: there may have been a few piercings and soul patches on display in Music City, but no one wore them with quite the same cool as Keith.

The video shot for 'It's a Love Thing', directed by Thom

Oliphant, also cast Keith in a fresh light: it was fun and upbeat, with a smiling Keith constantly in motion. Part of the clip was shot in the back of a New York yellow cab, with a tripod set up on the floor of the back seat and Keith squeezed into the corner, the camera inches away from his face. The stylist rode in the front seat alongside the driver, as the night flashed by their window. Producer Matt Rollings put in a cameo elsewhere in the video, sitting behind the desk as Keith did his thing in the studio.

The song wasn't a big hit, sneaking into the Top 20 of *Billboard*'s Hot Country Songs list, but it was a good enough start, hanging about the charts for 25 weeks. It was facing some stiff opposition, because the charts were dominated by the Dixie Chicks ('Ready to Run') and Alan Jackson ('Little Man'), among many other regular hitmakers. Keith's big breakthrough, however, was just around the corner, even though a drama involving his label's brightest star almost put the kibosh on that.

★

The storyline of Garth Brooks' recent invention, Chris Gaines, ran like this. Gaines, according to his biography, was born in Brisbane in 1967, having first come to notice in a band named CRUSH, who were major Beatles fans. (Keith had played his share of Beatles covers back in his cover band days.) Brooks/Gaines wore a soul patch, just like Keith, while the musical flavour of *The Life of Chris Gaines* crossed over to pop in much the same way Keith did with 'It's a Love Thing'. And they both recorded for Capitol.

Things grew even stranger when an ad for Keith's 'Love

Thing' appeared in the trade mag *Country Airplay Monitor*, right alongside some Chris Gaines editorial.

When Keith was asked by a reporter from Florida's *The Star* how he reacted to Brooks' project, he admitted it was 'a very strange and weird thing. I mean, what are the chances of Garth coming up with this character, who was born in 1967, raised in Brisbane, Australia, and is doing music similar to mine?'

Under the headline 'Angry rocker: I'm the real Chris Gaines', the tabloid suggested a 'major rift' had developed between Brooks and his Aussie labelmate. This was the worst possible thing to be dumped on Keith—Brooks' project may have been a bomb, but the man wielded massive influence, not just at Capitol but in most parts of music-loving America. To piss him off was a career-killer.

Keith, naturally, downplayed everything, insisting he'd been 'so taken out of context'. To which he added: 'I am certainly not angry or annoyed at Garth, as some media are suggesting.'

Finally, Keith felt compelled to call Brooks at home.

'It's complete crap,' he told him, 'a complete fabrication by some bored journalist.'

Brooks admitted he hadn't read the piece. 'Welcome to tabloid sensationalism,' Brooks said as he rang off—in short, 'forget about it', which a hugely relieved Keith did, in a heartbeat.

8

Shake-ups and breakthroughs

There'd been some major shake-ups at Capitol around the time of 'It's a Love Thing'—and inner-label politics could easily scupper the career of an up-and-comer like Keith, who'd only just avoided a showdown with King Garth. Cincinnati native Mike Dungan, who'd started out stacking the racks of his local record store, had taken over as president of Capitol Nashville from Pat Quigley, among whose final moves had been pumping a whopping US$25 million into promoting Garth Brooks' 1997 album *Sevens*, which sold nowhere near as strongly as its predecessors had.

Fortunately for Keith, Dungan was a true believer, who stated, a bit opaquely, 'In my 23-year career I've never met someone with such horizontal and vertical potential as Keith Urban.' Dungan never made it clear whether he was referring to the charts—something Keith hoped for—or the bedroom. Perhaps both.

But the label itself was in a mess, which may have explained some curious Keith Urban promotion campaigns. In keeping with the 'It's a Love Thing' theme, one promo

94

offered the winner a return airfare to Australia and a trip to wine country, where they'd be met and serenaded by Keith. But Keith drew the line at plugging his album at a baby store, as Capitol had proposed. He had his limits.

Jeff Walker was another expat Aussie, originally from Sydney. He'd been in Nashville since 1974, and in 1980 had founded a Nashville-based company called AristoMedia. He'd seen Keith play a lot when he was with The Ranch, and soon enough he was hired to handle Keith's publicity.

'My relationship with Keith was more professional than personal, although we did have some great conversations,' said Walker. 'I always understood that, deep inside, Keith was looking for something that he hadn't found at the time. He seemed personally restless and anxious to get to the next level. He was very driven, which is a good thing.'

In early May 2000, 'Your Everything' was released as the second single from *Keith Urban*. Keith and his label knew that this was the track to really break him as a chart act. The song may have been liberally coated in sugar, but Keith had sensed, back when he'd first listened to the demo, that it was right for him. As he admitted, as soon as he heard the line 'I want to be the hand that lifts your veil', he was sold. 'I was covered in goosebumps.'

The video for the song was shot by CMT/MTV regular Trey Fanjoy, marking the start of a highly productive working relationship with Keith (they've now shot seven videos together). 'She brings such a great vibe into her work,' Keith said of Fanjoy, who studied theatre in New York and worked in film production in LA. 'Organic yet stylish.' Fanjoy, a strong visual storyteller, was then one of the few women making videos in Nashville.

Keith understood the power of video, as he told a writer from the *Boston Herald*. 'We live in an age that is often so visually driven, particularly with television and video, and if that's a card that you can play, you're kind of foolish not to do it. But you have to balance that with not letting it get in the way of the music.' It helped, of course, that Keith was handsome, very camera friendly—and could really play. He was made for Generation Video.

The clip for 'Your Everything' featured a couple tying the knot—all shot in slow motion, of course—as Keith stood nearby, observing proceedings, singing his heart out. Bizarrely, not long after the song's release, Keith was setting up for a gig in Pigeon Forge, Tennessee, when he heard 'Your Everything' wafting out of a nearby church. Keith stopped what he was doing and walked over to the church, only to be stopped at the door by the father of the bride.

'But that's me singing the song,' Keith protested.

Eventually, a pleasantly surprised bride gave Keith the all-clear. 'I went in and sang it, and they loved it. I charged them $2000,' Keith laughed. 'I'm just kidding. It was $1500.'

Keith had learned a handy lesson at Pigeon Forge. 'Your Everything' would grow so popular among couples, especially with about-to-be-wedded couples, that Keith sold the sheet music at gigs. It's a shame he didn't write it; the song was the work of tunesmiths Chris Lindsey and Bob Regan. It was also a peculiar time for Keith to have a big romantic hit—in his own words, he was then 'as single as a dollar bill'.

Soon after its May 2000 release, 'Your Everything' started to appear on several *Billboard* charts (the music mag had more charts than a doctor's office) as its popularity on country radio grew. Keith knew how crucial this support was; while it was great to be praised by your peers—and such stars as the Dixie Chicks were doing just that—airplay was what kept you alive and kicking as an artist. 'Your credibility goes through the roof,' he said, as the single ascended the charts, 'when country radio stations start to support you.'

'Your Everything' became a major hit on *Billboard*'s Hot Country Songs chart, peaking at number 4. Over the previous 50 years, only a handful of Australian artists— Diana Trask, Olivia Newton-John, the LeGarde Twins, Jewel Blanch, Arthur Blanch and Helen Reddy—had made the *Billboard* country charts, but none had hit the Top 10. Keith was a trailblazer.

But 'Your Everything' was more than a country hit. It crossed over into the mainstream Hot 100, parking itself just outside the Top 50 (number 51, to be exact) and charting for sixteen weeks. It also reached the Top 20 on the Canadian country charts, as Keith's reputation spread across the border. The video too was a hit, topping the CMT video chart for two weeks. And the song was a stayer; in the year's end Hot Country Songs chart, it ranked number 15. Keith was now competing for chart action with the likes of Faith Hill, Dixie Chicks and Rascal Flatts, the biggest country acts of the new millennium.

In the wake of 'Your Everything', the *Keith Urban* album, which had debuted at a modest number 60, started selling strongly, while Keith began finding fans in unlikely locales. Record company research showed that Mormons loved Keith; his biggest market at one stage was Salt Lake City, Utah, followed by Seattle, the heartland of grunge and Kurt Cobain. Texans loved him, too—he was particularly big in Houston and Dallas. Keith was also making an impact in the key musical centres of LA, New York and Chicago. And, of course, 65 per cent of his estimated audience was female, mostly aged between 16 and 35.

Keith's breakthrough success came with a downside, as is so often the case with the music biz—in this case, seemingly endless inquisitions about the dark days that had led to his stint at Cumberland Heights. Rather than deflect, Keith opted for full disclosure, which endeared him even further to his American fans. After all, publicly admitting to addiction hadn't harmed the careers of such superstars as Johnny Cash, who in 1965 was busted at the US–Mexico border with a pharmacy's worth of pills; Glen Campbell, who seemingly spent much of the 1970s and '80s drunk, high or crashing his car; or Waylon Jennings, who during the 1970s had a US$1500-a-day cocaine habit. All had come clean, literally and metaphorically, about their high times, and got on with their careers.

Keith revealed to *USA Weekend* how, in the midst of one of his many binges, he woke up one morning at five o'clock and was 'crawling around on my hands and knees, looking for these little rocks [of cocaine] . . . drenched in sweat. It was the worst. [There was] major chaos in my life. I pushed everybody away.'

When he spoke with a writer from the *Winnipeg Free Press*, Keith was just as forthcoming. 'I was completely prepared to die, and I had no problem with it,' he said. 'I was heading straight down that road without a care in the world.' Speaking in hushed tones, Keith said that an 'inner power' had helped him get his life back on course.

Those close to Keith knew that he'd played it brilliantly. 'In this country it's better if you come clean and tell the truth about stuff like that,' figured Jewel Coburn.

'We've got a long history in country music of pills and booze,' said writer Radney Foster, whose songs Keith recorded. 'There's nothing new to country music about that. But I give Keith a tremendous amount of credit; it's difficult to be that honest.'

Not that Keith had a huge amount of spare time to consider how this all went down. In the wake of the success of 'Your Everything', he was constantly in motion. He hadn't toured in 1998 and 1999 and was itching to play live again. During July 2000 he opened shows for superstars Tim McGraw and Faith Hill, as part of their Soul2Soul tour, an arena extravaganza that had Keith playing short sets for crowds of 20,000 at such mega-venues as the Ice Palace Arena in Tampa, Florida, and the Philips Arena in Atlanta, Georgia, home of the NBA's Atlanta Hawks. Also in July he hooked up with Dwight Yoakam, king of the 'Bakersfield sound', a rowdy mix of twang and rock and roll, for shows at the Starlight Amphitheater in Oklahoma City.

Keith was playing infotainment-sized sets, rarely more than 30 minutes, usually solo, opening with 'Where the Blacktop Ends' and closing with 'It's a Love Thing'. The inclusion of 'Walkin' the Country' was the only nod to his past. His shows may have been brief, but Keith was building an audience, night by night, show by show. Keith had never shied away from the grind, and 2000 may well have been his most active year yet—by his estimation, during the year he undertook something like 250 radio station visits, as well as a never-ending round of press and TV interviews and hundreds of live shows, in-stores and radio performances. Keith also put in his first appearance at Nashville's annual Fan Fair, where I'd encountered him just two years earlier when his career had been stuck in neutral. A lot had changed since then.

'You never stop working,' Keith said from the frontline. '[But] you really end up being rewarded if you work hard.' That started to become tangible for Keith when he began spending a long time after gigs meeting and greeting fans at shows beyond Nashville. This was a first. 'The autograph lines have gotten longer and longer,' he told Australian writer Bruce Elder. 'We will often be in some little town and we'll stay for two hours.'

*

Perhaps playing 'Walkin' the Country' night after night had made Keith nostalgic for his recent past, because when he heard from Peter Clarke, his friend and drummer from The Ranch, suggesting they play some shows at one of their old haunts during September while he was holidaying in the States, Keith was in. And with one phone call, so was Jerry Flowers, who was still part of the Dixie Chicks' touring band. The Ranch was back in the saddle, at least for a couple of nights. Keith's friend and mentor Tommy Emmanuel, now Nashville based, agreed to open the gigs—and tickets for the two shows sold out in a heartbeat.

Keith let the 12th & Porter audience in on some history as soon as the trio took the stage on 20 September. 'It's been two years, three months and seven days since our last gig,' he announced, yet they threw themselves into the opener, 'Walkin' the Country', as if they'd never stopped playing. As the CMT website reported, The Ranch's raw power hadn't been diluted by Keith's recent pop makeover. 'The high-energy performance offered proof that the band hasn't lost its edge as a unit,' the reviewer declared,

Just weeks later, the paths of Keith and Tommy Emmanuel intersected yet again, this time in Sydney, when Emmanuel played at the closing of the Olympics and Keith did likewise at the Paralympics. This trip, like so many of Keith's homecomings, was a hit-and-run affair—eleven shows in ten days, as well as the usual helter-skelter rounds of press and publicity. But this time around was different: Keith was now a rising star in the States, with a Top 5 record and 'But for the Grace of God' prepped for release on his return. The theme of his conversations with the press shifted from 'When will it happen, Keith?' to 'So, Keith, how does it feel?'

However, he wasn't getting too carried away with his new-found success. 'There are no words for the feeling that haven't been used before,' he told a writer from *The Sydney Morning Herald*, 'but I am really focused on the next single. I am now really interested in justifying that success.'

When speaking with a reporter from Newcastle, Keith said that he dreamed of juggling lives in both Australia and Nashville—which was exactly what he'd one day go on to do. 'My goal is to buy a house in Australia, somewhere in Queensland probably,' Keith said. 'In an ideal world, I'd like to live in both places.'

But Keith's reality at that stage was a life in motion, with a tour schedule, his band and his tour bus his only constant companions. And, ideally, a chilled bottle of Coopers, which was his tipple of choice—so much so that his local liquor store in Nashville would import Coopers especially for him when he was home. He'd given up the cocaine pipe, but still enjoyed a drink.

The obligatory video for 'But for the Grace of God'—again directed by Trey Fanjoy—cast Keith as the brooding loner, alone in his apartment and then taking a walk down a lonely street, which suited the melancholy mood of the song perfectly. Curiously, the original version ended with Keith returning home to his lady love, but in the edit it was felt the actor cast in the video bore too close a resemblance to a member of his 'video band', so it was cut. It was just too confusing: was he getting it on with a woman in his make-believe band? Keith was destined to stay sad and single, at least as far as viewers of the video were concerned. It worked, because as one Youtube.com viewer neatly put it, 'Who else can sing as well as being eye-candy?' 'He's so gorgeous,' declared another. 'I love his voice. His hair. *His nose*. Everything about him.' You know you've made it when fans start declaring their love for your nose.

Sales of the single backed that up, as 'But for the Grace of God' became Keith's second bona-fide country hit when it appeared in October 2000. It even outstripped 'Your Everything', becoming Keith's first country number 1 on 24 February 2001—and the clip did likewise on the CMT video chart. 'But for the Grace of God' was the first chart-topping single by a Capitol country artist in two and a half years, ending a long dry streak for the label. Again, Keith crossed over into the *Billboard* Hot 100, the mainstream chart, peaking at number 37. In the year-end country chart for 2001, 'Grace of God' hit a high of number 16. All in all, Keith must have been hugely relieved he hadn't given up on the single, as he'd considered on the day of its writing in LA.

By Christmas 2000, the *Keith Urban* album had reached

gold status, with sales of 500,000; eventually it would hit a country chart peak of number 17.

Keith, clearly, was on a roll.

*

In early December, Keith played a showcase for Capitol Records. But this wasn't your typical showcase; this was a celebration of Keith's recent success—'Keithstock' in all but name. His mother, Marienne, flew over for the event, while Garth Brooks made an appearance. Keith hadn't seen Brooks since the confusion over Chris Gaines.

'How's it feel?' Brooks asked him backstage, referring to his golden year.

'I feel responsible,' Keith admitted. 'I just feel like I have to justify all this now.'

It was an oddly sombre comment from a guy enjoying his time in the spotlight, but Keith had a point. A lot of people had helped get him to this flashpoint in his career, everyone from his parents to Greg Shaw and the Coburns and Brian Harris and so many others. Some of them had invested not only their energy into Keith's career but their money, too. Keith understood he had a lot of people to repay, and the best way to do that was to build on his success, to keep on working, keep on moving up the ladder.

Yet Keith's next achievement, if you could call it that, was a curious sideways move. Since 1985, *People* magazine has published a Sexiest Man Alive poll. Although actor Pierce Brosnan was 2001's winner, Keith found himself on the year's list of new and notable hunks, alongside Russell Crowe, Heath Ledger and Steve 'The Crocodile Hunter' Irwin. They were grouped awkwardly together as 'Awesome Aussies'—it didn't seem to matter that Keith and Crowe were both Kiwis by birth. When asked about the accolade in a 2001 interview with *Australia's A Current Affair*—'Are you one of the sexiest men of the year?'—Keith laughed. 'Keep it in perspective. Steve Irwin was on that list, too.'

Around the same time, Keith's International Fan Club released its first newsletter, and in April 2001 Keith made an appearance in *Playgirl* magazine, his modesty covered by nothing more than a guitar. The shoot took place in the house of a Capitol Records exec, Keith spending much of the session in a robe and boxers, with a Beatles record playing and one eye on the clock. (He had a show in Tulsa that night.) 'I love getting dressed up and having my picture taken,' Keith admitted. 'It isn't hard work.'

Talk, inevitably, turned to women and Keith's personal life. He confessed to receiving some pretty raunchy offerings from female fans—photos of them posing in bikinis, with phone numbers written on the back. But Keith was still hurting from his break-up; he said that while his relationship with Laura Sigler had ended, he hadn't given up on them, not yet. 'Hopefully I can get that back again sometime.'

And how did his ex feel about the more personal moments on his album, songs inspired by what transpired between them?

'Well,' Keith said with a rueful chuckle, 'she knows now how I feel about her.'

But for the moment he was a free agent whose biggest love was music. 'I don't have a relationship, I don't have kids, I'm a bachelor, I rent my house and I'm pretty free to spend all my time on music.'

Appearing on *People*'s sexiest list was out of his control, but not so posing for the spread that ran with the *Playgirl* interview—a decision that Keith came to regret. A come-hither shot of Keith appeared on the cover of the magazine, sharing space with such attention-grabbing teasers as 'How to Make Your Own Dirty Home Movie'. It was hardly the move of a musician striving for credibility, although Keith did come to see the humour in the shoot, joking, 'Thank god I play guitar and not harmonica.' Still, there was at least one celebrity who was drawn to the images of Keith posing provocatively—Aussie actress Nicole Kidman, who'd just launched her latest hit film, *Moulin Rouge*, at Cannes. 'Who's *that*?' she had asked a friend. In time, she'd get to know Keith much more intimately.

9

Cleaning house and topping the charts

American music, and in particular country music, seems to binge on awards, which are crucial when it comes to selling records and building careers. There are the Grammys, of course, but also the Country Music Association Awards (the CMAs), the Academy of Country Music Awards (the ACMs), the CMT Music Awards (the CMTs) for videos and TV, as well as the American Music Awards, which features no fewer than five individual country gongs. Each year is an endless cycle of acronyms and pointy statuettes and red carpets and lively rivalries. (Travis Tritt had accused Billy Ray Cyrus at one award show of turning country music into an 'ass-wiggling contest'. When Cyrus won the American Music Award for Best Country Song the following year, he responded, 'Here's a quarter, call someone who cares!', quoting the title of a hit song of Tritt's.)

The Academy of Country Music had been honouring its greatest and latest for more than 30 years. In 2001,

Keith was in the running for Top New Male Vocalist at the ceremony held on 9 May in Los Angeles. The night was hosted for the first of many times by Reba McEntire, who'd just released her *third* greatest hits album, and whose eponymous TV series was soon to launch. The flame-haired McEntire—simply 'Reba' to her many fans—was a crossover star, a big deal.

Keith, wearing a pink shirt so vibrant it could have glowed in the dark, teamed with a pinstriped suit and just a hint of spray tan, was understandably chuffed when he was declared the winner. 'Wow,' he gushed, waving his trophy in the air, duly thanking his dresser, the Academy, country radio and God. 'I think that's the right order,' he chuckled. 'I love you all, thank you for supporting me.' It seemed as though giving himself up to a higher power while in rehab had done the trick. God was definitely on Keith's side.

Within days Keith was back on the road with country kings Brooks & Dunn, who'd helped give The Ranch a leg up just a few years earlier, a gesture Keith had never forgotten. Keith was now playing arenas—the Rose Garden in Portland, Oregon; the Verizon Amphitheatre in Charlotte, North Carolina; the Ice Palace in Tampa, Florida—that would, over time, become as familiar to him as 12th & Porter.

★

In June 2001, Keith enjoyed a rare night off, hosting a bash at Six Degrees, an upscale Nashville eatery, to celebrate his recent success. Barry Coburn was in the house, as was Kelly Brooks, Garth's brother and co-manager, and Amy Kurland, the owner of Nashville's Bluebird Café, a venue famous for its 'songwriter's circle' events, where both big stars and up-and-comers traded tunes and stories. Keith's buddy Steve Wariner told the gathering about their first encounter, when Keith suggested he 'fuck off'. When Keith's label boss, Mike Dungan, took his turn at the mic, it was all business: 'This record was never set up right,' he said, referring to both Keith's album and his predecessor, Pat Quigley. 'It was set up to fail. This record should be platinum.' (It did make it to platinum, but not until December 2003.)

Keith spoke more calmly, thanking producer Matt Rollings, who he called his 'spiritual guide', and revealing that they had made the entire album without having a single argument. Later that night, Keith spoke frankly with a reporter. 'There's a part of me that expected this to come sooner,' he admitted. After all, Keith had been convinced for much of his adult life that becoming a star in Nashville was his destiny.

There was more business to attend to, of course—there was always more business for Keith. A fourth and final single, 'Where the Blacktop Ends', was squeezed from his album, and it did solid chart business, reaching number 3 on *Billboard*'s Hot Country Songs list (the third Top 5 hit from the record), and a peak of number 35 on the Hot 100 chart in early September 2001. Its success coincided with a big change in the world of Keith Urban Inc.

Greg Shaw, Keith's manager and booster from all the way back in Brisbane in the mid-1980s, had stuck with Keith even when he was at his lowest; at one point, Shaw even borrowed money from his mother to keep Team Urban afloat. But he was out of his depth in the US. He'd actually stopped managing Keith when Miles Copeland took over but returned to help again in 1998 at Keith's request, after his stint in Cumberland Heights. Shaw's marriage had ended while managing Keith, no doubt irreparably damaged by the huge amount of time Shaw spent away from his young family. Keith was about to drop the axe on Shaw for good, and he handled it badly.

Keith called Shaw, who was briefly back in Australia for his son's birthday, and insisted he return to the States. 'Things are really heating up,' Keith said, which was undeniable. But when Shaw reached LAX, en route to Nashville, he called Keith to let him know that he was almost there—and then got the biggest shock of his life. He was out, fired over the phone.

'I could not even say goodbye to friends I had met with Keith,' Shaw said. 'I could not get my affairs in order. I was just sacked.'

Rob Potts of Allied Artists was one of Keith's closest Australian consorts, booking his tours whenever he returned to Oz, and sometimes going out on the road with him in the States. He knew Keith as well as anybody. 'Keith will remove you from your career in a heartbeat if he feels that's what he needs to do,' said Potts. 'But I think with Greg, he legitimately put his own life into Keith's career. His marriage fell apart, he lost his house; whatever reasonable inheritance he had would have gone into Keith's career. He was totally committed; it was an amazing thing. I don't think Greg ever gave up.'

Keith had also grown disenchanted with Miles Copeland. As Copeland's second-in-charge Ged Malone read the situation, Keith 'had been fed up with Miles for a while'. Keith knew that he needed someone embedded in Nashville, so Copeland was also cut loose from Keith's life. Malone was gone, too; his marriage to Jane Wiedlin ended and he returned to the UK, where he began managing rock band Simple Minds. Keith, who duly signed with Gary Borman, a heavy-hitter who managed Faith Hill and James Taylor, was clearing house.

Keith, to his credit, gave a very public nod to Shaw when he next returned to Australia in October 2001, primarily to appear at the Goodwill Games. Keith was playing an industry gig at Sydney's Fox Studios complex when he stopped mid-set and invited Shaw onto the stage. Keith thanked Shaw warmly and presented him with a framed gold record. He then spoke about, and downplayed, 'the rumours' regarding he and Shaw—essentially that Keith had burned him badly—and made it clear to the full house that he respected everything his friend and former manager had done for him. Keith stated that Shaw was a man who 'would walk through fire' for him.

Rob Potts was in the crowd that night. 'That was a public acknowledgement on Keith's part,' said Potts, 'his way of saying: "I don't care what all you wankers are thinking over here, Greg and I are still mates." There was a little bit of showbiz, but it was pretty real.'

Keith gave Shaw another public thank you when he collected an ARIA Award for Outstanding Achievement at Sydney's Capitol Theatre on 30 October. Amazingly, it was Keith's first ARIA (his Golden Guitar count, meanwhile, stood at five). The gong was presented by none other than Slim Dusty, the bushie icon who'd supported Keith back when the Tamworth establishment was unsure about the flashy young kid with the mullet and cut-off shorts. Dusty himself was a Special Achievement Award recipient, in 1996, and a winner that night for Best Country Album.

After running through a checklist of Keith's recent achievements, Dusty insisted that he remained 'a dinky-di Queensland boy'. This was followed by a lengthy video montage, featuring Keith as a pint-sized Caboolture kid cradling an oversized guitar, then throwing forward to recent footage. Pat Quigley, his former boss at Capitol, heaped on the praise, as did Steve Wariner and Jane Wiedlin, his 'Grace of God' co-writer. In voiceover, the names Garth Brooks and the Dixie Chicks were dropped. Heavily.

Slim Dusty then reminded the audience that a pre-teen Keith had once busked on the streets of Tamworth. 'He's come a long way since then,' said Dusty, not a man to waste words. 'The one and only—Mr Keith Urban.'

Keith had hugged a lot of people during the past few months—his arms must have ached from all the love he'd given and received at awards shows—but Dusty seemed a bit stunned when Keith went in for a hug when he took the stage.

Not only did Keith thank Greg Shaw, but numerous other locals who'd helped him get this far—Brian Harris, who'd first signed him ('a freakin' living legend', in Keith's words); Rob Walker, another early champion; and Chrissie Camp, his Aussie friend and publicist for many years, as well as his brother Shane, who was with him at the awards. Rob Potts also got a nod, as did Joanne Petersen, who'd snagged him a deal at MCA Music Publishing back in 1989, a deal that had kept him afloat when money was tight. Later that night, Keith strapped on an acoustic guitar and played 'Not Pretty Enough' with singer/songwriter Kasey Chambers, the

Nullarbor-raised daughter of a fox hunter and the Australian act most likely to emulate Keith's American success.

*

Keith had one more awards ceremony to wrap up 2001, his first golden year. Outside of a Grammy, a CMA Award was a very big deal, and Keith had been nominated for the Horizon Award, essentially a 'best newcomer' award. The Horizon Award had been won by the Dixie Chicks in 1998, by Brad Paisley in 2000 and by many other up-and-comers who had gone on to well-established country stardom. It was an almost guaranteed career maker. Keith's rivals were a mixed bunch; among them was Australian-born Jamie O'Neal, who'd been one of Kylie Minogue's backing singers for many years before signing with Mercury Nashville in 2000. Also in the running was seventeen-year-old Tennessee native Jessica Andrews, who was riding high on the strength of her second album, *Who I Am*. At 34, Keith must have felt like a senior citizen by comparison.

On 7 November, the morning of the awards, during an interview on Texas radio station KAYD 101.7, talk turned to the American flag, a particularly hot topic after the September 11 terrorist attacks just two months earlier. Keith had worn an ankle-length Stars and Stripes coat at a recent Brooks & Dunn gig, the Country Freedom Concert, where he sang 'Only in America' with the dynamic duo. Keith admitted to being very wary about donning the coat; he had to make sure it didn't touch the ground or show it any kind of disrespect that could have led to a serious backlash, or worse. Americans, particularly in the heartland, and most especially in the wake of 9/11, could get very particular about how Old Glory was treated.

'I'm not from here,' Keith explained when asked why he wore it, 'but I came here to pursue the American dream, and it's allowed me to be what I've become. It was my way of saying thank you.'

Keith also spoke about 9/11, which he saw as 'an attack on the Western civilisation and way of life'. Keith had been in New York not long before the attack, playing a set for radio station WYNY, which was broadcast live from World Trade Center Plaza. He was then given a guided tour of the Twin Towers. On the day of the strikes, Keith recalled, he was in Sarasota, Florida, as was President George W. Bush. 'I was having a vacation, for three days, that was cut short. I couldn't be disappointed because people were in a far worse situation to me.'

That night, Keith dressed boldly for the CMA Awards. He wore a striking Western-themed pants-and-jacket ensemble, coloured cream and black and studded with rhinestones, a dark motif winding its way down his entire torso. This was Keith's homage to the late Nudie Cohn, who'd been the go-to tailor for some of American music's finest. Cohn designed the gold lamé suit that Elvis Presley wore on the cover of his *50,000,000 Elvis Fans Can't Be Wrong*; the suit was by then valued at US$10,000. Gram Parson's Nudie suit famously featured a marijuana-leaf motif and an embroidered naked woman. Keith's outfit wasn't quite so outrageous, but you couldn't miss him on the red carpet.

'Well, whaddya know, prayers do work,' said a clearly delighted Keith, after his name was read out as the Horizon Award winner. 'I prayed so much for this.' He thanked his mother, Marienne, who was in the crowd, and Laura Sigler, who was briefly back in his life: 'I love you, thank you for coming out.' His label and country radio also got big shout-outs, as did Music Row, the business heart of Nashville, the base for most of the city's wheeling and/or dealing. 'I'm so proud and honoured to be working here,' Keith said as his one minute wound down. 'Thank you so much everyone.' During the night, Dann Huff was crowned CMA's Musician of the Year. Huff would come to play a key role in Keith's future.

Proving that pretty much everything was fair game when it came to getting his name out there, Keith appeared on a special edition of *Family Feud*, shot the day after the CMAs. Keith's team comprised the Dixie Chicks and country legend Buck Owens, and they were fundraising for St Jude's in Nashville, a children's research hospital that became Keith's charity of choice. Their opposition was tough: they were up against The Muppets.

'Hey Keith, Keith Urban, you're originally from Australia, and you've kayaked right over to Nashville?' said genial host Louie Anderson, as he introduced Keith, whose first Muppet rival was none other than Pepe the King Prawn. Keith, in a gesture that got a big laugh from the crowd, offered to use his chin to press the buzzer, given that Pepe could only use his chin—and the prawn duly beat him to the punch on the first question: 'Name a hobby that someone with a fear of heights should never take up.' 'This is the skydiving,' said Pepe, which was the top answer. Keith smiled, shrugged his shoulders, and conceded defeat. Pepe was one smart crustacean.

Keith knew all about momentum, and when he was on air at KAYD he'd mentioned that he'd been writing a lot, with a plan to get back into the studio before the end of the year. The *Keith Urban* album had run its course—and done its job. Having one successful record was great, but what Keith needed next was an even bigger and better sequel.

10

'You fucking hypocrite! You're not the guy in the song'

Rather than keep on keeping on with Matt Rollings, Keith agreed to work with a more seasoned producer on his next record. Forty-one-year-old Dann Huff was a Nashville native with music in his veins—his father, Ronn, was the pops conductor for the Nashville Symphony, while Dann had been the guitarist for Christian rock band White Heart alongside his brother David, who played drums. As a producer, Dann had worked some chart magic with Faith Hill on her 1999 album *Breathe*, which sold a staggering eight million copies. He'd also produced records by Lonestar and singer/songwriter Jewel and, intriguingly, worked regularly with ultra-heavy rock band Megadeth. And he played in a hard-rock outfit called Giant. Huff was versatile.

Huff was also a fine player, who'd recorded with Michael Jackson and played the solo on Kenny Loggins' 1986 hit 'Danger Zone'. He'd been voted 1995's Top Session Guitarist by *Guitar Player* magazine, and his recent CMA Award for

116

Musician of the Year was proof of his skill. But the relationship between Keith and Huff, which in time would produce commercial gold, didn't start out so well. Keith was unsure about working with a fellow guitarist, who he feared might 'force his guitar style on me. I thought we'd clash.'

Keith may have made the occasional compromise when it came to song selection and image, but as far as he was concerned, the guitar tracks on his records were his private domain. Yet on their first day in the studio, in late 2001, Keith was shocked to discover that Huff had already begun laying down some guitar. Keith, who was more than a little pissed off, hatched a plan. He hastily organised a showcase for that night and made sure there was only one name on the guest list: Huff's. The producer turned up to the gig and watched his new charge work his way up and down and around his Fender like a rocked-up Tommy Emmanuel. He hadn't known Keith was a master blaster on the guitar.

The next day, when they returned to the studio, Huff spoke with Keith: 'I guess you'll be playing the guitar from now on?'

Keith had proved his point and their misunderstanding was never mentioned again.

Keith also dug in when it came to the players and technical crew on the record. Huff had chosen his own preferred group of musos, but Keith said no, he had his own guys, among them woolly-haired drummer Chris McHugh—who, admittedly, had worked with Huff before—bassist Jerry Flowers and engineer Justin Niebank. They'd be playing on the record.

Keith and Huff had agreed initially to work on the one song, 'Somebody Like You', to see if they had the right chemistry. As soon as they got to work on the track, which Keith had co-written with writer/guitarist John Shanks, he was sold on Huff.

'It was like [working with] a music teacher,' Keith admitted. 'He came in and took hold of the class. I just stood there and went, "Wow, this guy is awesome."'

They did butt heads, though, during the recording of the song. Huff was a perfectionist, whereas Keith was more inclined to go with a great take, even if it wasn't technically precise. Huff insisted that Keith play the closing guitar solo over and over again, much to his annoyance. It was hot in the studio, and Keith, after repeated takes, was shirtless and yelling at Huff: 'It's the same solo!' Then, out of frustration, Keith began playing something slightly different, because, as he admitted, 'I was so fed it up with it.' That was the take that ended up on the record. 'I learned a lot from that,' Keith said. 'I also learned that we should always have air conditioning in the studio.'

Interestingly, 'Somebody Like You' had an unexpected effect on Keith's (soon to be ex-) girlfriend when he played her the finished recording. She didn't buy the 'love at all costs' lyric. 'You're a fucking hypocrite!' she roared at him, according to Keith. 'You're not the guy in the song.' She felt strongly that Keith refused to give all of himself to relationships—and Keith admitted that she was probably right. 'I was writing about the person I wanted to be,' Keith said when he spoke at the SXSW music seminar many years later.

Over time—the sessions continued until the northern summer of 2002—Keith and Huff would work together on six of the album's tracks, while Keith produced the rest of the LP. He'd had most of the songs in good shape when he and Huff started work, having cut demos with his touring band and engineer Niebank back in December 2001. These were the songs that made up the bulk of what would become *Golden Road*, despite the resistance of at least one executive at his label. When Keith first previewed some new songs for Capitol, he was told, 'No, I don't hear anything.' When Keith asked the staffer whether he meant there was nothing suitable for radio, he replied, 'No, I just don't hear anything you should put on your record.' Keith was, by his own admission, 'gutted', but was reassured by Niebank, who insisted that the songs were fine and the guy had no idea what he was talking about. 'That sounds very empowering,' Keith replied, and he continued making the record. Among the songs that Keith previewed was 'Who Wouldn't Wanna Be Me', which would reach number 1 in 2003.

Keith had again collaborated with some of the best writers in town, among them Rodney Crowell (on 'What About Me' and 'You Won'), who'd been a big Ranch fan, as well as Monty Powell on the track 'Who Wouldn't Wanna Be Me' and Paul Jefferson on 'You're Not My God'. (Jefferson had co-written 'That's as Close as I'll Get to Loving You', a number 1 in 1995 for country traditionalist Aaron Tippin.)

Keith was bingeing on pronouns; the album featured 'me' or 'my' in five song titles and 'you' or 'you'll' in another six. A rare exception—lacking both a pronoun and a co-writer— was 'Song for Dad', the most personal song that Keith had yet committed to disc. Keith had premiered the song in May 2002, a full five months before the album was released, during a benefit show in LA. It was a heartfelt, metaphor-free tribute to his eccentric, country music–loving father Bob, whose record collection had pointed him in the direction of Nashville.

'You tend to just punch your dad in the shoulder to tell him you love him, and it's the same for dads sometimes,' Keith said after the LA show. 'They're not sure how to tell their sons that they love them. The older I get, the more I realise I'm so much like my dad. I mean, I say the same things and I do the same things'—Keith had a habit of jingling his car keys and tapping his fingers on the table, just like Bob—'so, it just became something I thought a lot of people would get.'

There were other traits that Keith and his father shared that didn't get a mention in the song. 'My dad was an alcoholic, and I grew up in an alcoholic's house,' Keith admitted in his interview with US *Rolling Stone* in 2016. Keith would later describe himself as being 'alcoholically wired', a burden that only various stints in rehab really kept under control. 'Song for Dad' didn't go there; the only allusion to friction was a mention of the times Keith 'thought he was bein'/Just a little hard on me', but even that came with a caveat, as Keith explained that he now understood his father's tough love was his way of teaching him to 'become the man he knew that I could be'.

Interestingly, Keith didn't play the song to Bob until after that LA show, when he was sure it was ready. Clearly, telling his father how he really felt about their relationship, for better or worse, meant a lot to Keith. He expressed his feelings in other ways, too, buying Bob a Harley, which he proudly rode on the streets of the Gold Coast where he and Marienne now lived.

★

Keith rarely stopped to catch his breath in 2002. In between sessions for *Golden Road*, he toured frequently. During June he took part in a number of high-profile, multi-artist gigs, including shows with Alan Jackson and Martina McBride—where Keith snuck new songs 'Somebody Like You' and 'Who Wouldn't Wanna Be Me' into his short sets—as well as his second appearance at Nashville's Fan Fair, in mid-June. On 30 June, Keith fulfilled a life's dream when he shared a bill at Grant Park in Chicago with the Charlie Daniels Band, whose 'Devil Went Down to Georgia' had been a crowd favourite during Keith's human jukebox days. (Keith would play Daniels' hellfire fiddle part on electric guitar.)

In July, Keith headlined shows of his own, in Jackson, Mississippi, and Tallahassee, Florida, before rejoining his buddies Brooks & Dunn on 20 July for a major show at the 20,000-capacity Polaris Amphitheater in Columbus, Ohio, as part of their Neon Circus tour. But all this concert action was a prelude to Keith's next big move—his new single, 'Somebody Like You', which appeared on 23 July.

The slick, sun-kissed video for the single was again directed by Trey Fanjoy and offered a peek into Keith's upwardly mobile life. Keith's video co-star was stunning 27-year-old supermodel Niki Taylor, a *Vogue* cover star at seventeen and a former *Sports Illustrated* swimsuit calendar cover girl. During the clip, the pair made quite the golden couple as they hugged it out on a mountain top near Malibu, radiating some major heat for Fanjoy's camera. (The site for much of the video was the home of the son of famous architect Frank Lloyd Wright.)

The video for 'Somebody Like You' was a love-in, the perfect accompaniment for a song that was modern country-pop at its best, its upbeat, sensitive-New-Age-guy lyric teamed with Keith's heartfelt vocals and fiery guitar and 'ganjo' playing. (The ganjo was a six-stringed banjo tuned like a regular guitar, a favourite weapon of Keith's.) 'Somebody Like You' had all the makings of a smash hit. Its timing was impeccable, too, this being a summer when sex appeal was big and hunks in hats, everyone from Kenny Chesney to Toby Keith and Gary Allen, were dominating *Billboard*'s Hot Country Songs chart, and pretty much ruling CMT's video playlist. Keith, of course, was an outlier who, unlike the others, saw no need to hide his shaggy golden mane beneath a Stetson.

'Somebody Like You' became Keith's second country number 1 on the country singles chart, finally hitting the jackpot on 19 October 2002, part of a six-week run at the top and a 41-week stint on the charts. (It also reached number 23 on *Billboard*'s Hot 100 chart.) As the song went supernova, over time selling one million copies—it's nearing 150 million streams on Spotify—the steamy video gained loads of attention as it scaled the CMT chart. But Keith downplayed any relationship with Niki Taylor, falling back on some old standards: 'We're good friends,' he said. 'A mutual friend'—Taylor's stylist cut Keith's hair—'suggested we meet because Niki wanted to be in a video. The video is very earthy and organic. She just fit the bill so well.'

As it turned out, Keith and Taylor were a couple. They'd even gotten matching tattoos, which read *Amor Vincit Omnia*, Latin for 'Love Conquers All'. Taylor referred to Keith as 'Kiki'. (Like their relationship, Taylor's tattoo wasn't destined to last; she has since had hers removed—painfully, as she admitted.)

As 'Somebody Like You' climbed the charts, Keith appeared at Farm Aid on 21 September, just two weeks before his new album hit the stores. Farm Aid, a fund-raiser first hosted by Willie Nelson in 1985, was a big event—'kick ass music and a kick ass cause', in the words of onstage MC Matthew McConaughey. The 2002 event, staged in Pittsburgh, featured Dave Matthews, Kid Rock, Neil Young, Toby Keith and John Mellencamp. Fourteen years earlier, Keith had been a face in the crowd at Brisbane's Entertainment Centre watching Mellencamp and his band tear the place up; now he was sharing a bill with one of his biggest musical heroes, in front of a 25,000-strong crowd.

'His new album is called *Golden Road*,' said McConaughey as he introduced Keith, 'and it symbolises the journey that has brought him all the way from Australia to America and to Farm Aid.' With that, Keith and his four-piece band tore into 'Who Wouldn't Wanna Be Me' but in a far looser, jammier version than would be heard on the album, Keith cutting loose on his Fender, reminding the crowd he wasn't just some pretty face in faded jeans and a snug T-shirt. A slowed-down, grittier 'Where the Blacktop Ends' followed, Keith managing to stir up a little excitement among the mid-afternoon crowd, even riffing on The Beatles' 'Day Tripper' for a few bars. The obligatory 'Somebody Like You' was Keith's closer, now familiar enough to audiences that many of them were out of their seats and joining in the chorus.

Clearly, Keith didn't choose his opening song on a whim. Who wouldn't wanna be him?

★

Golden Road finally hit the stores on 8 October and was an immediate hit, shifting some 66,500 copies in the US in the week of its release. It made its way to number 2 on the country albums chart and a very healthy number 11 on the *Billboard* 200, which was the domain of such major mainstream acts as Avril Lavigne, Norah Jones, Tom Petty and Eminem at the time. Keith's buddies the Dixie Chicks were also in the Top 10 with their album *Home*.

Critical response to *Golden Road* was effusive. '*Golden Road* reflects Urban's maturity as an artist,' noted Jack Leaver, a writer at the *Grand Rapids Press*. 'Musically, *Golden Road* is a compelling experience, with many unique twists and turns.' Over at trade mag *Billboard*, Keith's new album was being flagged as his big breakthrough: 'Without question, *Golden Road* could very well be the one for the incredibly talented Mr Urban.' *USA Today* was even more emphatic. 'Throughout the album, Urban balances his instrumental chops with his country-pop sense as well as anybody since his idol, Glen Campbell . . . This Australian guitar slinger's career ascension seems assured.'

On the flipside, a writer for the *Chicago Sun-Times* questioned why Keith yelped 'whoo' no fewer than thirteen times over the course of the album's dozen tracks. 'A "Whoo!" yelp typically indicates exciting music,' their critic figured. 'That's why it is so incongruous here.' He was not a fan.

American TV was also taking to Keith like the mainstream star he was fast becoming. 'That is a million-dollar smile,' one admiring female talk-show host said after speaking with Keith. He put in appearances on ABC's *The View* and *The Wayne Brady Show* and, most crucially, on 17 October, *The Tonight Show with Jay Leno*, which drew some five million viewers, where Keith performed 'Somebody Like You'. Keith and Leno bonded over their love of fast cars and motorbikes. Keith also performed 'Somebody Like You' at the CMAs, on 6 November, which were broadcast on CBS.

Keith, who had turned 35 on 26 October, was seemingly everywhere.

His success hadn't been ignored at home, where the album reached the ARIA Top 30. Rob Potts, his close friend, felt that *Golden Road* captured the true essence of Keith as a musician. 'What it expressed is Keith's complete commitment to his own creativity, not tempered by anything . . . At the end of it, he's one of the greatest artists this country has ever produced.'

A crew from Australian *60 Minutes* trailed Keith as he hit the road in the US, reaching the west coast for a run of club and theatre shows in LA, Sacramento and Anaheim at the end of October. Keith's tour bus had grown in proportion to his increased popularity—he now travelled in a ride that comfortably housed twelve, a world away from the days of The Ranch, when band, gear and tour manager would be sardined into a beaten-up minibus. The middle bunk was Keith's private domain, as were the stubbies of Coopers in the well-stocked bar. In the little downtime they had, Keith and the band liked to drink beer and go bowling—Keith even carried his own bowling ball with him on tour.

Keith was in good spirits when it came time for his face-to-face interview with *60 Minutes*. 'I'm a bit of a show-off,' he said in an understatement, laughing. 'And there's something intrinsically wrong with that, don't you think, getting on stage and going, "Look at me! Look at me! Look at me!" You've got some serious issues.'

Keith revisited the usual subjects—being inspired by Johnny Cash back when he was a kid, his early struggles in Nashville, and drugs, of course. 'I wasn't in good shape,' Keith freely admitted. Of course, that had all changed with the huge success of 'Somebody Like You' and *Golden Road*. So, he was asked, had that improved his personal circumstances? Apparently not. 'I'm still single,' Keith admitted. And as for being rich, well, that seemed a long way off; Keith said he was now close to breaking even. Getting famous didn't come cheap. 'It's a big hole,' he said. *'A big hole.'*

11

Walking the *Golden Road*

As 2002 morphed into 2003, the Keith Urban bandwagon kept on rolling. After a run of dates in Las Vegas during December, his next single was readied for a late January release. 'Raining on Sunday' was the big ballad, *Golden Road*'s answer to his previous album's hit 'Your Everything'.

In some ways, 'Raining on Sunday' wasn't your typical Nashville creation. It was a co-write between Radney Foster, a regular at Jack's Guitar Bar when The Ranch was the must-see band, and Darrell Brown. Brown was an openly gay songwriter/producer, perhaps the first in Nashville, a city whose public image couldn't be any straighter—it was part of the conservative Bible Belt, after all. But, as Brown stated in 2018, he didn't experience any homophobia—at least not to his face.

'I never was in a room with anybody in Nashville that cared about any of that stuff,' he told *Variety* in 2018. 'Now, when I left the room, I have no idea, but like my mom said, what somebody else thinks about me is none of my business.'

As for the song, it came out of a bleak time for co-writer

Foster, who recorded it for his 1999 album *See What You Want to See*—produced by Brown. It was on that record that Keith first heard the track, which he loved (and duly told Foster). 'Raining on Sunday' contained less obvious lyrics and themes than the typical country song of 2003, when ruling the country charts were Toby Keith's 'Who's Your Daddy?' and Tracy Byrd's 'Ten Rounds with Jose Cuervo'. 'Sunday' was on another level altogether.

'I was in the middle of a lot of emotional turmoil, but was also a newlywed,' Foster said about the writing. 'I don't tend to write on Sundays but due to logistics I had to write on a Sunday afternoon—*a rainy Sunday afternoon*. I walked into Darrell's house, just goofing around, singing: "Raining on Sunday" and he went, "Okay, that's what we're doing; here we go." When you're in the storms of life, just a day to hide under the covers with someone is a good thing. An absolute escape.

'I thought that no one would record it but me,' Foster continued. 'The entire second verse is sort of mystical, about God and sex and Mexico, but not necessarily in that order. It seemed way too out there for anything that Nashville could ever deal with . . . I think it was gutsy of Keith to record it because of that second verse. He figured out a way to make it his own.'

Foster's lyric may have triggered a memory that Keith shared during his notorious *Playgirl* interview in April 2001, when he recalled a night that he and his partner had spent entwined in a hammock. 'A storm came over and we were being thrust around by the wind, watching the trees blowing above us. It was just beautiful. The rain started pelting down and we didn't move. We just stayed there and cuddled. It was great.'

When Keith recorded the song during the *Golden Road* sessions, he reached out to Foster. Songwriters are typically kept at arm's length by artists and producers—part of the unspoken demarcation that exists in Nashville—but not so in this case. Keith called Foster as the final mix was being readied.

'Come by the studio,' Keith said. 'Check it out.'

According to Foster, 'That's a rare thing; most of the time you hear [the song] after the fact.' And he was blown away when he heard the finished product. 'It was fantastic; the moment I heard it I just went, "Wow." I pretty much knew at that point that it would be a single, and that's very rare because there's such politics to that.'

'Keith made it his own. It got more anthemic when he did it,' Foster added.

Keith had always loved Mark Knopfler's 'outros' on Dire Straits records, and now he took the chance to create a stirring outro of his own, adding a lengthy, epic guitar solo to the song. Foster described it as 'arena rock in the best sense of the word'.

As Foster left the studio, he thought to himself, 'That's a smash.'

Upon its January 2003 release, 'Raining on Sunday' faced the usual stiff opposition—Alan Jackson, Tim McGraw, Brooks & Dunn and Martina McBride all had big hit singles in the charts. But backed up by another sexy, soft-focus video, yet again directed by Trey Fanjoy—whose camera couldn't get enough of Keith—'Raining on Sunday' began to scale *Billboard*'s Hot Country Songs chart.

Keith was preparing for the big media push when, suddenly and quite shockingly, he dropped off the radar, just as he was about to leave for New York. This forced Keith's people to cancel high-profile spots on morning talk shows. A hastily prepared press release stated that Keith was suffering from a 'persistent and serious vocal cord ailment' and had been advised by his doctor to say nothing for six weeks. Literally. More appearances were cancelled, among them a proposed Canadian tour and a showcase at Nashville's influential Country Radio Seminar.

Keith 'spoke' via a written statement. 'There are no words to express my disappointment'—the irony was completely unintentional—'but I know I need to abide by my doctor's instructions.'

The truth, however, was a bit more complicated. Keith had relapsed and was doing a second stint in rehab. His silence was self-imposed. Unlike his first stretch at Cumberland Heights, Keith didn't speak about it publicly until long after the event—not until 2016, in fact, when he mentioned it to ABC News Radio in the US, although Keith had alluded to it during a sit-down with Oprah Winfrey in 2010, when he said he'd done three stints in rehab. (His third relapse happened in 2006.)

When Keith finished his recovery at Cumberland Heights, he was given some advice: if he was to go back on the road, he'd best keep his own company. Backstage in the green room, or the headliner's bus, were best kept off limits. Way too many temptations.

Remarkably, despite his three-month absence, on the strength of the song and the video, 'Raining on Sunday' kept on rising in *Billboard*'s country chart. In May, just as Keith prepared to get back to live work, the song peaked at number 3, becoming his fifth Top 10 single on the trot.

No Australian country artist, not even Olivia Newton-John during her 1970s peak, had achieved that. Keith's *Golden Road* album, meanwhile, was fast tracking its way to sales of three million—triple platinum status. The LP stayed in the charts for a remarkable two years. And Keith's earlier hit, 'Somebody Like You', found a second life on the soundtrack of the hit Hollywood flick *How to Lose a Guy in 10 Days*, which starred Kate Hudson. Matthew McConaughey, who'd warmly introduced Keith at Farm Aid, was her co-star.

Even during his enforced absence, Keith was being heard and spoken about. Sheryl Crow told a reporter, 'The whole thing about him is attractive, the fact that he can play, and *he is attractive*. He's . . . he's downright cute.' Come 2004, Keith and Crow would be sharing a stage at the *Billboard* Music Awards, with her husband Lance Armstrong looking on. A few years later, when Keith married Nicole Kidman and set up house in Nashville, Crow was a neighbour—she and Kidman sometimes took off on 'girls' weekends' to the Bahamas.

★

Keith and fellow country star Kenny Chesney had quite a lot in common. Keith was just five months older than the Knoxville native, and they'd both done hard time in Nashville before becoming bankable commodities in 1999— Keith via the *Keith Urban* album and its various hit singles, Chesney with his album *Everywhere We Go*, which produced two country number 1 singles in 'How Forever Feels' and 'You Had Me from Hello'. And both were destined to wed

Hollywood stars—Chesney marrying Renée Zellweger in 2005, Keith marrying Nicole Kidman a year later.

Chesney, like Keith, owned the stage when he played. He was a showman, a man of the people, who saw his concerts as large-scale parties. And, again like Keith, he drew his share of female fans to his shows—he was considered a major hunk.

As for their 2003 marquee value, Chesney was one step ahead of Keith, having already hosted his first headlining tour two years earlier. But together they presented a very marketable package and Keith joined Chesney on his Margaritas & Señoritas Tour, heading out on 1 May 2003. The roadshow rolled into such cities as Toledo, Birmingham, Charlotte, Raleigh and Pittsburgh, where they filled the 23,000-seat KeyBank Pavilion. Keith was playing solo, just him and his guitar, but his sets were now longer than the hit-and-run shows of previous years. Typically, he'd play ten songs, most of them now familiar to audiences, and then close with a rip and tear through John Mellencamp's 'Jack & Diane'.

But Keith was playing it safe while touring—a wise move, given the name of the roadshow, and Chesney's fondness for having a good time all the time. Keith took the advice he'd been given at rehab and, by his own admission, was living like a hermit, steering clear of all possible temptations. 'I didn't go anywhere,' he admitted. After playing his set, he would all but run back to his bus. And that's where he stayed.

This didn't quite fit with Chesney's idea of life on tour. After a few shows, word got back to Keith that Chesney found his behaviour strange, a bit cold. He'd asked one of his team, 'What the hell is wrong with this Keith Urban guy, man? He just sits in his bus all day. He doesn't come say hi, he doesn't hang out.'

Keith felt it was best to come clean with Chesney, so he sat down with the headliner and told him what he'd just experienced and how he was doing his best to stay sober. As Keith recalled, 'We had a heart-to-heart about what I was going through . . . [and he became] a friend, right from that moment.'

Not only did the rest of their shows run smoothly—'the crowds were very sympathetic and compassionate', a grateful Keith reported—but he would cite them as some of the best he'd ever played, something he admitted to Tamworth taste-maker Nick Erby. 'We've talked about that a couple of times,' said Erby. 'It was just Keith and the guitar, and he loved that. He would come on and watch this crowd of 15,000, maybe 20,000 who'd come there to party with Chesney—and Chesney's music is all party music—and his biggest buzz was that he could shut them up and have them listen to him.'

A rock-solid bond formed between Keith and Chesney, forged during that emotional backstage sit-down. It was a bond that stretched well beyond their run of dates in 2003. When they holidayed together in the Caribbean early in 2004, they shocked fellow resort guests by taking to the small stage and rocking the bejesus out of classics from AC/DC and Aerosmith. And Chesney would talk Keith up whenever he had the chance. 'He wasn't somebody that came to Nashville with a karaoke tape looking for a record deal,' Chesney told a reporter from NBC. 'He's honest, and his music is honest.'

While on the road with Chesney, Keith spoke with a writer from the *Boston Herald*. He cited Steve Martin's *The Jerk*, one of his favourite films, explaining that when he first reached Nashville he felt just like Martin's Navin R. Johnson, who had no idea he'd been adopted by the African-American family that raised him. 'I always forget that I'm not black,' Keith explained. *Sort of.*

★

Just like his fellow Australian acts that had broken through in the US, most notably INXS and AC/DC, Keith never shirked a gig. The road was his home. The dates with Chesney took him through to the end of July 2003, when Keith set out as a headliner, the road taking him as far north as Canada for two weeks during September. While he wasn't yet drawing audiences like Kenny Chesney, Keith's following was growing—he was now filling 3000-seaters.

Yet when Keith returned to Australia in October 2003, it was in the role of support act, opening for 21-year-old country songbird LeAnn Rimes, a former child star who'd had her first major hit at thirteen. LeAnn Rimes had the type of chart success in Australia that still eluded Keith. Her 'Can't Fight the Moonlight' had been the biggest-selling single in Australia during 2001, outselling even Kylie Minogue's 'Can't Get You Out of My Head'. Promoter Michael Chugg booked a run of dates, covering the NSW regional centres Newcastle and Wollongong, as well as Adelaide, Sydney and Melbourne, and in Brisbane—a hometown gig for Keith—on 22 October. The venues were mid-sized, and most were comfortably filled, if not jam-packed, during the tour. Thankfully, there were only a few empty chairs at the Brisbane show, staged at the Entertainment Centre, drawing almost 5000 fans. It was the biggest crowd of the tour.

During these shows with Rimes, Keith took a moment

to remember one of his earliest mentors, Slim Dusty, who'd died on 19 September, at the age of 76, from cancer. (Dusty was granted a state funeral, a rare honour.) Keith had never forgotten the support Dusty and Joy McKean had given him back when he was frowned upon by conservative Tamworth tastemakers because of his non-conformist ways. In 1998, Keith had covered 'Walk a Country Mile' for a tribute album, *Not So Dusty*. Now he had the chance to express his respect for Dusty in a more personal way. Each night on the Rimes tour, Keith would sneak in a chorus of the Dusty classic 'A Pub With No Beer' and then quietly say 'God bless, Slim' before segueing into 'But for the Grace of God'. The local crowds loved it.

Keith's *Golden Road* had stalled at number 29 in the Australian charts. It wasn't quite a flop yet came nowhere near the success it had found stateside, where the LP was still charting a year after first entering the *Billboard* 200. Keith's peculiar situation back home was best summed up by an encounter he had at the US Embassy in Sydney. One of the security guards approached him, stars in his eyes, asking for his autograph. He said to Keith, point blank: 'I'm sorry that your success hasn't translated here.' Keith smiled a little uncomfortably and replied, 'Well, that's what I'm back here working on.'

A writer from *The Sunday Age* asked Keith about his brother, Shane. What type of life had Shane chosen? Years ago, when they were kids, Keith and Shane had spoken about the future and Shane had said he wanted to have a family, own a house, get a job—normal things that gel with the big dreams Keith nurtured. Now, as Keith revealed, Shane was living his version of the perfect life: he had a wife, two kids, a good home (in rural Murwillumbah, New South Wales). 'And he is absolutely as content as I've ever seen anybody.

'When you're touring, it's wonderful because you're always on the move,' Keith admitted. 'But anybody that's single recognises that the hard part is when the work's over . . . when everybody goes home.' That was the moment, Keith confessed, 'when you go, "Oh, that's right. This is my home, out here in the middle of nowhere."'

While in Australia, Keith claimed his second ARIA Award, this time for Best Country Album, which went some way to offsetting his disappointment at not being a household name in his own country. Keith's current tour headliner, LeAnn Rimes, presented him with the gong, along with chirpy TV host Rove McManus.

Looking smooth as ever in a dress shirt open almost to the navel, designer jeans and a suit jacket, Keith was in good spirits. First up, he thanked Delta Goodrem, the night's big winner, 'for not doing a country record this year'. He gave a shout-out to his Australian team—Rob Potts, Chrissie Camp—and the staff at Warner's, who distributed *Golden Road* in Australia. 'My goal is that this will be the first of many, many tours,' Keith said in conclusion, 'because I'm ready to come home.' The audience inside the Sydney Superdome lapped it up.

Delta jokes aside, it was a strange situation for Keith. ARIAs such as Best Country Album were secondary awards at best. Despite huge sales in the States, a string of charting singles and an ever-growing number of high-profile awards, Keith didn't rate a mention in the key ARIA categories. Best Male Artist Alex Lloyd may have had a huge hit with 'Amazing', but his achievements didn't compare with those of Keith, who wasn't even nominated. It seemed that recognition at home—real, genuine recognition of not only his success, but the journey he'd undertaken to get to the top—was some way off yet. If it was to come at all.

*

Keith wound down a rollercoaster ride of a year—chart hits and a smash album were great, his stint in rehab less so—with a night for friends and guests at B.B. King's Blues Bar in downtown Nashville, on 8 December. There was business to attend to: the third single from *Golden Road*, 'Who Wouldn't Wanna Be Me', had hit number 1 on the country chart in November, and there were gifts to be exchanged. Jewel and Barry Coburn, Keith's backers at Ten Ten, gave their mega-successful client and friend a black leather chair, a reading lamp and a journal. Monty Powell, Keith's co-writer on 'Who Wouldn't Wanna Be Me', presented him with a blazing red electric guitar, inscribed with the Latin phrase *Amor Vincit Omnia* that matched the tattoo on Keith's wrist.

'I'm humbled by everyone's support,' Keith said when he stepped up to speak, 'and I just really want to thank everybody that goes to bat for me. Because this is an industry where people pick and choose and change sides so fast.'

It had been a banner touring year for country music. The genre's nine leading acts had grossed a hefty US$266 million on the road; Kenny Chesney alone had grossed almost US$37 million from touring during the year, often with Keith as his opening act. Keith wasn't yet raking in such serious money—although his market value as a live act would soon skyrocket—but *Billboard*, in its year-end wrap up, tipped huge things for him. In its words, he was one of the handful of 'breakthrough acts [that] are moving up'. Headlining your own big tour, which Keith was yet to do, was where the real money was to be earned. *Billboard* hinted that was on the horizon.

Yet Keith wasn't ready for the white picket fence, as he admitted in yet another interview on the subject. 'I would love to be married,' he admitted. 'I would love to have children. But you have to make sacrifices in a relationship, and I feel that one would suffer—my relationship or my career.' And Keith simply wouldn't make any sacrifices that might harm his career. '[I wouldn't want] to give it up for anybody, or anything.' It was this total commitment to his work that derailed his relationship with supermodel Niki Taylor. 'His career got really busy, I got really busy and we never saw each other,' she said after they split.

However, as the new year dawned, Keith did make one concession to domesticity. After years of house sharing, renting and/or living in the back of the tour bus, Keith bought his first home, in Nashville. It was humble by the standards that he'd soon come to know, but it did cater for Keith's one absolute must-have: it had a space that could be converted into a music studio.

'That will come before anything gets furnished,' promised Keith, and he stayed true to his word.

12

'Keith Urban is the Australian heartthrob of American country'

Having success on the scale that Keith had been enjoying in Nashville was a wonderful thing, but being truly accepted by Music City required more than chart stats and sales figures. Despite the racier videos and sexy image of acts such as Keith, Nashville's music community, deep down, was a very conservative place, where traditional values still carried a lot of clout. And there were key rites of passage to be undertaken.

Nashville's Ryman Auditorium is known as the 'Mother Church of Country Music'—playing there is still the musical equivalent of a Catholic pilgrimage to Lourdes, or a reggae lover jamming with Rastas in Jamaica. Opened in 1892, and originally known as the Union Gospel Tabernacle, the Ryman was built ostensibly to provide a place for evangelist Reverend Sam P. Jones to spread the good word. But in 1943 it began hosting the legendary Grand Ole Opry radio show and over the next 31 years staged concerts from Elvis Presley, Johnny Cash, Patsy Cline and many other titans of American music, before the show moved into its own Grand Ole Opry House elsewhere in Nashville. As far as Music City's establishment was concerned, you weren't fully accepted until you'd played the Ryman, or—in the case of Johnny Cash, whose memorial service was held there in September 2003—been farewelled there.

Keith had come close in the recent past. While still in The Ranch, Keith, Jerry Flowers and Peter Clarke had backed Slim Dusty at the 'new' Grand Ole Opry House, on Dusty's invitation, during a visit to Nashville in 1997.

On 1 March 2004, Keith was invited to play the Ryman. It was his first live set in America since Christmas, as he'd been in the studio working on a new LP. While Keith wore his standard stage gear—T-shirt and jeans—he was fully aware of the gravity of the occasion. 'This is mind blowing,' Keith said from the stage, taking in the 2300-seat home of country music.

Yet in some ways, this was not your typical Ryman show—Keith's female fans made sure of that, screaming as he played, which didn't usually happen at such a sacred site. In one particularly bizarre incident, Keith was handed something from the crowd: a Ken doll–like figure, created in his likeness. *A Keith doll.*

'Thank you,' he smiled, looking a bit puzzled, 'but I think you've got too much time on your hands.'

Keith worked his way through an eighteen-song set, liberally peppered with fan favourites. When he broke into 'Somebody Like You', his biggest hit, much of the crowd leapt to their feet—again, not your typical Ryman audience reaction. Keith's buddy Jerry Flowers joined him onstage for two songs. They remained tight. Covering the show for CMT, Craig Shelburne was won over by Keith, describing his take on country 'slick yet appealing'. As for being a sex symbol, Shelburne admired the fact that Keith didn't milk it. 'To his credit,' he wrote, 'Urban doesn't play up the sexy thing in concert, which would likely alienate half his audience.'

Keith, clearly, was no fool. When he'd first started out in Nashville, he'd developed a rep as a muso's muso, and while his good looks and pop smarts had helped him rise to the top, he still wanted to be known as a credible player. Crucially, Shelburne made the point that unlike much of the current crop of country hunks, Keith had risen to prominence the hard way, 'through the Nashville club scene, where a sold-out show at the Ryman is viewed as the ultimate success'.

That night, it finally became official. Keith had paid his dues.

*

A few weeks later, Keith headed out again with his pal Kenny Chesney, playing arena shows throughout April and May in the US heartland—Illinois, Minnesota, Louisiana, Arkansas, Oklahoma, Georgia and beyond. These were the type of country music hotspots that would adopt Keith, when he graduated to headliner, like a native son.

By mid-June, Keith was back in his adopted hometown, taking part in the huge CMA Music Festival 2004, the former Fan Fair, which was hosted at Nashville's humbly named Coliseum, a 60,000-seat downtown stadium. Brooks & Dunn were the main attraction, but Keith had worked his way up the ladder. He was billed above the likes of fellow Capitol artists Dierks Bentley, whose recent self-titled debut LP had just gone gold, and Chris Cagle, a Louisiana native who'd cut four Top 10 country singles in the past three years. Even legends Vince Gill and Tanya Tucker performed prior to Keith.

Keith's five-song bracket on Sunday 13 June, which began with 'Who Wouldn't Wanna Be Me' and closed with 'Days Go By', a sneak peek from his new record in the works, was rapturously received. '[His] amazing Sunday night set proved why many consider him the format's latest superstar', noted a writer for *Top40-Charts.com*.

As exciting as that was, Keith was equally focused on a guest star playing that Sunday night—none other than Glen Campbell, whose classic hits had inspired Keith's odyssey when he was just a little kid with a big guitar. (Keith admitted that, when he was a young hopeful, 'I wanted to be Glen Campbell.') Before taking the stage, Campbell revealed that Keith had reached out and asked if he'd consider recording with him. He said he was 'flattered'—and readily agreed. 'He's a good player,' Campbell said. 'He's not a bad singer, either. He's good all round.'

At 68, Campbell, looking sharp in denims and a long-sleeved shirt, took the stage and effortlessly crooned 'Rhinestone Cowboy', 'By the Time I Get to Phoenix' and 'Galveston', also showing off his chops on guitar. Fanboy Keith watched from the wings, flashing back to the long-ago night in Brisbane when he'd met Campbell backstage and boasted about his own guitar playing.

★

Be Here was released in September 2004 and appeared to be built upon the time-honoured philosophy of 'don't fuck with the formula'. Just like *Golden Road*, the album offered a steady balance of big ballads, country-pop rockers and rootsier moments, and again, just like its predecessor, it comprised thirteen tracks. Producer Dann Huff returned, as did many of Keith's *Golden Road* co-writers, including Rodney Crowell, Darrell Brown and John Shanks.

Keith had admitted that Nashville writing rooms weren't the most inspiring places, and at least one new song had come to him in an unlikely place. In March 2004, Keith was sitting in a TV studio, about to appear on *The Sharon Osbourne Show*, when he started humming a melody. It was good enough for him to pick up his phone and record it on his home answering machine, fearful that it might slip away. Later on, Keith got together with Monty Powell, another regular collaborator, and banged 'Days Go By' into shape.

There was also the obligatory cover on *Be Here*. On *Golden Road* Keith had gone with 'Jeans On', a number 3 hit in Australia and the UK for Brit David Dundas (Lord David Dundas, in fact, the son of the 3rd Marquess of Zetland), a choice that he had grown to regret. There was more cheese in 'Jeans On' than in a toasted sandwich. 'My memory of it was much cooler,' Keith admitted well after he recorded the song. 'I recently heard the original again and it sucks.' For *Be Here*, he turned to the estimable Elton John/Bernie Taupin songbook, and covered 1971's 'Country Comfort', a twangy pop song that Keith loved as a teenager, although he confessed that his take owed more to Juice Newton's 1981 cover than Elton's original. 'Purists will freak out,' Keith said, 'but that's just the way it is.'

There was one new co-writer in Keith's world. Chicago-born Richard Marx had been a star during the MTV era, best known for his 1989 power ballad 'Right Here Waiting' and a very impressive head of dark, wavy hair. Not unlike Keith, Marx had been more a fan's favourite than a critic's darling—*Rolling Stone* used the words 'glib', 'sappy' and 'hard to take' in one review of his 1989 LP *Repeat Offender*, quite the achievement. Not that this prevented him from shifting about 30 million records worldwide at the time of writing. Marx had actually started out as a songwriter; his first break came when Kenny Rogers recorded his song 'Crazy,' a country number 1 in 1985. And it was in this role as tunesmith-for-hire that Marx got to work with Keith.

'We love big hooks and great melodies,' Marx said of their creative connection, although he admitted that words didn't flow so readily when he and Keith wrote together. 'When we start writing lyrics, I want to kill him and me in a murder-suicide pact. It's a lot of staring into space and our laptops.'

The pair first tried co-writing in Nashville, but little came of it, so Marx invited Keith 'out to the house', a sizeable spread on the outskirts of Chicago, on the shores of Lake Michigan. Keith had come to believe that his ganjo was blessed—it 'seems to be a good luck charm for me'—so he booked an extra seat on the flight to O'Hare and brought it with him. Once settled in the music room at Marx's house, Keith began to play his ganjo over the top of a drum loop, and the song 'Better Life' gradually emerged. Keith was so smitten with the tune that, for a time, it was the working title of his new LP.

'I thought of calling the album *Better Life* because everybody wants one,' Keith figured, reasonably enough. The title didn't stick but the relationship did; Keith would continue writing with Marx—nicknamed 'Skid' by John Farnham, another Aussie collaborator, although Keith called him 'Ricardo'—in the future.

During his Chicago visit, Keith and Marx drove to a Best Buy to stock up on cassettes. Though Marx had a million-dollar home studio, both he and Keith preferred to record their ideas on cheap tape recorders. When the pair reached the counter, as Marx recalled in his 2010 memoir, a customer walked over. After recognising Marx, she turned and asked, 'And are you Keith Urbane?' Keith smiled and replied, 'Almost.'

In the end, a higher force influenced the choice of *Be Here* as the album's title. At the top of Keith's reading pile was a 1997 pop-psychology bestseller named *The Power of Now: A Guide to Spiritual Enlightenment*. Author Eckhart Tolle, a German-born Canadian, implored his readers to 'feel the power of this moment and the fullness of Being. Feel your presence.' Depending on whom you believed, *The Power of Now* was either an essential guide to all things spiritual or a long-winded ramble, top-loaded with 'New Age mumbo jumbo' (according to one unconvinced Amazon reviewer).

'Realise deeply that the present moment is all you have,' wrote Tolle. 'Make the now the primary focus of your life.' Keith did just that, in the process becoming a Tolle convert—and there was a strong whiff of Zen to not only the title of *Be Here*, but such tracks as 'Days Go By'—with its 'You better start livin' right now' refrain—'I Could Fly' and 'These Are the Days'. Keith wasn't alone—singer/songwriter Jewel and American chat show queen Oprah Winfrey were true Tolle believers, Oprah spruiking his work on her huge-rating TV show. Self-help guru Deepak Chopra was won over sufficiently to endorse Tolle's book, which was translated into 33 languages and sold several million copies—exactly the kind of numbers that Keith and Capitol Nashville hoped to capture with *Be Here*.

*

Keith's growing public profile guaranteed broader exposure for *Be Here* when it hit the stores during the first week of September 2004. US *Rolling Stone* had been cool on Keith but they couldn't ignore him now, granting *Be Here* a review. Writer Jon Caramanica (who had stated that *Golden Road*'s 'You'll Think of Me', Keith's fourth country number 1, was 'the best breakup song of the year, in any genre'), noted how Keith 'turns the cruel lens on himself with "The Hard Way", the starkest track on *Be Here*'. Caramanica even mentioned John Mellencamp, although he felt that Keith didn't 'quite have the gravel pipes' of one of his biggest musical heroes. Still, it was a three-star review in a mainstream music mag with a huge circulation.

Bob Allen, writing for Amazon, poured on the praise. He saw Keith as 'kind of like contemporary country's Tom Cruise. The kid is just so unjustly talented, likeable, and good-looking that it's hard not to *hate* him.' The BBC's Sue Keogh took a more Anglocentric approach, calling Keith 'the David Beckham of country music'. *Billboard* rated 'Making Memories of Us', the biggest ballad on the album, as 'one of the more moving and romantic songs of his career'. A big rap.

'Days Go By', the album's lead single, generated yet another country number 1 for Keith, his fifth. As for *Be Here*, the LP shifted 148,000 copies in its first week—huge sales—and topped *Billboard*'s country album chart as well as leaping into the third position on the all-important *Billboard* 200. Its race to the top was only halted by Green Day's *American Idiot* and Nelly's *Suit*.

Now was the obvious time for Keith to set out on his first headlining tour, Be Here '04, which was sponsored by CMT. Keith still wasn't quite ready for the stadiums; instead, his tour hit smallish theatres, 2500- to 5000-seaters, with tickets in the US$30–35 price range. His first show was held on 8 October at the 3280-seat Emens Auditorium in Muncie, Indiana, where Keith packed the room to the rafters.

Away from the action on stage, the Be Here Tour featured a fan attraction known as CMT Cross Country, a 'star-studded red carpet' where punters could pose with their favourite stars—or at least life-sized cut-outs of their fave stars. A cardboard Keith was, naturally, a huge drawcard.

Keith's touring band comprised five Nashvillians: Mark Hill on bass, Steve King on piano and keyboards and stocky Chris McHugh on drums (who'd worked on all of Keith's Nashville albums), while between them Chris Rodriguez and Chad Jeffers did their best to play every stringed instrument known to humankind: acoustic and electric guitar, ganjo, dobro, mandolin, bouzouki, the works. This left Keith to focus on singing, busting out some serious guitar solos (and equally serious rock faces) and charming the hell out of audiences.

Together, Keith and the band generated enough energy to light a city. These were more straight-up rock-and-roll shows—punctuated by a sit-down acoustic set—than the country-pop heard on Keith's million-selling albums. Keith, who'd be sweating clear through his T-shirt within two songs, transformed *Be Here*'s 'Better Life' into a balls-out rocker worthy of any act on MTV. 'Raining on Sunday', meanwhile, not only inspired a hearty audience singalong every night, but opened *and* closed with a screaming guitar solo, which left Keith, and his fans, just about breathless. On the flipside, Keith stripped 'But for the Grace of God' down to just voice and acoustic guitar, with a little added percussion from drummer McHugh, leaving plenty of space for a loud audience singalong.

Subsequent gigs in Austin, Houston, Birmingham, Savannah, Atlanta, Pittsburgh and elsewhere either drew full or nearly full houses, and on 27 October Keith packed New York's venerable Beacon Theatre, which had hosted everyone from the Reverend Al Green to The Rolling Stones and southern rock greats The Allman Brothers Band. The tour then stopped in Milwaukee, Detroit, Cleveland and Louisville before Keith headed to Nashville briefly to spend Thanksgiving with his parents, who were visiting from Australia. Back on the road, just prior to Christmas, Keith and band played a two-night stand at LA's 2500-seat Wiltern Theatre, shows that were filmed for the *Livin' Right Now* DVD (another nod to Tolle).

'As you guys probably have figured out,' a grinning Keith, dripping sweat, told the LA crowd between songs, 'we're shooting a DVD tonight. So, if you're standing next to somebody you shouldn't be with, now would be a good time to move.'

Keith had clearly grown comfortable with these types of venues, advising the Wiltern audience 'to just make yourselves at home . . . it's your living room, we're just gonna

Keith on the banks of
Tamworth's Peel River, January 1990.
June Underwood.

Keith with Smoky Dawson,
Tamworth, NSW, January 1991.
June Underwood.

Keith in Tamworth, 1991. John Elliott.

Keith on the road with Slim Dusty,
Moree, NSW, 1993. John Elliott.

Keith in Brisbane, 1990.
John Elliott.

The Ranch, January 1998:
(LEFT TO RIGHT) Peter Clarke, Keith,
and Jerry Flowers. John Elliott.

Keith with his mother, Marienne,
at the BMI Awards banquet,
Nashville, October 2000.
©Billy Kingsley/USA Today Network.

Keith performs in Pennsylvania, June 2001. Steve Trager/Frank White Photo Agency.

Judges Keith Urban, Mariah Carey, and Nicki Minaj smile at a Fox panel for the television series *American Idol* at the 2013 Winter Press Tour for the Television Critics Association in Pasadena, California, January 8, 2013. REUTERS/Alamy Stock Photo.

Keith with Shania Twain and Billy Joel after being named Entertainer of the Year at the CMA Awards, November 2005, New York. ©Robert Deutsch/USA Today Network.

Keith performs at Burgettstown, Pennsylvania, May 2003. Steve Trager/Frank White Photo Agency.

Keith and Nicole Kidman
at the American Music Awards,
Los Angeles, November 2009.
Burning Karma/Wikimedia Commons.
https://commons.wikimedia.org/wiki/
File:Nicole_Kidman_Keith_Urban_2009.jpg

A very pregnant Nicole with Keith,
American Country Music Awards,
Las Vegas, May 2008.
Tsuni/USA/Alamy Stock Photo.

Keith and Nicole at the
US Open tennis, Flushing Meadows,
New York, September 2009.
Edwin Martinez/Wikimedia Commons.
https://commons.wikimedia.org/wiki/
File:Nicole_Kidman_.jpg

LEFT: Keith with *The Voice* contestant
Darren Percival, June 2012.
Eva Rinaldi/Wikimedia Commons.
https://commons.wikimedia.org/wiki/File:Darren_
Percival,_Keith_Urban_(7178843793).jpg

BELOW: Keith with *The Voice*
co-judges Seal, Delta Goodrem,
and Benji Madden, Sydney, June 2012
(LEFT TO RIGHT). Eva Rinaldi/Wikimedia
Commons.
https://commons.wikimedia.org/wiki/File:Seal,_
Keith_Urban,_Delta_Goodrem,_Joel_Madden_
(7178840681).jpg

Keith and Nicole at the Golden Globes, Beverly Hilton, California, January 2013. J. Deering Davis/Wikimedia Commons. https://commons.wikimedia.org/wiki/File:2013_Golden_Globe_Awards_(8378775681).jpg

BELOW: Keith with *American Idol* co-judges Jennifer Lopez and Harry Connick, Jr., January 2015. PictureLux/The Hollywood Archive/Alamy Stock Photo

Keith performs "The Fighter"
with Mel C, *Graham Norton Show*,
London, May 2017.
PA Images/Alamy Stock Photo.

Keith's jeans on display at the
Hard Rock Café in Nashville, 2015.
Michael Rivera/Wikimedia Commons.
https://commons.wikimedia.org/wiki/
File:Hard_Rock_Cafe_Nashville,_
Keith_Urban.JPG

Three of Keith's recent collaborators — rapper Pitbul (TOP LEFT), funk legend Nile Rodgers (TOP RIGHT) and pop superstar Taylor Swift (BELOW).
Eva Rinaldi/Wikimedia Commons (Pitbull), https://commons.wikimedia.org/wiki/File:Pitbull_the_rapper_in_Sydney,_Australia_(2012).jpg; Raph_PH/Wikimedia Commons (Rodgers), https://commons.wikimedia.org/wiki/File:Nile_Rodgers_Coachella18W1-174_(42013481142)_(cropped).jpg; Brian Cantoni/Wikimedia Commons (Swift), https://commons.wikimedia.org/wiki/File:TaylorSwift4.jpg

Keith with Mary Martin at the
Country Music Hall of Fame,
December 2015. It was Martin
who encouraged Keith
to persevere with Nashville
after his early rejections.
©George Walker IV/
USA Today Network.

Keith tears up after being named
Entertainer of the Year at the CMA awards,
November 2018, Nashville.
©Larry McCormack/USA Today Network.

Keith, Nicole and their daughters Sunday Rose and Faith Margaret, LA International Airport, July 2014.
WENN Rights Ltd/Alamy Stock Photo.

Keith snapping a selfie with fans at the CMA Fest, Nashville, June 2015.
©Mark Zaleski/USA Today Network.

Keith performs at the CMA Fest, Nissan Stadium, Nashville, June 2016.
©Larry McCormack/USA Today Network.

Keith Urban performs on the NBC *Today Show* at Rockefeller Center in New York City on August 2, 2018. UPI/Alamy Stock Photo.

provide the music', and Keith and his band did just that. Keith even took it to the people, wading into the crowd during a kick-ass 'Where the Blacktop Ends', his guitar, and probably his clothes, only saved by the diligent security guard who stuck to him like glue. Keith jammed so hard with Chris Rodriguez on 'You Look Good in My Shirt' that they both fell on their backsides, laughing all the way. Then, mid-solo, Keith bent down and posed for selfies with the phone-wielding ladies in the moshpit, which was three, maybe four rows deep with dancing, singing, laughing, sometime screaming female fans.

The more zealous Urban-ites in the crowd—who'd soon bond together under the fan club name Monkeyville, later shortened to The 'Ville—not only seemed to know every single lyric Keith uttered, but waved banners that spelled out their feelings pretty blatantly. One read 'All I Want For X-mas Is U'; another, simply, 'Marry Me'; yet another asked 'How's It Hanging Down Under?' One banner that read 'Kiss Me, I'm Getting Married' left Keith a bit confused. 'Are you asking your husband [to be] or me?' he asked, flirting outrageously, shielding his eyes from the glare of the house lights.

Told that the sign was directed at him, Keith invited the fan up to the edge of the stage for a snog. Oddly, two women claimed the sign was theirs, puckering up for Keith; he obliged them both. When Keith took a seat and gently crooned his way through 'Making Memories of Us', yet another wedding-song-in-waiting, screams almost drowned out his vocals. The slightly stunned look on Keith's face said it all: Gladesville's Bayview Tavern was never like this.

Soon after, when Keith filled the Ford Center in Oklahoma City, Malisa Morsman, a journo from *Tulsa World*, noted that many of his female fans didn't just see Keith as a sex symbol but as a male role model, the perfect metrosexual. 'Undoubtedly, these were moments in which the majority of the female audience took a minute to sigh, bask in the ambience and wonder why their dates could not be as perfect as the incredibly romantic Urban.' Keith, wrote Morsman, was 'the Australian heartthrob of American country'.

Keith was now also a highly bankable live proposition; his graduation from must-have opener to headliner was complete. The nightly gross for these late-2004 *Be Here* shows ranged from US$100,000 to a very healthy $195,000 for a one-off at the 6500-capacity Maverik Center in Salt Lake City, Utah, on 7 December. He filled the 6500-capacity Pensacola Bay Center in Florida (grossing $201,000, a tour peak) and the 5600-seat Hertz Arena in Estero, Florida (a further $182,000). Keith's two nights at the Wiltern generated almost $250,000 all up. With a hit single and *Be Here* lodged in the charts—it would eventually sell four million copies in the US alone, and another 200,000-plus in Australia, his biggest seller so far in both countries—Keith had hit a new peak without, seemingly, any recent offstage blowouts or relapses.

Life was good—great, even—but Keith's world was about to be turned upside down.

13

'I swear that she floated across the room. It was out of this world'

Australia Week was an annual schmoozefest held in January in the US, honouring Aussies who had succeeded on a global level in such fields as film, music, theatre, travel, food and wine, fashion and business. A partnership of the Australian Consulate in Los Angeles, the Department of Foreign Affairs and Trade, Tourism Australia, AusTrade and Qantas, the 2005 event was to be staged in the City of Angels from 15 to 23 January. The key event was the Penfolds Black Tie Gala, known simply as G'Day LA, where the success of three prominent Aussies was to be acknowledged, but without much of the pomp of typical awards shows. According to Mel Gibson, a 2005 honouree, 'It's really just an excuse to get loaded.'

The G'Day LA honourees were to be actors Gibson and Nicole Kidman, and songbird Delta Goodrem. While

Gibson and Kidman were huge stars, having just been seen in *The Passion of the Christ* and *The Stepford Wives* respectively, Goodrem, while a big name in Australia, had made next to no impact internationally. It was an odd decision, clearly designed to boost her profile in the US.

Keith's situation, however, was vastly different. A second single from *Be Here*, 'You're My Better Half', would soon hit number 2 on the *Billboard* country chart, while the album was still selling by the thousands. And Keith was about to be nominated for the Male Vocalist of the Year gong at the upcoming Academy of Country Music Awards, a huge accolade. No Australian musician had come close to what he'd achieved over the previous five years.

Kerry Roberts, who was part of Keith's team back in Australia and a colleague of Rob Potts, began to push for Keith to be honoured at G'Day LA. Roberts was a former employee of Channel 9—the network was involved with the event—and she still had some pull there. Roberts lobbied them, stating that Keith richly deserved the honour. He was, after all, one of the biggest country music stars on the planet. Eventually the decision was made: Keith was in, Goodrem out.

The event was held in the ballroom of the Century Plaza on 15 January, in front of an invited crowd of 1000, staged amid a strange collection of yellow-and-black road signs warning of kangaroos ahead and posters depicting red sandy deserts. It was Hollywood via Ken Done with just a hint of Mambo. The mix of expats attending included Keith's buddy Tommy Emmanuel, actors Geoffrey Rush and Cate Blanchett, Olivia Newton-John and the foreign affairs minister Alexander Downer, as well as media mogul Rupert Murdoch. Also in the house was Cameron Daddo, a friend of Keith's—they'd recorded together back in Australia—and actor Julian McMahon, at the time starring in FX TV's hit series *Nip/Tuck*, who turned up with his mother Sonja, the widow of former prime minister William 'Billy' McMahon, on his arm.

When Keith and Nicole Kidman walked the red carpet, the contrast between them couldn't have been more apparent. Keith turned up in a black velvet sports jacket and a mostly unbuttoned white collared shirt, sporting his trademark three-day growth. Kidman, who'd taken more than a passing interest in Keith's risqué *Playgirl* shoot, was coolly elegant in a fringed, glittery black dress, cut just above the knee, her hair a golden blonde. Keith was the rocker, Kidman Hollywood royalty.

Just before the official proceedings began, a VIP cocktail hour was held in a nearby green room. Keith was speaking with Rupert Murdoch; nearby, Kidman was chatting with Alexander Downer and Kerry Roberts. When Murdoch was called away, Keith found himself standing alone, feeling a bit awkward.

Roberts noticed this and asked Kidman, 'Have you met Keith?'

'No, I haven't,' she replied. Together they walked over to Keith and introductions were made.

Keith related the events of this first meeting many years later when he spoke with Oprah Winfrey. He said that he'd been intimidated when Kidman entered the green room. She was otherworldly. 'I swear that she floated across the room,' he said. 'It was out of this world. There was a moment when . . . I plucked up the courage to say hi, very nervously, trying to be all cool.'

When they said their goodbyes, Keith stopped for a moment, unsure if he should have said more. 'I think she wanted to spend more time with you,' someone mentioned to Keith, glancing in the actor's direction.

Keith admitted that this left him 'dumbfounded'. 'Why me?' he asked himself. After all, Kidman was still on the mend from a public—and acrimonious—divorce from Hollywood superstar Tom Cruise, which, in her own words, left her in a 'very wary, very damaged' state. And while Keith may have been big news in Nashville, 37-year-old Kidman was something else altogether: she was a global superstar who'd won an Oscar in 2003 for her role in *The Hours*, and who'd earned more than US$10 million from her film work in the previous year alone. She'd just been paid $3 million by Chanel to appear in a four-minute ad.

Kidman was also from good stock, part of a well-heeled family based on Sydney's upscale North Shore. Her father, Antony, was a biochemist and psychologist; her feminist mother, Janelle, was a card-carrying member of the Women's Electoral Lobby; her sister, Antonia, was at the time a TV presenter. The Kidmans were from a different planet than the Urbans. Kidman was a UNICEF Goodwill Ambassador, for goodness' sake. Why would she be interested in some country singer whose dad used to work at the Caboolture tip?

Keith came clean about this in 2018 when he spoke with Andrew Denton. 'I thought she was way out of my league . . . I'm a kid from Brissie . . . not in a million years did I think somebody like that would be interested in me.'

Back in the green room, Keith, ignoring his doubts for the moment, took a deep breath, walked over to Nicole, apologised for being a little short and, as he told Winfrey, 'It went from there. We just really clicked.'

Nicole later revealed two key things. In the wake of the Cruise drama, she longed to 'meet a normal guy'. She also thought Keith wasn't interested in her when they met. 'I had such a crush on him,' she told TV host Ellen DeGeneres. 'He wasn't interested in me.' Keith insisted that wasn't the case and that he 'just didn't let on'.

At the time, though, their careers were calling: Nicole was off to New York to play photographer Diane Arbus in the film *Fur*, while Keith was due back on the road within weeks, as the Be Here Tour kept rolling well into April, including his first headlining tour of Australia.

*

One of Keith's biggest heroes was John Fogerty, the co-founder and songwriter of trailblazing roots rockers Creedence Clearwater Revival. Keith knew Fogerty's music inside out; such standards as 'Proud Mary', 'Lookin' Out My Back Door' and more had been in high demand when he was playing the pubs and clubs and beer barns of Australia. These songs were seared into Keith's DNA.

In late 2004, Keith had been introduced to Fogerty at a Bruce Springsteen show, and plans were quickly put in place for them to appear on an episode of the series *CMT Crossroads*, which paired like-minded musos to chat and play. Previous episodes had matched Lucinda Williams with Elvis Costello, and Willie Nelson with Sheryl Crow. The show was filmed in Hollywood, five days after his Australia Week honour, and Keith couldn't believe his luck. 'When you're standing next to the guy who wrote "Bad Moon Rising"—and he's singing "Bad Moon Rising"—you're like, "Oh, wow. This is pretty damn good right here."'

Early in the shoot, Keith sat down with Fogerty and rattled off all the Creedence songs he had played back in his cover-band days: 'Down on the Corner', 'Lookin' Out My Back Door', 'Who'll Stop the Rain', 'Bad Moon Rising', 'Have You Ever Seen the Rain'—'and "Proud Mary", of course', Keith added, as if it was the most obvious thing on earth.

As great as the moment clearly was, it was also slightly awkward for Keith. While the pair generously traded songs, Keith would be the first to admit that even his biggest hits, 'Days Go By' and 'Somebody Like You', weren't classics to rate with 59-year-old Fogerty's best, such as 'Down on the Corner' or even the later 'Centerfield', a comeback hit in 1985 with a snaky guitar riff similar to 'La Bamba'. (Both Fogerty songs made the day's set list.) Keith's songs were popular, but Fogerty's best were on just about every jukebox and classic rock playlist in the country.

Still, Fogerty was gracious. When Keith announced what 'a huge honour' it was to share the stage with him, Fogerty smiled and said that 'it's a huge instruction to play with you, sir'. Sure, Fogerty at his CCR peak didn't have a stylist and publicist waiting backstage, but he could sense that Keith was a kindred spirit, a torch-bearer for the type of music he'd created with Creedence, made even more clear when they plugged in together. Fogerty appeared genuinely inspired, watching open-mouthed as Keith ripped up 'Walkin' the Country', hitting the strings of his guitar with raw power. When they tore into Creedence's 'Rambunctious Boy', the pair jamming on acoustic guitars, it was hard to believe that this was the first time they'd played together.

They then got into a discussion about making radio-friendly music. It was no crime, as far as either was concerned. 'I love hearing my songs on the radio,' Keith confessed to Fogerty, who nodded agreeably. 'I like writing hooky songs that are catchy and people want to sing along with. It's a wonderful way to make music. I love it.' Fogerty felt exactly the same way. Why write songs if no one was going to hear them?

By the end of the show—which aired on 19 February—they were old pals, Fogerty thanking Keith loudly and proudly from the stage. Keith returned serve, describing Fogerty as a 'legendary and awesome damn good bloke'. Then, to make his point even more strongly, Keith tweaked the lyrics of the closing 'Somebody Like You', singing 'it sure feels good to finally be playing with John Fogerty tonight'. The studio audience, who were now on their feet, went crazy.

It had been a hell of an LA trip. Keith had met a Hollywood princess, then he'd buddied up with one of his idols. And it wasn't the last Keith would see of either Nicole Kidman or John Fogerty.

*

In April 2005, after finally summoning the courage to call Nicole, having gotten her number from a mutual friend, Keith collected her on his Harley and they rode up to the bucolic hideaway Woodstock, a couple of hours north of New York City, where the legendary 1969 festival—'three days of love and peace and music'—had been staged. They settled in for a romantic picnic.

'I was a goner,' Nicole confessed to a writer from *WSJ Magazine*. 'I mean, *c'mon*.'

When he spoke with Oprah Winfrey about his earliest times with Nicole, Keith said he surprised himself by asking Nicole something he'd never asked anyone before.

'How's your heart?'

'It's open,' Keith recalled her saying.

'What a great answer,' Keith told Winfrey, looking back. 'Instantly it made me ask myself, "Is mine?"'

Kidman turned 38 soon after, on 20 June, and Keith stood on the stoop of her New York home at 5 a.m., clutching a bunch of gardenias. Nicole was lovestruck, as she readily admitted. 'That is when I went, "This is the man I hope I get to marry."'

Keith-and-Nicole sightings soon became regular occurrences. They were seen together in Greenwich, Connecticut, the leafy home of everyone from David Letterman to Keith Richards. Then they attended a Tommy Emmanuel concert in Nashville, their first 'public' outing. Backstage, Keith caught up with expat Aussie Jeff Walker, who'd been Keith's publicist during his early days at Capitol. He introduced Walker to Nicole, then pulled him aside.

'She is the love of my life,' Keith confessed. It seemed that he was a goner, too.

Walker had been with Keith during his darkest days and could see he was a changed man. 'I was really happy for him and them both.'

It wasn't just Keith's love life that was in good shape. 'Making Memories of Us', the third single from *Be Here*, topped the country charts in May. And it was proving to be another banner year for awards. In mid-May Keith flew to London to play his first-ever UK show, at a venue called the Scala in London, then he travelled to Ireland to do some press. He was in Belfast when the Academy of Country Music Awards were staged at the Mandalay Bay Resort and Casino in Las Vegas. The time difference wasn't doing Keith any favours—he needed to be up at 1.30 a.m. for the video link—but he'd soon forget about his lost sleep.

Wearing a purple T-shirt that proclaimed 'Thank God I'm a Country Boy', Keith looked genuinely stunned when *Be Here* was declared Album of the Year.

Keith asked, 'Can you guys hear me alright?' and the roar of the crowd back in Las Vegas proved that they certainly could. 'This is fantastic,' Keith continued. 'The best wake-up call I've ever had.'

Soon after, Keith was up for an even bigger gong, the coveted Top Male Vocalist award. When he was declared the winner, Keith thanked God and 'everyone in my team that looks after me', and gave a special shout-out to Tim McGraw, who'd given him a good-luck ring when they'd performed 'Sweet Home Alabama' at the Grammys in February. There, Keith had been nominated for two awards, but missed out. Not this time. 'Thank you, brother,' Keith smiled, looking way too good for a guy who should have been asleep.

On his return to the US, Keith and Nicole resumed their romance. Soon enough, they had pet names for each other: Keith was 'Hank', Kidman was 'Evie'. (They'd later use these names for their own fashion line—shoes, boxers, belt buckles, PJs and the like.)

During the summer of 2005, when throat problems forced Keith off the road and Nicole wasn't shooting, they were seen regularly in and around Nashville. They hung out at the

Country Boy Restaurant in Leiper's Fork, and then, closer to town, shared desserts at MaggieMoo's ice cream parlour or got caffeinated at Starbucks—his a black coffee, hers a green tea. It seemed that the relative anonymity of Nashville suited them as their relationship grew. Paparazzi weren't as prominent or as aggressive in Nashville as they could be elsewhere in the country.

Jewel Coburn, Keith's friend and former music publisher at Ten Ten—he'd shifted his publishing to the bigger Universal Music Group—was one of many Nashville insiders who sometimes bumped into them around town. The 'Kurbans' (as they'd soon be dubbed) were doing their best to resemble just another country couple, wearing baseball caps and casual clothes, shopping, drinking coffee, enjoying not being famous for a little while.

'They're very down to earth,' Jewel Coburn said at the time. 'I think they feel comfortable here in Nashville. It's a big country town, really, in many ways. The countryside is beautiful and the people are pretty normal. It's not like LA or New York.'

Radney Foster, the co-writer of 'Raining on Sunday', backed this up. 'The culture of the people here is that they leave you alone. LA is filled with guys trying to work out how to make 500 bucks selling a photo. Nashville isn't filled with people like that. Part of it is demand, too: do people really want to see Martina McBride buying her groceries?'

Even though it was becoming apparent that theirs was a love thing, Keith still downplayed their romance, at least when speaking with the press. Bruce McMahon, a writer for Brisbane's *Courier-Mail*, joined him on the road in the US, and Keith was happy to talk up his new million-dollar home in Nashville—'a real find'; his current musical loves (newies from the Kings of Leon and The White Stripes, and classics from Cold Chisel and AC/DC); and his great year so far ('2005's been the best'). But as for Nicole, Keith said only this: 'No, we're just mates. That got blown out of proportion.'

When a journo from the *Hamilton Spectator* pushed a little harder, asking, 'What's with you and Nicole, anyway?' Keith showed a clean pair of heels. 'Keeping your private life private is definitely a challenge,' he replied, 'but it's one I'm maintaining as best as I can.' And then he coolly changed the subject.

When he guested on TV's *Good Morning America*, playing a live set in New York's Bryant Park in early August, the crowd, and the banners, were out in numbers. 'Keith You're a True Urban Legend', read one. 'I'm Here To See My Mom's Boyfriend', stated another. The hosts were more than a little gushy, too. But when host Robin Roberts mentioned the cover of *Country Weekly* magazine, which had declared Keith to be 'Country's Hottest Bachelor', he looked a bit sheepish.

'To be a sex symbol—to be country music's sex symbol—how do you do it, Keith Urban?' she asked, as the crowd screamed.

'You'd have to ask Tim McGraw that question, I don't know,' Keith replied.

And what about the chatter in the tabloids concerning Keith and a certain fellow Aussie? How did he feel about that?

'I don't read 'em,' he replied. 'I don't read 'em, and neither should you.'

*

Keith turned 38 on 26 October, and he and Nicole dined at the upscale 1789 Restaurant in Washington, DC, where she was on location. Keith learned just how upscale the venue was when the maître d' discreetly handed him a sports jacket to comply with the dress code.

Keith was in the midst of another hot streak, coming off a string of dates in August and September in bigger venues, including the 20,000-seat The Gorge in Grant County, Washington, which he very nearly filled on 10 September, and generated almost US$600,000 at the box office. A few weeks earlier, Keith had drawn 8000 fans to the Erie County Fair in Buffalo, the largest crowd in the fair's concert history. A fourth single from the *Be Here* album, 'Better Life'—Keith's co-write with Richard Marx—was his latest country number 1, reaching the top spot on 22 October. A fifth and final single, 'Tonight I Wanna Cry', would hit number 2, becoming Keith's twelfth single to reach the Top 5 on the *Billboard* country chart.

Livin' Right Now, the concert film shot the previous December at the Wiltern in LA, had been granted a limited cinema run in late September, a real accolade in a time of straight-to-DVD releases. Keith also appeared in a TV and print campaign for clothing company The Gap, rocking, in an accompanying limited-edition CD, Billy Thorpe's 'Most People I Know Think That I'm Crazy'. (When he got news that 'Thorpy' had okayed using the song, Keith was thrilled. 'God bless him,' he stated. 'I'll have to go wash his car or something.')

During late July Keith had reconnected with his square-jawed buddy Kenny Chesney for a gig at Heinz Field in Pittsburgh, and they drew a remarkable 54,133 punters, the biggest-ever paying country-music audience. A TV special of that concert was scheduled to air in a few weeks on CMT. Keith was everywhere: the charts, the record books, the gossip columns—and perhaps Hollywood was next, according to a whisper doing the rounds that he'd been signed to Paramount to make his movie debut. (Nothing ever came of this, as intriguing as the thought was.)

Keith's expanding bank balance and media profile, however, didn't matter so much at his birthday dinner in DC. During the night he proposed to Kidman, and she accepted. Yet the public denials still came thick and fast. Soon after they were spotted together in Boston, near where they were staying at the chic XV Beacon Hotel. A writer from *People* magazine contacted Nicole's publicist, asking if the engagement whispers were true. 'I have not spoken to Nicole about it,' came the reply. 'I cannot tell you either way.' Keith's 'people' were equally noncommittal. 'Right now, it's just a rumour,' they insisted, a tad unconvincingly.

But a couple of weeks later, when the Be Here Tour, now a year in, reached New York, Nicole sat in the front row at Irving Plaza, brazenly blowing kisses to Keith, a hefty rock gleaming on her left hand. When asked about its origin, she replied: 'My fiancé gave it to me.' Time for denials and obfuscation was over. Keith made his own statement by having her initials—NMK (the M was for Mary)—tattooed on his right wrist, obscuring the 'Love Conquers All' tatt from his time with Niki Taylor. (Keith later had 'Mary' tattooed on the fingers of his right hand.)

Keith's hot streak hadn't ended yet. The night after the second of two Irving Plaza shows, on 15 November, Keith was in the house for the 39th CMAs, staged at Madison

Square Garden. His pals Brooks & Dunn were hosts. Keith, who had flown his mother in especially for the event, was up for three key awards: Music Video of the Year, for 'Days Go By'; Male Vocalist of the Year; and the night's closing (and biggest) gong, Entertainer of the Year. Interestingly, of all the nominees for the latter award—Keith's 'rivals' were Kenny Chesney, Alan Jackson, Toby Keith and Brad Paisley—Keith was the only one to dispense with the seemingly obligatory Stetson. He wasn't just reshaping country music; he was also updating its dress code. (Soon enough, acts such as Dierks Bentley, Luke Bryan and Sam Hunt would also go hatless.)

Ten-gallon hats were in fact the topic of discussion between the show's hosts, Shania Twain—whose most recent album, *Up!*, had sold eleven million copies in the US alone—and Billy Joel, as they stepped forward to announce Entertainer of the Year.

'I don't even own a cowboy hat,' said Joel.

'Billy, we love you just the way you are,' deadpanned Twain. The audience groaned.

When Keith's name was called out, he buried his head in his hands and was engulfed in an embrace from his mother. Before Keith could reach the stage, Chesney, who'd won the award in 2004, grabbed him in a bear hug, ruffling his hair, huge smiles on both their faces. The bond between the two was palpable.

'I'm completely weirded out,' admitted Keith, who was sporting what could have passed for a six-day growth. He duly thanked voters, his record company, his mother and Chesney—'for being so good to us and for teaching me so much about entertaining'. Then, almost with a wink, he gave a shout-out to 'Hank and Evie', before getting the big wind-up. Keith waved the trophy above his head, flashed a smile and disappeared backstage.

When Keith was asked in the press room about his relationship with Nicole, he remained shtum. 'Well,' he said, trying his best to be polite, 'I'm very grateful for this award and I'd hate to use up such valuable time discussing my personal life.'

It had been a hell of a night—a hell of a year, in fact, even though it was far from over for Keith. He had a run of big shows through December, in Kansas City, St Louis, San Diego, Phoenix, San Jose and Fresno, in rooms that ranged from 7000- to 13,000-seaters, generating up to US$400,000 a night. Every house was full.

Yet being crowned Entertainer of the Year worried Keith. He genuinely feared that he'd peaked, that his purple patch might have been over. 'I was terrified,' Keith admitted in an interview with Sirius XM. 'I thought, well, that's it, that's the end of the career. It felt too much too soon.'

How wrong he proved to be.

14

'I make out with my husband and pretend it's Keith Urban'

Way back in 1978, Keith appeared on TV performing a Dolly Parton song, 'Apple Jack'. Given all that had happened in the past year, let alone the past three decades, Keith must have thought of it as a moment from a different life altogether. But in early February 2006, his past was about to collide with the present.

Keith was playing at Nashville's annual Music City Jam, an invites-only affair that kicked off the highly influential Country Radio Seminar. Midway through his set, Keith strummed an acoustic guitar as his band locked into an oddly familiar riff. 'All we need is a female singer,' Keith said knowingly. With that, Dolly Parton strolled onto the stage and powered her way through one of her standards, 'Jolene'. She and Keith then sang 'Two Doors Down', another Parton tune.

Parton was in a typically chatty mood afterwards, joking about her upcoming 40th wedding anniversary and how she maintained the heat in her boudoir. 'I make out with my husband and pretend it's Keith Urban,' she chuckled, before adding a cheeky aside directed at the man himself. 'And there's nothing you or your leggy girlfriend can do about it.'

Of course, talk about Keith and that 'leggy girlfriend' of his hadn't ceased one bit over the past months. Keith, however, was back in the studio with Dann Huff, working on songs for a new album. But he was juggling recording with another run of sold-out shows throughout February—as well as comparing schedules with Nicole—and admitted that it was making his head spin. (Which might explain, when asked about the sound of his new record, Keith replied: 'Polka.')

'The odd part is, when you're making a new record, you're going out on tour and doing all these old songs. And your head is very much in the new record,' Keith said. 'So that very side of it is very discombobulating.' Keith had given his fourth solo record for Capitol a working title of *Love, Pain & the Whole Damned Thing*. It was a perfect commentary on his life, which he was living at hyper speed.

That pace increased even more at the Grammys on 8 February, which were staged at the Staples Center in LA, when Keith won the award for Best Male Country Vocal Performance. During the ceremony, Keith performed his winning song, 'You'll Think of Me', while seated on a glass stage several metres above the audience. Once he'd gotten that out of his system—'You'll Think of Me' was a hefty emotional purge—Keith then played guitar and sang with Faith Hill, another winner on the night, for Best Country Collaboration (with her hat-wearing hubby Tim McGraw). Finally, a Grammy—Keith's first.

★

In May 2006, Keith and Nicole reconnected briefly in New York, where Kidman, just back from inspecting the damage wrought by Hurricane Katrina, was attending a United Nations gala. Keith may still have been publicly playing down their relationship, but not so Nicole. When asked if her 'boyfriend' would be attending the gala, she corrected her interviewer. 'He's actually my fiancé. I wouldn't be bringing my boyfriend.'

An official announcement was released and quickly consumed by a hungry media: the couple were to be married in Australia on 25 June, at the Cardinal Cerretti Memorial Chapel, a stately sandstone pile located on St Patrick's Estate in the harbourside Sydney suburb of Manly. The chapel was renowned for its acoustics, although muso Keith's thoughts were likely to be elsewhere on the day.

Of course, now that there was no denying their relationship, the couple was exposed to the occasional sleazy attack. A *Daily Mail* piece, sensitively titled 'Nicole and the Crack Addict Cowboy', quoted various 'friends' whose observations drove home the story's 'message': this wasn't a relationship built to last, and what the hell was such an angel doing with this scruffy country rocker?

'Keith is still wild and always will be,' said one 'source'. 'He has looked into hell.'

A 'musician friend' of Keith's spilled on the singer's womanising ways: 'He's never been one to turn down a polite offer.' The same friend predicted that the Kurbans would last six months, tops. Some 'friend'.

A not-so-subtle comparison was drawn between the couple and the brief marriage of Keith's pal Kenny Chesney and actress Renée Zellweger, which came undone after just four months. They'd met in the same month as Keith and Kidman, January 2005, marrying that May on a beach in the Virgin Islands. (Julia Roberts had also married a country musician, Lyle Lovett, and that union didn't make two years; they divorced in March 1995.)

'Surely a girly heart-to-heart with Renée Zellweger,' the *Daily Mail* piece concluded, 'might persuade Nicole that a home on the range might be more than she bargained for.'

Zellweger did just that, albeit indirectly, advising Nicole to 'beware of cowboys' during an interview with a US newspaper. Nicole didn't respond, although—as Keith would one day admit—she did express some doubts in the weeks leading up to their wedding.

'She was worried about getting married to me, understandably,' Keith revealed, but more so because of his history of addiction, and the demands of their careers, not his womanising. 'I was trying every way I could to reassure her that I was born to be her man,' Keith said. 'The only thing I could do was reassure her, comfort her, be strong.'

There was one other thing Keith could do—write a song for his fiancée (with a little help from regular co-writer John Shanks). It was called 'Once in a Lifetime'. 'It's a long shot, baby/I know it's true,' Keith sang, 'But if anyone can make it/I'm betting on me and you.'

Nicole cried when she heard the finished version. This marriage might well be for keeps.

Meanwhile, a reporter from Perth's *Sunday Times* tracked down Greg Shaw, Keith's former manager. It was clear that Shaw still felt some resentment towards Keith and the manner in which he'd been 'cast aside', in his words. Shaw spoke frankly of how Keith would play shows while wasted—'He hated letting people down'—and tried to define his role during Keith's darkest days. 'I was not the one taking drugs . . . or buying [Keith] drugs. I was the guy telling him to treat people nicely and be responsible for his behaviour.'

Greg Shaw was not invited to the wedding.

Nor was Amanda Wyatt, a twentysomething Nashville party girl who sold her 'Keith and Me' story to *The Mail on Sunday*. Her so-called exposé was based on a few flimsy 'facts': she had a backstage snap of herself and Keith, she said that she knew the security code for his house, and was familiar with his cologne and body wash. 'Keith was always high on something,' she said. '[He said to me] I have this huge gaping hole inside of me I just can't fill.' She talked of his 'sexual' text messages and his longing for a child. 'Maybe he came to Nashville and partied with me because he could do things with me he couldn't do with Nicole,' Wyatt figured. She maintained that their relationship had continued right up until the time of Keith's engagement. 'Keith is a guy who has everything,' she told a reporter, 'but he is never truly happy.'

As dodgy as Wyatt's story seemed, it still scored plenty of reputation-damaging column inches. Keith was now tabloid fodder.

★

Controlling the message was paramount for both Keith and Nicole, something that Father Paul Coleman, who was to conduct the marriage ceremony, learned very quickly. He innocently told a reporter that the service would be short, sweet and simple, and that the couple was 'very much in love'.

Soon after, the padre was quietly told to 'cool it' by the team running the big event, headed by Nicole's publicist, Wendy Day. Day had been down this road before, having corralled the media during the marriage of Russell Crowe, another high-profile client, to Danielle Spencer in April 2003.

A few days prior to the wedding, some twenty photographers, who had set up camp outside the Kidman family home, started to stir when the garage door began opening. But they were very surprised by what they saw. Two unfamiliar women stood there, carrying a slab of beer and some water bottles. Sitting on top of this gift was a note: 'Enjoy! Nicole and Keith.'

Earlier in the day, the assembled paparazzi had sung 'Happy Birthday' to Nicole—she turned 39 on 20 June—via the intercom. They had flowers for the birthday girl, who emerged, smiling. 'Thank you for the flowers and the singing,' she said, before heading back inside. Nicole had history with 'paps', having famously clashed with photographer Jamie Fawcett in January 2005. She and Keith played this situation beautifully.

Come 25 June—the day before Bob Urban's 64th birthday—and dozens of police officers and security guards patrolled the area outside the chapel, aided by some local volunteers sporting 'Nicole and Keith' T-shirts who helped with traffic control. But the mood was more village fete than celebrity wedding, despite the media scrum and interested onlookers.

The invited guests soon began heading inside the chapel. Among them were Nicole's adopted children, thirteen-year-old Isabella and eleven-year-old Connor, who'd flown in from Tokyo by private jet. Hollywood was represented by Naomi Watts, Russell Crowe, Hugh Jackman and Baz Luhrmann. But they were outnumbered by music folk: Capitol label head Mike Dungan, Keith's attorney Ansel Davis and his financial adviser Mary Ann McCready all flew in from the US, as did Keith's manager, Gary Borman, and Anastasia Brown, who had worked with Keith during his days with The Ranch. Keith's producer Dann Huff was there, along with his engineer, Justin Niebank, his drummer, Chris McHugh and co-writers Darrell Brown and Monty Powell. Kylie Minogue was also in the house, as was Angie Marquis, who'd started out with Keith in their duo California Suite.

Among Keith's groomsmen were Marlon Holden, his old friend and bandmate from Queensland, and his brother Shane, who was best man. Antonia Kidman was her sister's maid of honour; her bridesmaid was daughter Isabella, while her niece Lucia was a flower girl.

Keith, who had spent his buck's night watching a soccer game at the Sydney Football Stadium, arrived in a silver BMW and ducked in a side door, looking slightly uncomfortable in a black tux and white vest. He was barely noticed by the crowd outside the chapel, or by the media choppers that hovered above the site. However, when those helicopters spotted the bride's ride, a cream Rolls Royce, they swooped, seemingly as one—it was like a scene straight out of *Apocalypse Now*.

None of this seemed to rattle Nicole, who emerged wearing a white Balenciaga gown. She was her usual sleek, stylish self, clutching a bouquet of white roses and working the crowd as she would an audience on opening night, oblivious to the commotion overhead. 'You are beautiful,' one onlooker called out to Nicole. 'You are all beautiful,' she replied, as she headed inside the chapel, which was decorated with thousands of lit candles, white lilies and white orchids.

In a service that Hugh Jackman described as 'a natural, loving, real Aussie wedding', the Kurbans said their vows—Keith stated, 'You make me feel like I'm becoming the man I was always meant to be'—and then it was over, seemingly in a heartbeat. At 6.25 p.m. the chapel bells tolled for five minutes and everyone within earshot knew that the knot had been tied.

The reception was held in a huge marquee, walking distance from the church.

The Urban/Kidmans chose Etta James' 'At Last' as their wedding song and had taken dance lessons so they could impress their 230 guests. But what the onlookers didn't expect was a snippet of Skyhooks' 'You Just Like Me Cos I'm Good in Bed', which blasted out of the speakers halfway through the song. 'Just to keep it real,' laughed Keith, who was proud of their ruse. 'The guests were very surprised.'

Later on, Keith's fellow Kiwi/Aussie Neil Finn serenaded the newlyweds, and then Keith stepped up to the stage and sang 'Making Memories of Us' while looking deeply into his new wife's eyes. It was as though the guests had somehow faded away for those few minutes. It was the second time in recent history that Keith had made his feelings known to Nicole via song.

When it came to the press, the couple played it like their wedding vows, keeping the message short and sweet. They issued a statement that read: 'We just want to thank everyone in Australia and around the world who have sent us their warm wishes.' *People* magazine was already working on their next cover, running the official wedding shot, which showed the couple cheek to cheek. 'DREAM WEDDING!' the mag declared. 'He cried, she cried—all about the couple's romantic candlelit ceremony.'

Rob Potts and Kerry Roberts, two key members of Keith's Aussie team, were wedding guests, and they thought it reasonable to provide 30-second grabs to the press, although they said little more than how wonderful the newlyweds looked, and how some people chose the chicken, others the fish. But this didn't play especially well with the machine that ran the respective careers of the newlyweds.

Not long after Keith and Nicole returned from their Pacific Island honeymoon, Keith to continue working on his new record in Nashville, Nicole to shoot a film in Kosovo, Rob Potts received a terse message from Gary Borman: 'Can you please take my artist off your website.' End message.

Potts, to his credit, held no ill feeling towards Keith. As ruthless as this was, given their long association, he understood it was a flexing of managerial muscle. It wasn't personal. 'I intrinsically believe Keith is a lovely person,' Potts said in 2008.

*

Keith's marriage altered the way in which the broader public viewed him. Before he met Nicole, he was a big name in country music circles but not so well known elsewhere, a situation that seemed to suit him just fine. Nicole, however, was a global superstar, whose every move and every role were monitored closely by the general public. Keith was now part of her much bigger world. The life of the Kurbans, over time, would be scrutinised in much the same way as the lives of other celeb couples, such as Angelina Jolie and Brad Pitt— aka 'Brangelina'—or Victoria and David Beckham. It was a big adjustment for Keith.

Admittedly, Keith played a minor role to his more famous wife. While not quite a human handbag, he was typically referred to as the 'husband of Nicole Kidman', her 'other half', 'Mr Kidman' and all the rest of it. Harsh comments were made about them. 'Physically they have always made a slightly odd couple,' sniffed the *Daily Express*, 'she the graceful, elegant Hollywood star and he the shorter, scruffy, tattooed "Urban cowboy" [with a] history of addiction.' (To her credit, it seemed that Nicole got Keith away from the spray tan, which had rendered him a strange shade of orange more than once in the past.) In some circles, Keith was a celebrity by association, as unfair as that was considering his achievements. Even when Keith sat down with Elton John for an *Interview* magazine story, John's first question was: 'Some of [your new songs] seem to be specifically about Nicole.'

Yet it was Keith who drew a huge amount of public attention to the couple, for all the wrong reasons, within a few months of their wedding.

★

It had been helter-skelter business as usual for Keith after he took his vows. Two weeks on from the wedding, he was back out with Kenny Chesney for a stadium show at LP Field in Nashville and come 13 July he was playing to his own full house in Ontario, Canada, with his wife watching from the wings. A few nights later, back in the US, Keith began his set by playing 'Days Go By' as he ran down a 20-metre-long catwalk that led him deep into the crowd. Even the pouring rain didn't prevent the 30,000-strong crowd from going gaga. Keith snuck in Creedence's 'Have You Ever Seen the Rain' as a nod to the unkind weather gods.

Keith was well and truly back on the rollercoaster, with more dates to play and a new album to complete. The title had been altered to *Love, Pain & the Whole Crazy Thing* so as not to upset fans who might take umbrage at the word 'damn'. 'Once in a Lifetime', the song he'd written to reassure his fiancée that they were the real deal, had been released as the lead single in late August, and created a new record when it became the highest debuting song in the 62-year history of *Billboard*'s Hot Country Songs chart, coming in at number 17 on its first appearance. It stayed in that chart for 20 weeks and over time sold some 500,000 copies—a gold record. It was yet another hit, Keith's thirteenth Hot Country Top 10 on the trot. Each of these songs had also broken into the mainstream Top 50; 'Once in a Lifetime' peaked at number 31. It also breached the Australian Top 20, reaching number 18.

During a muggy Nashville day in August, Keith had previewed his new album—still a few months away from its official release—to a writer from *Billboard*. Keith periodically put in calls to his wife during the interview, blowing kisses into the phone and saying, 'I love you.' Keith pointed out that he and Nicole liked to travel together whenever they could; he missed not having her in town. 'You don't want something cool to happen to you and not have the person you love there to share it with you,' Keith said, reasonably enough.

In mid-October, Nicole was in Rome promoting her Diane Arbus biopic *Fur*, and spoke warmly about Keith to the press. 'I love being married to my husband,' she said. 'It's the best thing I've ever done.' Meanwhile, Keith had just been photographed for the cover of his new album by high-end fashion photographer Max Vadukul, and had been voted the sexiest man in country music in a poll in the *Country Weekly* mag. But a couple of weeks earlier, when he played a show at the Fox Theater in Atlanta, something was clearly up. He seemed physically drained; there was a faraway look in his eyes, totally out of character for a focused performer who was always very much in the moment.

Then, according to at least one person who knew Keith well, he slipped. It was just one night, one boozy Cognac bender, but that was enough. Clearly, his upcoming new album, and all it would entail, was weighing on Keith, but he was also adjusting to his new, higher-profile life. And, according to some reports, he also had to cope with the added pressure of a prenuptial agreement that, in short, stated clearly that he shouldn't get fucked up—which was precisely what he did. (Both newlyweds denied that any such prenup existed.)

Despite going through 'the program' twice, Keith didn't have a sponsor, a fellow recoveree to whom he could speak and unload. He didn't attend AA meetings. Keith had no support group, nobody he could depend on to get him through the rough patches. He wasn't properly equipped to cope with his addiction.

'I went off the rails,' Keith said. 'I hadn't conceded to myself that I needed help and a new direction in my life.'

When Nicole learned about Keith's bender, she booked a

flight back to the States and reached out to some of Keith's closest friends and allies, mostly from Nashville, and arranged an intervention. Soon enough, Keith was sitting in a room surrounded by his wife and a group of people who genuinely cared for him. 'The love in that room in that moment was just right,' Keith told Oprah Winfrey. 'To see love in action in that way . . . I'd never experienced anything like that before.'

He was completely humbled. 'I was very, very blessed to have Nic call an intervention on me,' he would tell *Rolling Stone*. In his own words, he was ready 'to make a decision which road I was going to take, once and for all'.

Keith had a show booked at the Mohegan Sun Casino in upstate Connecticut, but rather than plugging in and playing, he packed his bags and checked into the Betty Ford Center at Rancho Mirage, California, on 19 October. (Fellow rehab-er Tommy Emmanuel said that Betty Ford was right for Keith. He believed it had a 'really good, solid program'.)

As Keith described it, 'The night I went in, it was total surrender.' His mantra—which sounded a lot like one of his lyrics—was 'Let's do it and let's do it right this time.' Keith even left behind his guitar, as he had done during his time at Cumberland Heights. It was a massive sacrifice for such an obsessed musician. But part of his rehab was the need to discover who he was away from music, which had defined him pretty much all his life. As Keith would tell a reporter, 'I had to find out, "What am I doing and why do I do it?"'

A post from Keith appeared on his website, which read: 'As you've likely discovered by now, last night I voluntarily admitted myself into a treatment centre. I feel calm and optimistic about the future and with finally coming to terms with the reality of my condition.'

He may have been a wreck, but Keith understood clearly what personal peril he was in. 'I'd caused the implosion of my fresh marriage,' Keith later admitted. He would have understood if Nicole had upped and left, he said—as devastating as that would have been. But for the grace of god, she didn't. Instead, she contacted her publicist, Wendy Day, and advised her, 'Wendy, I'm standing by Keith and that's all I have to say.'

In an unfortunate turn of events, Angus Hawley, Nicole's brother-in-law, also entered rehab soon after Keith, spending several weeks at the Sydney Clinic, which specialised in drug addiction and mood disorders. He and Antonia Kidman separated soon after.

*

No crisis is complete without a formal press release, and one was duly issued on Keith's behalf by his Nashville publicist, Paul Freundlich. It read: 'Keith Urban voluntarily admitted himself to a treatment rehabilitation center last night with his wife by his side.' Keith was then quoted: 'I deeply regret the hurt this has caused Nicole and the ones that love and support me. One can never let one's guard down on recovery, and I'm afraid that I have. With the strength and unwavering support I am blessed to have from my wife, family and friends, I am determined and resolved to a positive outcome.'

Everything related to Keith's upcoming album—live shows, personal appearances, interviews—were put on hold indefinitely. Messages of support came from the obvious sources—Keith's label boss, Mike Dungan, said, 'we just want him to get healthy'—and some less obvious sources. Country great George Jones, a notorious hellraiser once known as 'No Show Jones' (until he got sober in 1999, after almost dying in a car crash), was asked what advice he had. The 76-year-old Jones said that Keith should look into the damage booze and drugs had done to his career, and to his life. That would be a hell of a wake-up call. There was a caveat, though: 'It's hard to give the younger artists advice that they are going to take,' said Jones, 'because they are still young in life.'

But Keith had more than his career to lose this time if rehab didn't stick; his marriage was also at risk. And by his own admission, he was 'ready' for rehab, probably more so than he had been for his two previous stints. Keith said he was hell-bent on shaking off 'the shackles of addiction' and extended his stay from one month to two, while Nicole holed up in LA with fellow Aussie and friend Naomi Watts. Nicole's sister Antonia, who was pregnant, also joined her.

Keith was so involved with his recovery, in fact, that a few weeks in, on 6 November, when the CMA Awards were staged in Nashville, he had completely forgotten, despite receiving several nominations.

The audience in Nashville, however, hadn't forgotten about Keith, even though he was missing in action. When his Song of the Year nomination was announced, for 'Tonight I Wanna Cry', the cheer that went up inside the Gaylord Entertainment Centre was the loudest for all the contenders (even though Keith didn't win). Clearly, he had the support of all the key figures in Music City, some of whom understood all too well what he was going through. Up-and-comer Joe Nichols, who'd hit big with the oh-so-subtle 'Tequila Makes

Her Clothes Fall Off', had recently been in treatment, as had the troubled Mindy McCready (who committed suicide in 2013) and Trace Adkins, who went through rehab in 2002 after crashing his pick-up truck while on a bender. Keith wasn't alone.

Keith was also in the running for Male Vocalist of the Year, one of the key CMA Awards, which, in the words of elegant, shiny TV star Eva Longoria, who presented the award, 'celebrates the amazing men of country music'. The crowd rose to its feet when Keith was declared the winner. Keith's old friend Ronnie Dunn, who would appear on Keith's new album on the track 'Raise the Barn', stepped up to say a few words on his behalf, ending with a simple: 'We love you, Keith. Good luck, brother.'

Back at the Betty Ford Center, a staffer walked into Keith's room. 'You just won something,' he said to Keith. 'Male vocalist? CMAs or something?'

'Really?' Keith replied, more than a little shocked.

'Yeah. Off to bed.'

With that, the staffer closed the door to the room and turned off the light.

Keith turned to his roommate. 'Hey, I just won Male Vocalist of the Year.'

'How weird is this?' Keith thought to himself, lying there in the dark.

15

'Abstinence is the ticket into the movie. It's not the movie'

Keith's commitment to recovery was essential for his health and his marriage, but it caused big problems for his career, especially when he decided to extend his stay at Betty Ford by another 30 days. His new album was ready to roll, but Keith wasn't there to flog it, which was a huge dilemma. Keith's label boss, Mike Dungan, may have stated that 'we just want him to get healthy', but there was business to attend to, especially given that Keith's album was one of Capitol's key releases for the silly season. Keith had been booked to appear on the *Today* show and *The Tonight Show with Jay Leno*; he was also expected to play at a big football game. These were major cogs in the promotional machine, but when it became apparent that Keith would remain in treatment, all these appearances were cancelled. His label decided to release the album on 7 November, sans Keith—and hope for the best.

They couldn't have dreamed of a better result: state-side, *Love, Pain & the Whole Crazy Thing* moved a hefty

270,000 copies in its second week. Only Josh Groban, with his album *Awake*, and the various-artists pop collection *NOW 23* prevented Keith from topping the *Billboard* 200 album chart. The record would continue charting for a year, shifting one million units by the end of the year, becoming his third platinum LP on the trot—and debuting at number 1 in Australia.

Love, Pain was a transitional record. Keith would later admit that he was trying to 'expand outwards'—that is, get beyond the boundaries of his previous records—'but I just wasn't able to do it. Very frustrating.' There were some interesting twists: legendary arranger/conductor David Campbell (the father of indie rock great Beck) was brought in to work his magic with strings, and other new tricks—drum loops, digital-age bleeps and blips, and the rest of it—and he gave the record a very contemporary sheen. ('Urban crossover?' asked *Billboard* magazine when they ran a feature on the album.)

Keith had recently name-checked some seemingly unlikely influences, including such masters of dance and groove as Pharrell Williams, Dr Dre and the Dust Brothers. 'They're extraordinary,' said Keith. While his latest record was hardly hip-hop, it wasn't strictly country-pop, either.

'The album is further proof of Urban's ability to stretch the genre to the breaking point by bringing in more of modern pop's elements, while remaining firmly within Nashville's good graces,' wrote AllMusic's Thom Jurek. 'The man writes honest, beautifully crafted songs that are adult enough to ponder, tough enough to rock, and tender enough to pull—not tug—on the heartstrings.'

The big ballads were now even bigger: 'I Can't Stop Loving You' channelled the spirit of Queen's epic 'Bohemian

Rhapsody', with a closing guitar solo that Brian May would not have sniffed at. The Queen connection was not coincidental, given that Freddie Mercury was one of Keith's idols; Keith also loved the band's no-such-thing-as-too-much approach. In fact, the entire *Love, Pain* album was big—only a few of its songs checked in under four minutes. Another sweeping ballad, 'Stupid Boy', rolled on for more than six. Keith, clearly, had gone widescreen.

'Stupid Boy' came with a curious backstory. One of its writers was Nashville newcomer Sarah Buxton; the 'stupid boy' of the title was her ex. Keith loved the song and played it to Nicole.

'I need something like this on my record,' he told her.

'Why don't you just do that song?' she replied.

Keith initially baulked at the idea—'I can't say "stupid boy"'—but Nicole replied, 'No, you're looking in the mirror singing this song.'

Keith could have been offended but instead he was sold, and was very impressed by Nicole's instincts, stating, 'I should really give her an A&R credit on this album'. And the song would prove incredibly rewarding for Keith over time, winning him a Grammy, his second, at the 2008 awards.

★

Keith was permitted leave from the Betty Ford Center, and there were occasional sightings in the latter months of 2006: he lunched with Kidman at the Polo Lounge in Beverly Hills, and they both headed to Australia for Christmas, the couple's first homecoming since their June wedding. It would make for an interesting return to Oz—one of Keith's uncles,

Brian Urbahn, upon hearing that Keith was back in rehab, told a reporter, 'Well, he's done it before, hasn't he? It didn't fix him. Why should it work the second [*sic*] time?' Keith was just about ready to prove to such doubters that he was on his way to 'wellness'.

It turned out that Keith's recent travails perhaps hadn't been as widely followed back home as they were in the US. While onboard a Qantas flight, an attendant innocently offered him a glass of wine. One of Keith's entourage stepped in, snapping: 'He doesn't drink!' Qantas felt the need to issue a press release, stressing the point that the attendant 'genuinely did not realise who the passenger was', which begged the question: if they *had* known it was Keith Urban, would they instinctively have known that he was on the wagon? And it also unintentionally hinted that when it came to mainstream Australia, maybe Keith wasn't a household name, or at least an instantly familiar face, just yet.

Upon returning to the US, Keith disappeared, once again, through the Betty Ford Center's gates, finally signing out in mid-January 2007—and this time with a sponsor. Rather than sitting through a series of uncomfortable post-rehab interviews, he cut a video while in Los Angeles that was posted on his official website on 22 January. Looking much fresher than he had a few months earlier, Keith seemed by turns contrite, humbled, frank and positive during a lengthy address that, despite his occasional lapses into recovery-speak, had all the intimacy of a confession.

'I just wanted to take a moment today to talk a bit about the last three months,' he began, looking straight down the barrel of the camera. 'On October 19, I checked into the Betty Ford Center in Palm Springs, California, with the support of my wife and family and friends, for what I thought was going to be a 30-day stay.'

Keith insisted that there hadn't been some 'big cataclysmic event' that triggered his relapse. Rather, he said, it was an accumulation of small things 'that were telling me very loud and clear that I was a long way from my program of recovery, and they were making my life unmanageable'.

Keith acknowledged that he could have chosen a better time to fall off the wagon, given the imminent release of his new LP. He also spent his 39th birthday 'inside' and missed out on a big bash that Nicole had planned for him. He missed Thanksgiving, too. But, as Keith explained, there was a reason he didn't emerge after the planned 30 days.

'That first 30 days, I learned what they say in there: abstinence is the ticket into the movie. It's not the movie. So, learning about abstinence was one thing, but then there was all this other area of my life to start learning about. So, 30 days became 60, 60 days became 90 . . .'

Support was a big part of 'the program' and Keith said that he had that, in spades. 'I felt very, very, loved, and I felt very supported, and [it] made the time go by. I never felt alone.' Keith said his 90 days inside were 'one of the most impactful times of my whole life'. During his recovery, cards, letters and hundreds of emails—'when I finally got to my laptop and I could retrieve them all'—poured in from well-wishers. 'I just didn't expect that kind of support,' he said. 'I truly didn't, and it helped so much. Especially through a lot of the lonely days.'

'But my wife stayed extraordinarily strong and loving,' he said in conclusion, 'and my friends and family were there, and, man, it's just been really overwhelming. I feel so much gratitude, and it feels really good to have gone through it and be where I am right now.'

And where, exactly, was that? Getting back to playing, of course. Keith was still very much addicted to the adulation of his fans. 'Because where I am right now is starting on that road to getting back to doing what I love—which is playing music . . . I look forward to seeing you guys very soon. And from the bottom of my heart, thank you, and God bless every one of you.'

In almost every way, the video was the perfect way for Keith to reconnect with his fans: taking the path of 'full disclosure', laying it all out there for his audience, most of whom readily and warmly embraced the 'new Keith', if record and subsequent concert tickets sales were any gauge.

Certainly, his post-rehab return to Australia in March 2007 was seen by many as a second coming. Although this was a small-scale tour—he'd play the arenas when he returned in a few months' time—when Keith and the band plugged in at Sydney's Metro Theatre on 21 March, the audience reaction was ecstatic. Fans waved banners—'We Love You Keith' was a favourite—and cheered for songs both old and new with such zeal it felt as though Keith had returned from the dead.

The show was a 'secret' showcase that had originally been set down for the week in October 2006 when Keith's world had fallen apart. In the crowd at the Metro was a mix of true believers, some of whom had been Keith followers so long they could recall the time he was berated by Bernard King, as well as newer fans and the usual music biz players who nursed free beers and whispered off-colour jokes about how Keith looked like he could use a drink. Judging by the level of energy generated by the band—featuring Keith's long-time bandmate Jerry Flowers—and the look of pure joy on Keith's face, he seemed very much like a guy who was glad to be back doing what he was born to do: play live.

Keith had every reason to be pleased: not only had his marriage survived the recent crisis, but he and Nicole were about to upgrade to a fourteen-acre dream home in Franklin, one of Nashville's tonier areas. He also had a hit record lodged in the charts and the unconditional devotion of millions of fans. It was time to get back to work.

*

When Keith and the band got back on the road for a run of dates that took them through June and July 2007 (they'd go on to play some 80 shows during the year), Keith was now easily filling mid-range venues, from 9000- to 12,000-seaters, in such Urban-friendly hotspots as Fresno, St Louis, Milwaukee, Omaha and Des Moines. The thirteen-gig summer stretch generated an extremely healthy US$6.6 million in ticket sales, tangible proof that all of Keith's recent turmoil hadn't encouraged his devoted fans, the Monkeyville community, to move on to someone perhaps a little more wholesome. Keith was bigger than ever. His live 'guarantee'—essentially, what it cost to book Keith and his band—would soon be a staggering US$487,500 per show.

While pushing his latest record, Keith got embroiled in a trademark dispute with, of all people, Keith Urban, a painter from New Jersey. The latter Keith Urban had registered the domain name www.keithurban.com, much to the chagrin of Keith's team, who were using www.keithurban.net. The tricky part, of course, was that Keith's actual surname was Urbahn, unlike his New Jersey counterpart; the painter had fair claim to the domain name, at least in theory. But the bitterest pill, at least according to the suit that Keith's people filed in the US District Court in Nashville, was that Keith Urban of New Jersey had failed to mention on his site that he wasn't the 'other' Keith Urban of musical renown. The suit requested that the site be shut down and that the domain name be returned to its 'rightful' owner, and that Keith Urban of New Jersey not operate a website that suggested any kind of relationship with the singer.

The 'other' Keith Urban countersued, stating that the first lawsuit was 'baseless and is a tool to intimidate him'. Eventually, Team Keith wrested the domain name away from the New Jersey painter, but not before some inventive subeditors did their best to out-pun each other: 'Will the Real Keith Urban Stand Up' wrote one blogger. 'Keith Urban v. Keith Urban' read a tagline at the Smoking Gun website. While it all seemed a bit silly, it was proof of the kind of detail-oriented, client-first machine that Keith had behind him. Keith Urban had become a brand.

★

Keith and Nicole had hinted strongly that they intended to spend more time in Australia, and Keith, accordingly, returned for his third trip for 2007 in October. He'd intended to perform at the 2006 ARIAs but had been otherwise engaged at Betty Ford. Perhaps the year's delay was worthwhile, because when Keith returned for the 2007

ARIAs he blew the roof off the place—with a little help from a like-minded muso.

John Butler was a 32-year-old former skate punk, an American expat who'd become a big drawcard in the local roots/folk music world, renowned for lengthy jams and left-leaning politics. At the ARIAs, Keith stepped up with Butler's band, The John Butler Trio, and ripped a hole in their song 'Funky Tonight', Keith and Butler trading riffs like old sparring partners, Keith on electric guitar, Butler on acoustic. The crowd was quickly on its feet and a moshpit formed at the foot of the stage. In the VIP section, the camera cut to Nicole, lost in the music, her eyes closed. The song built to a furious finish, Keith and Butler banging their instruments together, wringing feedback out of their guitars, as the crowd inside Acer Arena—both punters and industry guests—went nuts.

The ARIAs were not known for spur-of-the-moment funky jams—more spontaneous events tended to happen at the show's many after-parties. But 'Funky Tonight' lived up to its name. It was so good, in fact, that their performance was rush-released as a digital download and reached number 11 on the ARIA singles chart.

It had been a big night for Keith. Not only had he reminded Australian audiences—and the ARIAs drew a sizeable TV audience—that he knew his way around the guitar, but he was also up for Best Country Album. One of his fellow contenders was former 'rival' James Blundell, still a big name in country circles, who'd tried to crack Nashville several years earlier. Blundell had looked on admiringly as Keith became more and more famous stateside. He bore no grudge. The way Blundell read it, 'Keith had the good sense to keep his mouth shut and work out who was who, while I'd alienated all of them . . . telling them, "Fuck it, I'm not changing."'

When supermodel Megan Gale read out Keith's name—it was his third ARIA—Keith smiled, planted one on Nicole's cheek and made his way to the stage as the crowd lit up, yet again. He was a popular winner, no doubt about it.

'It means so much to win this award here in my home country,' Keith said, his voice almost drowned out by screams from eager fans down front. He thanked his record company, his fans, and 'everybody that played the album, turned their friends onto it'. Crucially, he added, 'And it wouldn't exist without my wife. She was the inspiration for it. I dedicate this award to you, baby.'

The arena crowd, once again, went crazy. Newcastle rockers Silverchair may have won six awards, including Single of the Year, Album of the Year and Best Group, but to many Keith made the biggest impression on the night. And, of course, he looked like a million dollars while doing it, be it in T-shirt and jeans while jamming with Butler, or in black suit during the night's formalities.

All this made the obvious oversight even more bewildering: why wasn't Keith nominated for any of the major ARIAs? He'd now had sixteen singles in the mainstream US charts—more than Silverchair, Missy Higgins or any of the night's other big winners could ever imagine—and had sold more records than any Australian act this side of INXS. It was passing strange that he'd had more mainstream acceptance in the US than in his own country. 'He's one of the greatest artists this country has ever produced,' stated Rob Potts. 'International success, ten million-plus records, redefining an American music genre—huge achievements.' But still no Best Male Artist ARIA.

The only downside of Keith's latest return to Australia happened just prior to the ARIAs, as he rode his motorbike to an AA meeting in the eastern suburbs of Sydney. A photographer recognised Keith and gave chase in his car. Keith sped up, and while trying to avoid an oncoming car making an illegal U-turn he was forced to drop his bike on the road. Keith was shaken but unhurt and continued on to his meeting. Afterwards, he was reasonably sanguine about the incident. 'It was the result of one person's desire to do his job and my desire to maintain my privacy,' he stated. The photographer, Keith made a point of mentioning, helped him to his feet when he took a tumble and didn't take any shots of the incident.

★

Barely a year had passed since the release of *Love, Pain & the Whole Crazy Thing* before there was another Keith Urban record on the shelves: a greatest hits collection. Its slightly clumsy title was *Greatest Hits: 18 Kids*. With two additions—an earnest cover of Steve Forbert's already earnest 'Romeo's Tune' and a new cut called 'Got it Right This Time (The Celebration)'—the album was a traditional best-of containing Keith's biggest hits culled from his three hit albums: 'Days Go By', 'Somebody Like You', 'Where the Blacktop Ends' and the rest of his, erm, kids.

The fact it emerged so soon after *Love, Pain* suggested that the latter had run out of steam faster than earlier albums. But it had done its job, generating four hit singles—'Once in a Lifetime', 'Stupid Boy', 'I Told You So' and 'Everybody', which was still in the charts when the hits compilation was released. And over time, *18 Kids* would, too, provide great returns for Keith and his label, selling 1.2 million copies in the US, 140,000 in Australia and another 100,000 copies north of the border in Canada, where Keith's star continued to rise.

By late January 2008, Keith had set out on yet another jaunt to promote his best-of, the 30-date Love, Pain & the Whole Crazy Carnival Ride Tour—the rejigged tour name being a nod to his fast-rising support act, *American Idol* winner Carrie Underwood and her new album *Carnival Ride*. But there'd been even bigger news on the home front. Keith had spoken openly about his desire to become a father, and in early January 2008 it was official: a little Evie or Hank was on the way. Outside of their families, Nicole's publicist Wendy Day was the first person to get the news and she swiftly prepped the official announcement: 'The couple are thrilled,' it read.

Not surprisingly, the media went into overdrive. When the Kurbans turned out for a day of tennis-watching at the 2008 Australian Open, the TV cameras spent more time monitoring their movements than the on-court action. Compare-and-contrast shots of Nicole's stomach, taken days apart, became a common sight in even the more credible dailies as Australia's latest royal couple prepared them-selves for parenthood. All the time, water cooler discussions focused, somewhat cruelly, on the big question, 'Is she really pregnant?' It seemed hard for people to digest that someone as Hollywood-thin as Kidman could actually conceive a child. And, if so, *would the kid be born with stubble*?

A reporter buttonholed Nicole as she and Keith were leaving a Sydney restaurant; she said they were 'very excited'. Asked if she knew the baby's sex, Nicole smiled and replied: 'Secret.' Even her mother Janelle was doorstepped by eager press. 'Very pleased, very pleased indeed,' she told a group of reporters. 'Nothing else would make me come out from the pool onto the front doorstep.'

In seemingly every photo taken of the expectant couple, they positively glowed. And for good reason: when Nicole married Keith, she feared that she couldn't conceive a child. While married to Tom Cruise, she'd suffered an ectopic pregnancy, which led to their decision to adopt. Nicole then miscarried as their relationship imploded—she was about three months pregnant at the time.

There was also the matter of her ticking maternal clock, Nicole having just turned 40 (although her grandmother had given birth to her mother at the age of 49). The now pregnant Nicole took no chances, pulling out of a film called *The Reader*, which she was to shoot with director Stephen Daldry (they'd filmed *The Hours* together, which won Nicole her Best Actress Oscar). The baby was due sometime in the middle of 2008.

Nicole had discovered she was pregnant while filming the blockbuster movie *Australia* in the Kimberley with director Baz Luhrmann. Keith, who was on tour in the US as filming took place, had a three-day break and flew back to Australia to be at her side during her first ultrasound. 'We had lunch and then I got on the plane and flew back,' Keith revealed in a conversation on *The Bobby Bones Show*.

Nicole found out that at least seven babies were conceived during the making of the film. 'There is something up there in the Kununurra water because we all went swimming in the waterfalls,' she said. Nicole believed they'd been wading in 'fertility waters'. As soon as she mentioned this in an interview, the site was overrun by couples hoping for children.

★

Keith's status as a top-tier live act continued to grow. On 13 February 2008 he headlined Madison Square Garden in New York, where he'd been crowned CMA Entertainer of the Year back in November 2005. The New York gig was a huge achievement for Keith, another career milestone. Not only did the famed venue host 12,500 fans (who coughed up nearly US$1 million at the box office), but its legend was large. George Harrison had staged his Concert for Bangladesh at the 'Garden' in 1971; 30 years later, another Beatle, Paul McCartney, headlined the Concert for New York City, staged just weeks after the 2001 terrorist attacks on the city. Away from music, the Garden was the home of the New York Knicks and the Rangers—and it was where Muhammad Ali and Joe Frazier slugged it out during the legendary 'Fight of the Century' in 1971. It was a sacred site for New Yorkers.

At the Garden, Keith was supersized: as he and the band played, his image was displayed on a massive screen—almost 150 square metres—that ran the entire length of the stage, his every move captured by a flying video camera suspended from the ceiling. Keith opened up with 'Once in a Lifetime', lit up with the first of many guitar solos. Early in his set, Keith strode down a catwalk and stopped to play 'Raining on Sunday', then he walked a little further to a small circular stage for a brief set. During 'You Look Good in my Shirt', Keith, very much a man of the people, made his way through the audience, playing and singing as he went—at the end of the song he signed his guitar and handed it to a gobsmacked fan. He wrapped up a big night with a three-song encore: 'Got it Right This Time'—which he dedicated to Nicole for Valentine's Day, operating on Australian time—'Better Life' and 'Everybody'.

Okay, it wasn't quite Garth Brooks in Central Park—Keith wasn't *that* famous—but to fill the Garden and get jaded New Yorkers off their seats and on their feet was a monumental achievement. 'It could be the best concert I've seen,' gushed a writer from *Entertainment Weekly*. 'It's not necessarily that Urban does anything new, it's more like he does everything right.'

Covering the show for *The New York Times*, Kelefa Sanneh accepted that Keith's celebrity marriage 'raised his profile among non-country fans', but also rated his work highly, wondering out loud why Keith's songs were 'mainly absent from rock and pop radio stations'. It was a fair comment, given that most of Keith's singles made their way into *Billboard*'s Hot 100 mainstream chart, and that the music he made wasn't strictly country by any stretch.

'For years,' Sanneh continued, 'Mr Urban has seemed like someone who should be more famous than he is; somehow the more famous he gets, the more true that seems.' As far as Sanneh was concerned, Keith was 'the all-American rock star Jon Bon Jovi has always wanted to be', even though, as Sanneh noted, Keith wasn't a local. High praise.

Keith's tour then headed in the direction of the US west coast, where he filled the 20,000-seat Honda Center in Anaheim, California. After a brief pause, he was back in Australia in late March for a hit-and-run tour: two concerts at the Hordern Pavilion in Sydney—where he recalled his nights playing Sydney gigs where 'six people would turn up and we knew five of them'—and shows at the WIN Centre in Wollongong, the Botanical Gardens in Hobart, Portsea in Victoria, and his debut appearance at the annual East Coast Blues & Roots Music Festival (now known as Bluesfest), staged at Byron Bay on 20 March. While in Byron, he stayed with Joanne Petersen and her family.

During the encore of his Wollongong show, Keith surprised the audience when he began playing the familiar riff to Dragon's 1978 number 1 'Are You Old Enough?' While it might have been familiar to almost everyone in the WIN Centre, it was a mystery to his all-American band, who were left to follow Keith's lead when he launched into the song proper. Judging by the smile on his face—and the rowdy audience singalong—Keith was having a blast. And he wasn't done with covers; after asking the crowd, 'You don't want to go home, do you?', he tore up Steve Miller Band's 'The Joker'. 'I'm a picker, I'm a grinner/I'm a lover, I'm a sinner,' Keith sang, sharing a mic with bassist Jerry Flowers and guitarist Brad Rice, grinning broadly, as they jammed their way deep into overtime.

*

As the birth of his first child grew ever closer, Keith reconnected with Kenny Chesney when the man with the big hat played a massive outdoor show at LP Field in Nashville on 5 July 2008. (Box office take? A handy US$4 million.) This was a huge day of music, eight hours in all, featuring such acts as LeAnn Rimes and Gary Allan, even rocker Sammy Hagar, sometimes seen out front of Van Halen. (The large-living Hagar had drinks served mid-set by a bikini-clad waitress.) Chesney invited Keith to play a set to the appreciative audience of 50,000. It was to be Keith's final show before fatherhood, although judging by the way he played, pre-baby nerves didn't appear to be an issue.

Wearing a shirt that proclaimed 'Someone Went to Florida and All I Got Was This Lousy T-shirt', Keith stormed the stage and ripped into 'Days Go By', followed swiftly by 'Where the Blacktop Ends' and 'Who Wouldn't Wanna Be Me'. He and the band were in great form, a well-oiled machine. By the time of 'You Look Good in My Shirt', Keith was down the front, in the audience, getting among the people, as security looked on and hoped for the best.

Never one to miss out on a big moment, Keith introduced 'You're My Better Half' with a simple dedication: 'This song,' he announced, 'is for my very, very, very, very, *very* pregnant wife.'

Backstage, a fit-to-burst Nicole smiled along, cradling her not-inconsiderable baby bump—a sight that silenced any remaining doubters as to whether she was actually carrying a child. Before heading home after Keith's 60-minute, eleven-song set, the couple climbed into a golf buggy, waving at his fans and their well-wishers before disappearing into a waiting limo.

The day before, Keith and Nicole had been in a Borders bookstore in Nashville, stocking up on reading material— *Pocket Dad: Everyday Wisdom, Practical Tips, and Fatherly Advice*, among other titles. But the Kurbans had also been doing some more substantial shopping of late, having bought another American home, a sizeable spread in Beverly Hills, some 370 square metres in all, which they picked up for a cheeky US$4.7 million. Nicole's friend Naomi Watts was a near neighbour.

They were also about to drop more than A$6.5 million on Bunya Hill, a stately Victorian mansion built in 1878, set on more than 100 acres in the pristine NSW Southern Highlands—and almost A$6 million on a waterfront pent-house apartment in Sydney, with sweeping views of the Harbour Bridge. (They'd go on to buy another apartment in the complex and convert it into a private gym.) A Manhattan condo would be next for their property portfolio. But the couple would spend their early days as parents in Nashville.

The baby was due any time now, and the troops were gathering. Nicole's mother Janelle had arrived in Nashville, along with Nicole's sister Antonia, herself the mother of four. All was in place; everyone was ready.

16

'A little ray of sunshine in the shape of a girl'

Sunday Rose Kidman Urban was born in Nashville on 7 July 2008. She weighed a notch under three kilos. The baby was named after Sunday Reed, who'd been a muse for the Australian artist Sidney Nolan. Kidman's father Antony heard about Reed and spoke with Nicole, saying that 'Sunday strikes me as a nice name for a woman'. Nicole agreed. Coincidentally, Nicole had also recently attended an exhibit of Nolan's work; a quote from the painter was scrawled across a wall in the gallery that registered with both her and Keith. It read: 'When you are young you are given a good view of life, because of your closeness to birth.' The child's middle name, Rose, was a nod to Keith's late grandmother.

During her labour, Nicole, who'd stayed in shape during her pregnancy with yoga and spin classes, listened to a hand-picked soundtrack, a curious blend of her husband's music and the easy listening of sexagenarian flautist Sir James Galway. Keith, who'd brought a little celebrity dazzle to the

Lamaze lessons he took to prepare for fatherhood, was by her side throughout the birth, and he broke the news soon after.

'We want to thank everybody that has kept us in their thoughts and prayers,' Keith reported on his website. 'We feel very blessed and grateful that we can share this joy with you.'

Once again, the couple carefully controlled the message, just as they'd done with their wedding. ('Nothing to hide and everything to protect' was how Keith described their media stance when it came to family matters.) Only one shot of the parents with their new baby—a tasteful black-and-white snap—was released to the media.

Sunday Rose was nicknamed Sunny, although sometimes her mother would call her 'Keith-ette'. When Keith spoke about his daughter with chat show host Ellen DeGeneres, he joked about how her accent might sound, given that she was to be raised by Australians living in America's South. 'Maybe she'll say, "G'day y'all."' Keith later referred to his daughter as 'a little ray of sunshine in the shape of a girl', neatly lifting a lyric from Axiom's 1970 Oz-pop classic.

Father Paul Coleman, who'd united the couple in holy matrimony in 2006, was given the job of baptising the child when she was deemed ready to travel to Sydney a month after her birth. While in Sydney, Nicole made a request during an interview with radio station 2Day FM, asking that the media give them 'a little space' during their visit, and not impose on them while they did their best to be normal people, of sorts, doing normal things. Keith backed this up when he spoke. 'I get the interest there is. But at the same time, it's our little girl. She's just awesome . . . cute little thing.' He added: 'I'm not looking forward to having to go on tour.'

But Keith, as always, had business to attend to, and was back on the road by 19 July, playing in Philadelphia. He was in a playful mood, slipping in a snippet of Elton John's 'Philadelphia Freedom' after his opener 'Days Go By', as a nod to the city of brotherly love. Keith then invited his band-mates to take a brief turn at the mic: Jerry Flowers belted out a little of Brooks & Dunn's 'Believe'; Chris Rodriguez opted for something sexier, Marvin Gaye's 'Let's Get It On'; while Brian Nutter went for stadium rock, choosing Journey's 'Lights'. This became a regular feature of subsequent shows. Sometimes Nutter opted for Boston's 'Rock & Roll Band', while guitarist Brad Rice would croon John Anderson's 'Swingin''.

This run of dates wound down at the Grand Ole Opry House in Nashville, where Keith appeared in a celebration of Country Music Hall of Famer Marty Stuart, who was turning 50. Throughout the night Keith played a few songs, joining Stuart on a version of Hank Williams' 'I'm So Lonesome I Could Cry'. Stuart was a man with an impressive mane of grey hair and an even more impressive knowledge of the American country music songbook. He had also been Johnny Cash's son-in-law, when he was married to Cindy Cash in the 1980s. Another big name, and yet another Keith admirer.

Somewhere in between all this activity, Keith struck up a friendship with a member of the CMT hat-wearing brigade (and fellow guitar nut), Brad Paisley. The 35-year-old West Virginian had a bit in common with Keith: he too was from working-class stock and had started young, mastering his first guitar, a Sears Danelectro Silvertone, when he was barely eight years old. A publishing contract—in Paisley's case, with EMI—kept him afloat before his recording career proper began in 1999 (the same year Keith released his first US album). And Paisley, again like Keith, was a CMA Horizon Award winner, in 2000. A string of platinum and multiplatinum albums, and sold-out arena tours, followed.

Paisley was cutting a primarily instrumental album called *Play* and he reached out to Keith, suggesting they get into the studio and 'do something really cool that people are going to talk about and want to hear'—nothing arty. Paisley had two suggestions. His first idea was that they write together and hope to come up with what Paisley described as 'a real fast guitar instrumental and try and blow people's minds', just as Keith had done in the past with 'Clutterbilly' and 'Rollercoaster'. His second pitch was that they record a funny, good-natured song called 'Start a Band'.

While he may not have written the song—it was the work of Dallas Davidson, Ashley Gorley and Kelley Lovelace, a trio who'd written dozens of country hits—Paisley, just like Keith, had done his time in garage bands during his slow rise to the top. Paisley called Keith and read out the lyrics to him. 'Just get you a guitar and learn how to play', Paisley recited to him over the phone, 'Cut up some jeans, come up with a name'.

'He cracked up when he heard it, because we've both been through this so much in our lives,' Paisley reported, 'just our attempts to be cool as guitar players you know, and wanting to fit in.' It might have reminded Keith of his days in Caboolture when he had sprayed his pretend band's name—Rock Fever—on the wall of the family garage. As for Paisley, 'Start a Band' reminded him of the Eagles, but the rockier side of the band, when Joe Walsh and Don Felder would trade licks and harmony guitar parts. Perhaps there was a little Creedence in the mix, too.

When Keith and Paisley recorded the song in the northern summer of 2008, the results were so good that they decided to release it as the first (and only) single from *Play*, in mid-September. Judging by the goofy interplay between the pair, shooting the video for the song was as big a blast as the actual recording of the song. It had been a long time since Keith had been the hired hand and he was revelling in the freedom. All he had to do was remember the lyrics and cut loose on his Fender, he and Paisley, no slouch on the guitar himself, jamming like schoolkids. (Their younger selves were even portrayed by kids during the 'story' part of the video.) To top it all off, the song was a hit, reaching number 1 on *Billboard*'s Hot Country Songs chart—Keith's ninth, Paisley's thirteenth—and reaching the mainstream Top 50.

The vibe between the pair was so good that they played the song to open the 2008 CMAs on 12 November, the crowd making some serious noise when they both strutted to the edge of the stage, playing loud and fast. Earlier in the song, Paisley had snuck in the riff from Derek & The Dominos' 'Layla', and at the end, he and Keith threw in a bite-sized chunk of Deep Purple's 'Smoke on the Water'. It was classic-rock nirvana.

Paisley co-hosted the CMAs with Carrie Underwood. Midway through the show, Paisley, a guy who knew his funny bone from his humerus, introduced Keith to play a new song, but did so with a noticeable pout. 'Earlier in the show you might remember that the next performer and I were a duo. Apparently, he's now decided that he wants to go solo. Fine. Go ahead. See how you do on your own.' Then, joke over, his face broke into a big smile. 'My pal, Keith Urban.' Keith played 'Sweet Thing', another song inspired by his relationship with Nicole, who was seated in the front row of Nashville's Sommet Center, having just completed filming her second musical, *Nine*. ('Sweet Thing' was also, in part, a tribute to one of Keith's favourite cars, a 1969 Ford Mustang, a recent birthday gift from his wife.)

Later on, Keith missed out on the Male Vocalist of the Year award, but any pain he felt was softened considerably by the winner—Paisley, of course—who, prior to his acceptance speech, ran into the crowd, grabbed Keith and hugged him hard, almost bowling him over. It was a love-in, a musical bromance.

★

'Sweet Thing' was the first taste of Keith's new album, *Defying Gravity*, which was due in March 2009. Just weeks before the album dropped, Keith made one of his more unlikely cameos. At most awards shows, Keith was typically teamed with someone like-minded—Faith Hill at the 2006 Grammys, Brad Paisley at the recent CMAs. But for the 2009 Grammys, which were staged at the Staples Center in Los Angeles, Keith lined up with the very Reverend Al Green, a true soul legend, as well as R&B hitmakers Boyz II Men and Mouseketeer-turned-sex symbol Justin Timberlake. Together they played Green's immortal 'Let's Stay Together'. Keith was in the backline, playing a rock-solid rhythm guitar in an almost exclusively African-American band—and then delivered a convincing solo later in the song. This was a whole lot more Sunday gospel than Grand Ole Opry, yet Keith seemed right at home.

As for his new album, Keith had started work in mid-2008 with a very familiar team—co-producer Dan Huff, co-songwriters John Shanks, Darrell Brown and Monty Powell, drummer McHugh and bassist Flowers—but the magic didn't happen. Nothing from those early sessions made the finished record.

Keith had a theory about what went wrong. 'I just don't like doing demos, I think,' he told *Billboard* magazine. 'I like to create a song in a much more organic process. I like to keep everything very spontaneous.'

None of this stopped 'Sweet Thing' from racing to the top of the Hot Country chart and, like many of Keith's hit singles, crossing over into the mainstream, reaching number 30 on the *Billboard* Hot 100. (It would also win him another Grammy, his third, for Best Male Country Vocal Performance.) It seemed that Keith could have released a single of him yodelling, gargling or burping his daughter and it would have blazed through the charts.

But critical response to *Defying Gravity* was mixed when it was released in the final days of March 2009. *Rolling Stone's* Mark Kemp gave the record a limp two-star rating, considering it a backward step from the more ambitious *Love, Pain & the Whole Crazy Thing*. 'Keith Urban plays it so safe,' he wrote, 'you'd think he got a musical lobotomy when he went to rehab.'

Kemp may have not chosen his words too delicately, but he had a point: much of the album replicated what had worked for Keith in the past. He was taking no chances. Keith had transformed Radney Foster's 'Raining on Sunday' into a major hit in 2002, but this time his cover of Foster's 'I'm In' didn't stand up to a previous version, cut by twins The Kinleys back in 2000. And much of the record came and went without leaving any kind of emotional impression. It was impeccably played, skilfully produced, but ultimately a bit empty. As for the track 'Standing Right in Front of You', it seemed that perhaps Keith was channelling the New Radicals' 'You Get What You Give' a little too much for comfort.

Entertainment Weekly was more generous with their review of the album. 'He's taken such an aggressive header into the fluffy clouds of romantic optimism,' wrote Whitney Pastorek, 'that he should have just mailed Van Morrison a couple bucks and called this thing *Love, Love & Crazy Love*. Get thee behind him, cynicism!' The PopMatters website took a similar tack, describing the album as 'pure romantic make-believe, wish fulfillment. It's a soap opera and romance novel rolled up in one.'

It certainly didn't require a degree in forensics to figure that many of the songs were inspired by the recent upturns in Keith's life: the birth of his first child, his ongoing romance with Nicole, his many and various career highs. The titles alone—'My Heart is Open', 'Only You Can Love Me This Way', 'Thank You' et. al—gave the game away. But they weren't his best songs, nor was he willing, lyrically, to step outside the safety zone of banalities and clichés. Keith actually spilled more on his life, his feelings and thoughts during sitdowns with Oprah and Ellen DeGeneres.

Still, Keith took an upbeat approach when he began promoting the album. 'I'm very grateful for where I'm at in my life,' he told a writer from *VOA News*. 'We just went in to record this album and it turned out to be a very uplifting and a very joyous record.' On April Fool's Day he made two key TV appearances, on *The Ellen DeGeneres Show* and NBC's *Today*, singing 'Sweet Thing' and 'Kiss a Girl'—a song with a nagging earworm of a guitar riff—on both shows. Ellen's audience, in particular, lapped it up and Keith soon became a regular on the DeGeneres couch.

Sales-wise, *Defying Gravity* defied criticism. It sold almost 200,000 copies in its first week of release and was Keith's first album to debut at number 1 on the all-genre *Billboard* 200 album chart. (*Be Here* and *Love, Pain* had both peaked at number 3.) In its opening week, the album outsold Prince (*Lotusflow3r*), jazz queen Diana Krall (*Quiet Nights*)—he even beat out the *Hannah Montana* movie soundtrack. No further proof was needed: Keith Urban was a mainstream powerhouse.

*

Taylor Swift was the fastest rising star in country music. The nineteen-year-old was a native of West Reading, Pennsylvania, who was named after singer/songwriter James Taylor. Hearing Shania Twain for the first time, as a pre-teen, was a huge moment for Swift. By the age of eleven she was travelling to Nashville with her mother Andrea, clutching a demo tape that contained her covers of Dolly Parton and Dixie Chicks songs. Eventually, the Swift family relocated to Music City and in 2005 she signed to Big Machine Records. Swift's self-titled 2006 debut was a massive hit, reaching number 5 on the Billboard 200 and charting for three years. No other album released in that decade charted for that long.

When Swift teamed up with Keith for the Escape Together World Tour, her second album, *Fearless*, was another huge hit, on its way to global sales of ten million. And when she was stage-bombed by rapper Kanye West at the 2009 MTV Video Music Awards, her place as a bona fide star was set in stone. Swift was not only an award-winner, a role model for young women and a very credible singer/songwriter, she was also a meme. And nothing said 'celebrity' in 2009 quite like trending madly on social media.

After a one-off on 17 March at the Houston Rodeo, the Escape Together tour—whose other guests included Sugarland, Dierks Bentley and veteran Glen Campbell— really kicked into gear on 7 May 2009 in Connecticut, rolling on until early August. In the wake of the devastating global financial crisis of 2007–08, Keith ensured that some tickets for each show were priced at just $20. 'It's easy to see that people out there are hurting,' Keith said, reasonably enough. Yet this would still be the biggest tour of his career, production wise, with five large video screens, a 330-square-metre stage and a crew of 60. Keith was now a stadium act, a major headliner, playing 15,000-seaters night after night.

Keith and the band had put in two weeks of rehearsals before heading out, and he spoke with a reporter about the amount of detail required to pull it all together. 'It's like painting rivets on the Harbour Bridge,' he figured. 'For me, it's all about the stuff that connects everything, the things in between songs.'

The rapport between Keith and Swift was unmistakable from the get-go. Some nights she'd join Keith on stage and let loose while he played 'Somebody Like You', shaking her mane of blonde hair, headbanging wildly. By the time the roadshow reached Kansas City, Missouri, on 9 August, Swift had a surprise in store for the headliner. It was Swift's final date of the tour, and she wanted to leave an impression: Keith was about to be pranked.

As Keith began playing 'Kiss a Girl', a crowd favourite, Swift and her band strutted on stage dressed as 1970s cartoon rockers KISS—face paint, platform boots, spandex pants, topknots, the works. A few members of Swift's entourage, dressed as human Hershey's Kisses, followed them on stage—after all, the song was called 'Kiss a Girl'. Keith tried to keep a straight face while Swift and the others pranced and preened around him, wisely retreating to the rear of the stage when Swift briefly took over the lead vocal. Then the entire ensemble formed a line at the front of the stage and pulled off—almost—some choreographed rock moves. The Hershey's Kisses, meanwhile, had baskets of their namesakes that they threw out to the eager and slightly bewildered crowd.

At the end of the song, as the audience erupted, Swift removed her wig, shook her hair free, blew the crowd a kiss and shouted, 'I'd like to thank Keith Urban for a great tour!' And with that she was off into the wings, leaving Keith in mild shock—although Swift did join him again a few songs later for the finale, 'Somebody Like You'. This time, however, she wasn't dressed as Ace Frehley.

As with most of the people Keith connected with strongly over the years—Brooks & Dunn, Brad Paisley, Kenny Chesney, the late Slim Dusty—that first tour wouldn't be the only time he worked with Taylor Swift. And Keith could see, plain as day, that Swift was set to become an even bigger star than she already was in 2009. 'She was a blast on the road,' he later told a reporter from *Entertainment Tonight*. 'People have asked me, "Could you sense that she was going to be who she became?" And I was like, "I think everybody knew that." You could see it clearly. She was playing way past where she was. She was way into the future. You could tell.'

★

'Giving back' was a tradition in the country music world. Since 1985, Willie Nelson, John Mellencamp and Neil Young had co-hosted the huge fundraiser Farm Aid, in which Keith had appeared in 2002. Garth Brooks co-founded Teammates for Kids in 1999, animal lover Miranda Lambert ran various events, and in 2005 Dierks Bentley started his Miles and Music for Kids motorcycle rides and concerts. Dolly Parton, who'd one day pour money into vaccine research, ran the Imagination Library, which provided free books for kids around the world. Many other high-profile country acts participated in similarly civic-minded events.

Keith did more than his share of charity-related work as his star power and influence increased. He'd never forgotten how the Red Cross, the Salvos and Goodwill had helped his family when their home burned down in Caboolture, and he frequently donated his time, and anything else he could offer, to St Jude's children's research hospital in Nashville. He also maintained an ongoing relationship with treatment centre Cumberland Heights, even though he was no longer quaffing Cognac or snorting coke. 'But for the Grace of God' wasn't just one of his early hits, it was almost a mantra for the now very sober, AA-abiding Keith.

In mid-October 2009, Keith reached the end of the

American leg of his current tour. His final US show for the year was the inaugural 'We're All for the Hall' benefit, staged at the Sommet Center in Nashville. This fundraiser was designed to raise cash for Nashville's Country Music Hall of Fame and Museum, which had first opened its doors in 1967. Vince Gill, who was married to Christian pop million-seller Amy Grant, was the president of the museum board and did a lot of heavy lifting when it came to preserving the city's musical legacy. Gill helped organise the gig.

Keith had played tourist at the Hall of Fame during his first Nashville trip in 1989 and was a true believer. He loved the place: the displays; the handwritten lyrics, where first-draft lines had been erased and scribbled over; the lavish costumes; and the collection of guitars, of course. 'I love all of the history,' he told *The Boot*, 'and how people got to work with one another.' Keith figured that country music history was worth preserving. 'It's really important to remember that influences go back further than a decade.'

When Keith took the Sommet Center stage with his band on the night of 13 October, he made a promise to the 14,000-strong crowd: 'This will be one of the greatest open-mic nights ever seen in Nashville.' He wasn't kidding. For a modest $25, the audience got to witness sets from Keith, Vince Gill, Faith Hill, Taylor Swift—who donated the rhinestone-studded acoustic guitar she was playing to the museum to be auctioned—Little Big Town and Lady Antebellum. An online audience of more than one million streamed the show.

Musical chairs was theme of the night. Keith was joined by Brad Paisley to rip into 'Start a Band', the pair wandering off into the audience as they played, Keith heading left,

Paisley right, providing punters with a close-up look at their techniques. Keith then joined Gill and an all-star band, swapping guitar parts with Gill, another fine picker. At one point during Keith's hour-long set, he traded his electric for an acoustic. 'This is an example of the music that influenced me and brought me to this country,' he said by way of an introduction. He then played Dolly Parton's 'Coat of Many Colors'.

Praise came thick and fast. Gill said Keith was 'one of my favourite musicians on the planet', and joked that they should form a band, which they'd call Over Yonder and Down Under. Taylor Swift announced, 'I would love, in my lifetime, to say I stood on a stage with Vince Gill and Keith Urban as my guitar players and sing a song'—and that duly happened when they played her hit 'Love Story'. It was another musical love-in. Keith was making a habit of big nights like this.

The entire line-up took the stage for the finale, jamming 'Lay Down Sally', with Keith, Gill and Dann Huff combining in a formidable three-guitar attack. (Monty Powell, Keith's lucky co-writing touchstone, even joined in on vocals.)

Just before the lights came up, Gill turned to Keith and asked, 'This thing turned out all right, didn't it?' 'It's getting there,' replied Keith, his tongue wedged so firmly in his cheek he might have choked. They promised to return in a year's time (which they did, continuing annually until 2016). The event raised about US$500,000 for the museum. In August 2018, Keith and Nicole donated a whopping A$100,000 to the Farm Aid telethon, an Australian drought relief appeal, and then a further A$500,000 for Australian bushfire assistance in January 2020.

Keith was also giving back in other, less public ways. Brantley Gilbert was an up-and-coming country singer songwriter, a pastor's son. A high school jock, Gilbert had been boozing since his teens, getting to the point where he'd drink in the morning to stave off hangovers. When he was nineteen, in 2004, he got into an argument at a party and punched a friend, who then drove away. Gilbert set off after him in his truck; inevitably, he ran off the road, flipping his vehicle several times before hitting a tree. A judge ordered Gilbert to group therapy and AA.

When Gilbert scored a songwriting deal and moved to Nashville, he was still running wild. He'd turn up to writing sessions with a laptop bag containing two bottles of whiskey and a pistol. In late 2009, Gilbert released his debut album, *A Modern Day Prodigal Son*, but a bout of pancreatitis landed him in hospital, and then Cumberland Heights. After a rough few days, Gilbert figured that because he was now able to walk to the shower without crawling, he was ready for the outside world. He told his counsellors he was signing himself out.

'Just wait one more day,' he was told. 'There's someone we'd like you to meet.'

Reluctantly, Gilbert unpacked his bag. The next day he came face to face with a recovering addict—Keith Urban.

Gilbert was angry at first. 'These fuckers are pulling out all the stops,' he thought to himself.

'What's going on?' an unfazed Keith asked in a calm voice.

Gilbert talked about the booze, the guns, the car wreck— and his fears. 'I don't think I can do my job,' Gilbert admitted to Keith. 'I don't know if I can ever play a song at my shows without being fucked up.' He was worried that if he stopped drinking, his music would lose its edge. Keith explained that he, too, had felt that; his first sober shows were among the scariest of his career. Yet he'd got through it okay. 'And,' Keith added, 'I'm a better writer, performer and human being without drugs and alcohol.'

Keith's confession registered strongly with Gilbert. 'My whole world flipped,' he admitted. 'I was like, "All right."'

Gilbert remained in Cumberland Heights for a week and emerged a better man. He'd subsequently thank Keith for his help and guidance—and for his recovery. 'If it weren't for him,' Gilbert told *The Tennessean* in January 2017, 'I'd probably be dead.'

In 2011, Gilbert's career exploded when he scored back-to-back country number 1 hits.

Keith refused to go on the record about his counselling work at Cumberland Heights. He may have been a public figure, but some things remained very private.

17

'The most autobiographical song I never wrote'

Floods of an almost biblical proportion hit Tennessee in May 2010, while Keith was in Hawaii with Nicole, who was shooting a film called *Just Go With It*. Over 36 hours between 1 and 2 May, some 35 centimetres of rain fell on Nashville, doubling the previous soggy record. Twenty-six people died in the carnage, while nearly 11,000 homes were either damaged or destroyed. Floodwater swamped the Grand Ole Opry House, along with many other Nashville businesses and buildings of historical import. Damage ran into the billions of dollars' worth.

Tennessee is known as The Volunteer State, and that really proved to be true when the big clean-up began. Keith dug deep and made a substantial financial contribution to the city, and also spoke with his peers about benefit shows. 'I've experienced first-hand what it's like to lose all that sort of thing,' he told CNN.

But Keith suffered some losses himself. One of the

many businesses deluged was the music storage facility at SoundCheck in Nashville, where Keith kept about 50 of his favourite guitars, some more than twenty years old, as well as amps and concert gear. He managed to salvage a guitar with strong sentimental value from the carnage. It was a 1988 Telecaster that he'd named Clarence in honour of Clarence Odbody, the angel in the 1946 film *It's a Wonderful Life*—it was Keith's lucky Fender. He'd bought it in New York for US$2500 back when he was hoping for a miracle of his own. He'd since used it on every album he'd recorded, in photo shoots, the lot. 'So it was really important for me to salvage that guitar,' Keith said. (Over time, 'Clarence' was painstakingly nursed back to life by a Nashville luthier, as were other guitars from Keith's collection.)

Keith's loss was a huge problem because he was going to start recording a new album just days after the rivers rose and flooded the city. He was forced to borrow a couple of axes from his guitar tech, and also use guitars that were already in the studio. Ultimately, though, when Keith eventually completed his new album, which he titled *Get Closer*, he figured that there had been an upside to losing his gear in the big wet. 'It certainly took me out of my comfort zone,' he told NPR. 'There's something quite liberating about it, too . . . Not having all my instruments to reach for was creatively liberating. It allowed everything to be spontaneous and fresh.'

Keith's knack for great collaborations hadn't abated. He teamed up with his buddy and fellow guitar-slinger John Mayer, a devotee of hair metal *and* Stevie Ray Vaughan, during a remarkable episode of *CMT Crossroads* that aired in June 2010. But in mid-May 2010, Keith put in what was possibly his finest one-off yet, fired up by the flood disaster in his adopted hometown. He put in a rollicking take on The Rolling Stones' 'Tumbling Dice' on Jimmy Fallon's *Tonight Show*. Keith took the stage with his regular band, plus three back-up singers and Chuck Leavell, who'd been playing keys with the Stones on record and in concert for the past 30 years. Keith and the ensemble were surrounded on the set by fans, who enthusiastically sang every note right along with them. It was rousing stuff, and heartfelt, too, with Keith ad-libbing lyrics about the Nashville floods, singing, 'The rain's been comin' down in Nashville, Tennessee.' Host Fallon almost fell over himself racing onto the set to shake Keith's hand when the song ended. (Three years later, Keith got to jam 'Respectable' with *the* Rolling Stones at the Staples Center in LA, trading licks with Keith Richards and vocals with the preening, prancing Mick Jagger. Another dream fulfilled.)

Keith wasn't done yet. A few weeks after his appearance on Fallon's show, during the CMA Music Festival at LP Field in Nashville on 11 June, he and the band, again with a trio of female voices (and added brass section), pulled off a stirring cover of The Beatles' (via Joe Cocker) 'With a Little Help from My Friends', as images of Nashville's devastating floods flickered on the screen behind them.

'No Flood Can Stop This Party' proclaimed a banner held by a member of the crowd, and Keith proved that to be true. 'You are the best,' he declared as he left the stage, sweat pouring off him, and the audience roared their approval. It was the perfect song for the occasion.

★

Get Closer was released on 16 November 2010. The centre-piece of the record was a slow burner called 'Right on Back to You', which opened with the sound of rolling thunder and tumbling rain—it was as though someone had left a tape running during the floods. Keith would admit that the deluge and its aftermath did have an impact on his music, although this song, a co-write with regular partner Darrell Brown, was straight out of the songwriter's handbook. He and Brown started out with the classic image of a guy clashing with his girlfriend, jumping in his car and driving off into the distance, but then something happened, as Keith told NPR.

'He pulls over to the side of the road; he's saying to himself, "Why do I always run? And it's not because I don't love this person. It's actually because I love them so much . . ." It's in that moment of realisation that it's the fear of the love, not the lack of it, that has him turn around and go back to get even closer with her.'

The song was moody, evocative, and again hinted at the significance of Nicole in his life, even though Keith, true to form, resisted naming names. But during another track, 'Without You', he did seem to refer to the joy his daughter Sunday Rose, now almost eighteen months old, brought him when he sang, 'Along comes a baby girl, and suddenly my little world/Just got a whole lot bigger.'

But that was about it for clear and distinct references to his offstage life—and even then there was a twist. Keith revealed to Randy Lewis, a writer from the *LA Times*, that 'Without You' was the 'most autobiographical song I never wrote'. It was in fact the handiwork of writers Joe West (the son of Sarge and Shirley West, America's first Black country duo) and Dave Pahanish. A friend had given Keith the heads-up about the song—and he freely admitted that if he'd attempted to write it himself, the lyric would have turned out to be vastly different. 'I would have filled it with metaphors and analogies, where this is perfectly sound and beautifully put.'

This reluctance to disclose too much of himself was something he got into with Randy Lewis. 'Nic and I both deal with that,' he admitted. 'Even in the film choices she makes, people will ask, "Is that what's going on in her life?" For me, I'm looking for the feelings that resonate with me, for a multitude of reasons.' The very title of Lewis's *LA Times* feature, 'Keith Urban reveals a piece of himself on "Get Closer"', made it clear that full disclosure was not for Keith Urban, at least when it came to his music.

Get Closer was a surprisingly precise album—the original version contained just eight tracks and ran for only 33 minutes. It was one of the shortest albums released by a country star in the CD age. (A deluxe limited edition, sold via Target and Target.com in the US, added three more studio tracks and some live cuts.) And it didn't do the same business as its predecessors. It sold 162,000 copies in its first week, debuting at number 7 on the *Billboard* 200—but didn't reach platinum status until April 2017. Keith's peers were suffering similar downturns: Kenny Chesney's 2007 LP *Just Who I Am: Poets & Pirates* sold 1.4 million copies within a year but his follow-up, 2008's *Lucky Old Sun*, sold about half as many in its first twelve months. Brad Paisley shifted one million copies of 2007's *5th Gear*, but his subsequent record, 2009's *American Saturday Night*, only reached 561,000. It was barely a gold record, a failure by his standards.

It'd be easy enough to say that Keith's declining sales simply meant that he'd peaked a few records back, but that wasn't quite the case (as his later creative rebirth would prove). But the emergence of file-sharing platform Napster in 1999 and then iTunes in 2003 reinvented the way music was consumed. Until 2007, the biggest retailer of recorded music in the US was Walmart, with its miles of aisles of CDs. By 2008, it was iTunes. Physical record sales in the US declined by US$1.3 billion in 2009, to $6.3 billion, whereas digital music sales grew by $363 million, although how much of that money found its way back to artists was less clear than a deal with a major label. Spotify wouldn't launch in the US until July 2011, but a major change was in the air. Established artists like Keith needed to find new ways to generate the revenue they once had simply by releasing a new record, hitting the road hard and maybe flogging a few tour T-shirts on the side.

Critical response to *Get Closer*, however, was generally positive. *The Boston Globe* gave it a thumbs-up, as did *Entertainment Weekly*, *The New York Times* and the *LA Times*. Writing on roots music website Engine 145, Blake Boldt figured that the album's 'eight uplifting songs [offered] one cohesive message: love is grand . . . Settling down, he's learned after all, has finally set him free.' Jonathan Keefe, a writer at *Slant*, acknowledged that whatever edge Keith's music had once had, it had faded since 'he started writing most of his songs about how amazing it is to be married to Nicole Kidman'. But he also felt that *Get Closer* 'owes less to . . . Phil Collins than has his recent output', which could only be a good thing.

★

When it came to spreading the word, Keith did take a new approach when *Get Closer* was released. On 15 November he set out on a day trip promoted as 'Get Closer to Keith'. First up, he surprised New Yorkers with a pop-up performance at Penn Station—the day after R&B star Rihanna had done something similar in nearby Times Square. Keith, dressed in basic black, entertained the morning shift, doing his thing in the thick of the Tuesday morning commute. He played for 30 minutes to startled fans and curious onlookers.

Then Keith hopped on a Philadelphia-bound Amtrak and disembarked at 30th Street Station, where he quickly set up and did it all over again. 'It's always about playing for me,' Keith said, 'in any setting evidently.' While he had once played inside the Tamworth Airport terminal, rocking out on the baggage carousel, a train station was a first. 'Good acoustics,' Keith noted afterwards. 'It was cool.'

Keith staged a similarly impromptu gig soon after, outside the Taco Diner in Dallas, the night before a much grander appearance at half-time during an NFL Thanksgiving Day clash between Dallas and New Orleans. Keith, clearly, was developing a taste for unusual gigs, because on 30 November he headed to Edmonton in Canada for yet another pop-up show, this time at the Ice Palace in the West Edmonton Mall, one of the world's biggest malls.

Keith took the stage at 6 p.m. with his acoustic guitar— there were about 3000 people crowding him from all sides; some had been waiting for nine hours. Teenagers, mothers with babies, rusted-on fans, middle-aged true believers barely able to control their excitement—they were all there, holding their phones aloft. Keith welcomed one especially eager fan, a seventeen-year-old named Mitchell Lavigne, to sing 'Kiss a Girl' with him, and what he lacked (desperately) in vocal chops he made up for in karaoke skills, precisely mouthing the lyrics whenever Keith took the mic. 'Keith Urban has very good-smelling breath,' Mitchell told the gathering, as he flashed a huge smile and left the stage. Keith almost fell over, he was laughing so hard. He stayed on to press the flesh and sign autographs for 200 contest-winners after his brief set, which didn't just feature his hits but also songs from Johnny Cash ('Folsom Prison Blues') and Steve Miller Band ('The Joker').

Next stop was Sydney. On 15 December, after making a cameo with Nicole on Oprah Winfrey's Sydney Opera House special, Keith strolled a few blocks up to Pitt Street Mall for another unplugged set. This time about 2500 people turned up, filling every inch of the square, stopping lunchtime foot traffic stone dead. Keith was a big drawcard in the CBD.

Keith managed to find the cheekiest kid in the crowd, fifteen-year-old Luka from Parramatta, who came on stage with his own acoustic guitar and bespoke plectrums. On Luka's request, they agreed to play 'Put You in a Song'. 'This'll look good on my résumé,' Luka told Keith, as he had his guitar miked up and they got cracking. Luka didn't lack confidence; in fact, he was downright cocky, strumming confidently and then sharing the mic with Keith as the crowd got very enthused. 'Just know that I'm not singing this *about* you, Luka,' Keith said, mid-verse. 'Your résumé's looking pretty good right now!'

Keith's time with Oprah (it was always simply 'Oprah') was his second time in recent weeks with the talk-show titan. The Opera House chat was a love-in, bright and breezy, the happy couple playing to the big crowd and talking up all things Australian, but Keith's earlier interview with Oprah back in late November had been very different. He went deep in a way he still wasn't quite willing to do in song.

With Nicole in the front row looking on, Oprah had quickly turned the conversation to Keith's downward spiral that had led him back to rehab in 2006. There was a lot of talk about higher powers, open hearts, 'conceding to your innermost self'—they were both quoting from the self-help handbook. But Keith, to his credit, was totally sincere, openly discussing the events of the 2006 intervention and how he immediately surrendered, telling the group to 'put the cuffs on' and get him to Betty Ford as soon as humanly possible.

Keith brightened up considerably when talk turned to his daughter, Sunday Rose; this was far safer territory. Had parenthood changed him, Oprah asked? Hell yeah, Keith readily admitted. 'The more I get out of myself and be aware of other people . . . my life actually gets fuller and fuller.'

Later on in the show, his interrogation over, Keith played 'Put You in a Song', the cameras frequently cutting between him and Nicole—it was as though he was singing only to her. Perhaps he was. Keith certainly played up to it, standing directly in front of Nicole as he tore into a guitar solo. The studio audience, naturally, went gaga, even more gaga than a typical Oprah crowd, who, frankly, could make quite a ruckus.

*

Keith might have spilled about pretty much everything while speaking with Oprah, but one family secret remained unspoken: the Kurbans' second child. Once again, they stayed totally in control of the message—it was a shock when news broke that Faith Margaret Kidman Urban had been born at the Women's Hospital at Centennial in Nashville on 28 December 2010. The response from *People* magazine said it all: 'It's a girl—and a huge surprise!' A few days earlier, the couple had attended the Golden Globes and hadn't uttered a word about the impending birth.

'Our family is truly blessed, and just so thankful,' Keith posted on his website, 'to have been given the gift of baby Faith Margaret. No words can adequately convey the incredible gratitude for everyone that was so supportive during this process'—and then the reveal—'in particular our gestational carrier.'

Those five words were the giveaway—Faith had been born via surrogate. This put Nicole in a very exclusive motherhood group: she had adopted two of her children, carried and given birth to one child, and had a fourth by surrogate. 'I'm one of the few people in the world to have experienced so many different forms [of motherhood],' she told the BBC. The surrogate would remain a part of the family's world; she was simply referred to as 'Aunty Sheila'.

Faith was born via what is known as gestational surrogacy, which meant that she wasn't biologically related to the surrogate mother. Rather, the embryo was created by IVF, using Nicole's eggs and Keith's sperm, and then transferred to the surrogate, who carried the baby until giving birth.

Five weeks passed before the public got their first glimpse of baby Faith, when Keith shared an iPhone shot of mother and child. Keith beamed with pride. 'She looks just like her, don't you think?'

★

On 13 February 2011, Keith claimed his fourth Grammy, again for Best Male Country Vocal Performance, for his hit ''Til Summer Comes Around', the fourth single from *Defying Gravity*. (While he may have won for his vocal, Keith's fluent, lyrical guitar solo was the feature of the track.) Keith had now won as many Grammys as the Bee Gees and Olivia Newton-John—and his achievement rated barely more than a few sentences in the Australian media.

Backstage at LA's Staples Center, Keith was in a particularly buoyant mood. 'It feels amazing,' he smiled. He admitted to having a thing for Katy Perry's monster hit 'Teenage Dream'; in fact, all the Kurbans were fans. 'We had it in the car, and we'd just play it as loud as the stereo would allow . . . We love that song.' Keith rubbed shoulders with Canadian pop sensation Justin Bieber for the first time on the night—'No, I don't have Bieber fever,' he admitted politely—but he did love the cross-generational performance that teamed Bob Dylan with Mumford & Sons and The Avett Brothers. It was a highlight of the night.

As he was leaving, Keith was asked his advice for aspiring musicians. Interestingly, rather than opt for an easy sound-bite, he quoted from Joseph Campbell, an American thinker and academic best known for the 1949 book *The Hero with a Thousand Faces*.

'Follow your bliss, Joseph Campbell says. That's the way to do it.'

Typically, Keith kept on moving, playing almost 90 dates in 2011, most of them for his Get Closer World Tour. His headline run took him across the US and Canada then back to Australia for a seven-show run during April, which included a return to Tamworth, where he filled the city's

5000-seat entertainment centre on 12 April. A few weeks after returning to Nashville, on 15 May, Keith was presented with his own star on the Music City Walk of Fame, a huge honour. He was sharing space on the Demonbreun Street pavement with Elvis Presley, Roy Orbison, Loretta Lynn and other American music legends. Keith had already been made a member of the Grand Ole Opry, another big accolade. Both were firsts for an Australian act—and yet he still hadn't been inducted into the ARIA Hall of Fame back home.

However, by the end of the Get Closer tour, Keith's bliss was dampened by the discovery of a polyp on his vocal cord. Surgery was required to fix the problem, which he underwent in mid-November 2011. Just prior to his operation, when news broke of Keith's condition, the office of his manager, Gary Borman, was deluged with cards, gifts, get-well messages and flowers for his star client.

Keith wrote a heartfelt thank you on his website. 'I can't express enough my gratitude to you guys; it feels like family.' Keith fell silent for a few weeks after his surgery—literally, because he couldn't speak—as whispers began to spread of a very new gig for him: TV talent-show 'coach'.

18

'It was an experiment that went terribly wrong. I'm glad Randy was there'

Australian TV producers were quick to seize on the runaway success of singing competition *The Voice*. Ground zero was *The Voice of Holland*, which began airing in 2010, and some 30 franchises were soon in production, most notably in the US, where the show premiered on NBC in December 2010. Originally known as *The Voice of America*, it was shortened to simply *The Voice*. The original American 'coaches', whose job it was to offer wisdom and guidance (and sometimes Kleenex) to the show's many singing hopefuls, were CeeLo Green of the duo Gnarls Barkley and Maroon 5's Adam Levine, as well as pop star Christina Aguilera and country hunk Blake Shelton. Ultimately, the winning contestant would be decided by the viewers' votes.

The ratings for that first US season were big, with about twelve million viewers tuning in each week. The winner,

Javier Colon, a 33-year-old from Stratford, Connecticut, pocketed a handy US$100,000 and a recording deal with Universal Republic Records.

By May 2011, press stories were emerging that an Australian version of *The Voice* was in the works, helmed by Shine Australia, who'd had local success with adapted reality hits *The Biggest Loser* and *MasterChef Australia*. Channel 9 would broadcast the show. Various names were mooted as possible coaches, among them Pink, Gwen Stefani, Dannii Minogue (who'd already filled a similar role on *Australia's Got Talent*) and Vanessa Amorosi. But in mid-October 2011, the *Herald Sun* broke the news that Keith was one of the four coaches hired for the show, along with Delta Goodrem, Seal and Joel Madden from rock band Good Charlotte. It was an interesting mix—the Aussie diva, the international pop star, the tattooed punk and the Nashville-via-Caboolture cowboy. Seal was the senior member of the group at 49 years old. Keith only agreed to sign on when Nicole said to him, 'I think it could be fun.' Until then, he hadn't been so sure.

Keith wasn't available to speak about his new gig, mainly because he was preparing himself for surgery on his damaged throat. But it was made very clear that he'd be in good voice when the 'blind auditions' stage of the show began shooting in mid-February 2012, at Sydney's Fox Studios. The show itself would premiere on 15 April. Huge ratings weren't just hoped for, they were expected. Keith's family would jet in and out during the production, staying with him as much as they could, much to his relief.

'It's authenticity, that's what I'm looking for,' a very serious Keith stated during promos for *The Voice*, his own voice now fully restored, perhaps even improved by the surgery. 'It's all about the voice and I love that we get a chance to connect with that before anything else.'

But, as he admitted in an interview with *A Current Affair*, the competitive process of *The Voice*—contestants singing to the back of the coaches' chairs, and crossing their fingers that one of them would turn around—would have been too much for him when he was starting out: 'I could not do that.' He also knew *The Voice* would be a tough gig: there were 120 hopefuls, but he and his fellow coaches could only spin their chair twelve times each. 'It's a really awful feeling not being able to turn for people.' That comment summed up Keith the Coach—he was the voice of positivity, always supportive and encouraging. He knew what it was like to be judged; after all, he'd suffered the wrath of Bernard King all those years ago.

'Coaching' aside, *The Voice* gave Keith a chance to step way outside of his country-pop safe space. No one could have ever imagined he'd perform 'Crazy' with Seal, Delta Goodrem and the illustrated dude from Good Charlotte, but he did just that during the opening episode of the show. Totally unexpected.

One of the singers Keith 'turned' for was Darren Percival, who first appeared in the fourth 'Blind Audition' on 22 April, singing 'Jealous Guy'. 'Beautiful!' Keith roared, slapping his thigh enthusiastically, as he turned his chair to face Percival (although Seal had been the first to do so). Urged on by the crowd, the other two judges did likewise. Percival was on his way.

Percival was not your typical TV talent show aspirant: aged 40, he was a father of two, bearing a passing resemblance to *Grand Designs* host Kevin McCloud. He'd spent much of his life as a jobbing musician, performing jazz and big-band music, most notably as part of trumpeter James Morrison's touring band, which he'd joined straight out of school. In 2003, under his stage name Mr Percival, he recorded an album, *Falling Around the Sun*. It went nowhere, and by 2007 he was playing the club circuit and stripping things back to just his voice and a few electronic pedals, which he'd use to record loops and beats and melodies. Bobby 'Don't Worry, Be Happy' McFerrin, whom Percival had studied under in New York, was a big inspiration.

When Percival learned he'd landed a spot on *The Voice*, he had $18 in the bank. He badly needed a break. Having Keith on his side was huge.

Percival, a crowd favourite, made it through two more rounds, then the quarter-final and semi-final. In the final, aired on 18 June, which drew a TV audience of 3.2 million, Percival was voted runner-up. The winner was twenty-year-old Karise Eden, the product of a troubled family, who strived to be the next Janis Joplin. Keith had been the first to turn his chair when she debuted a week earlier than Percival, singing James Brown's 'It's a Man's World'.

Percival collected $30,000, but just as importantly found a true believer in Keith. And they connected person-ally: both were fathers of two young kids, and they'd paid plenty of dues to finally claim a slice of the spotlight. When they sang Keith's 'Without You' together on *The Voice*, it felt as though they'd been singing together for years, not weeks. They remained tight after the show, too; when Keith returned for some Australian shows in January 2013, he invited Percival, on his way back to clubland, to the stage to sing Bill Withers' 'Ain't No Sunshine' and Peter Allen's

'I Still Call Australia Home'. The bond between them was strong.

The Voice had been a big success, but Keith made it known that it was a one-off, at least for the time being. A much bigger TV gig had appeared on his radar.

*

Keith had been offered a role as a judge on Season 12 of *American Idol* in July 2012, taking over from Aerosmith's Steven Tyler. It was an offer that he just couldn't refuse: the payday was somewhere in the vicinity of US$3–4 million. Until now, it had been a gig for pop or rock stars or industry types—Paula Abdul and Randy Jackson had been judges, along with pot-stirring perennial (and music biz exec) Simon Cowell—but Keith was the first country artist to be an *American Idol* judge. The series began airing on the Fox network in mid-January 2013.

Keith, however, couldn't have imagined what he was getting into, especially when sparks started to fly between two of his co-judges, strong-willed pop legend Mariah Carey and hip-hop troublemaker Nicki Minaj, early on during the 37-episode series.

It was in Charlotte, North Carolina, that things got really uncomfortable. An auditionee named Summer Cunningham casually mentioned that she'd 'done the country thing', as if it was some passing fad—which didn't sit well with Keith, who typically kept things fair and upbeat. Mariah Carey stepped in, asking Summer to reveal more about her musical past. 'Why are we, like, picking her apart?' interjected a clearly annoyed Minaj, swaying backwards in her chair. Minaj turned on Carey and the show's fourth judge, Randy Jackson, accusing them of speaking disparagingly about pop music. ('Not you, Keith,' she made clear.) Carey and Minaj then began speaking over the top of each other, as the temperature in the room rapidly increased. Jackson and Keith both tried to play peacemaker, but with little effect.

A bewildered Cunningham left the room, soon followed by Minaj, who declared, 'Maybe I should just get off the fucking panel.' Production was swiftly shut down for the day, and within hours the leaked, uncensored video almost overloaded the TMZ website. 'I was the UN,' Keith said afterwards, playing nice. 'It's a very alive, a very invigorating work environment. Lots of passion.' It was the most Keith had said about the show to date; frankly, it had been hard for him to get a word in on set.

It was hardly the last time the two women drew swords—after one particularly volatile exchange, Carey said she feared for her own safety and beefed up her security detail for the rest of the series. Even president Barack Obama bought into their beef, insisting that they would 'sort it out'. Their clash, of course, generated handsome ratings for the show—*Idol* drew anywhere from eleven million to eighteen million per episode.

It was a tough gig for Keith. He admitted that he sometimes felt 'like a scratching post' when seated between Minaj and Carey. 'It was an experiment that went terribly wrong,' he said in 2015. 'I'm glad Randy was there.' Occasionally, the smile on his face seemed very forced; perhaps he was distracted by Minaj's wacky wig collection or her cringe-worthy attempts at a British accent. It could have been the peculiar nicknames—'Collard greens', 'Finger licking good', 'Frog Killer'—she bestowed on *Idol* hopefuls.

Clearly, Keith was still learning how to be a judge, but soon enough he'd find his groove as part of a very different panel. Fortunately, it was the last *Idol* saw of duelling divas Minaj and Carey. One season had been plenty.

*

Keith's TV profile had interrupted his recording career; when he closed the final episode of *Idol* on 16 May 2013, singing 'Where the Blacktop Ends' with runner-up Kree Harrison, it had been almost three years since *Defying Gravity* was released. He needed to get back into the studio.

Fuse, as his new album would be titled, was a radical shake-up. Rather than stick with the one producer, lucky touchstone Dann Huff, Keith decided to record with a few different producers. This got way out of control over time; in the end he worked with eight producers or production teams. Among his new collaborators was Benny Blanco, a wild-haired 25-year-old Virginian with even wilder musical ideas. Blanco had worked with solid-gold pop star Katy Perry—on 'Teenage Dream,' no less, the song loved by the Urban family—and Britney Spears. He had also co-written and co-produced Maroon 5's huge hit 'Moves like Jagger', but his approach was by no means mainstream.

Blanco was the type of producer who saw the studio as a sonic wonderland, who didn't see the need to use traditional instruments played by humans when computers could do the job. He operated on a totally different level to the long-established Music City system, the world of seasoned 'Nashville cats' who seemingly played on every record made in the city. Keith also brought in Mike Elizondo, whose roots were in hip-hop, having co-written Eminem's 'The Real Slim Shady' and 50 Cent's 'In Da Club'. Clearly, these people were not Nashville regulars— then again, neither was Stevie J, who Keith had worked with back in 1999.

'I'm just seeing what comes out of me working with those guys,' Keith told *Billboard*'s Gary Graff.

Keith's new buzzword was 'diversity', not only in the type of music he was making but in how he was creating it. Mavericks like Elizondo and Blanco impressed him: 'All these guys play lots of instruments and they program and play synths and they can build an entire track just on their own.' This was a whole new world for the platinum-plated country star—and ballsy, too. It would have been easy for Keith to stick with the safe and familiar, which had helped him sell millions of records, but he opted to up his game. 'I can keep making the same record,' Keith told US *Rolling Stone*, 'but I don't want to do that.'

Keith had well and truly moved on from 'But for the Grace of God' and the sound of a sobbing pedal steel guitar. Fuse standouts like 'Shame', 'Heart Like Mine' and 'Cop Car', tracks heavy with programming and digital-age tricks, were very contemporary, and unapologetically commercial.

Elsewhere, Keith's guitar riff on 'Good Thing', while a little closer to his roots, sounded filthy enough to warrant an X-rating. That turbocharged track was the result of Keith and Elizondo working as a production and recording team of two, whereas an ensemble of eight musos, including Keith, contributed to the deluxe-edition track 'Gonna B Good',

Keith playing electric and acoustic guitar, slide guitar, bouzouki, ganjo—and a baby sitar. Keith was really mixing it up. Even a big ballad like 'Come Back to Me' sounded vastly different to the weepies that had been huge hits for him in the past. It might have been a sad song, but it was also sonically adventurous, swamped in keyboards and sonic textures. Keith imagined the character in 'Come Back to Me' to be the same guy from his 2006 hit 'Stupid Boy', just a little older and a lot wiser.

Not only had Keith gotten wise to hip-hop, pop and R&B, he'd also been inspired by U2's *Achtung Baby*, the Irish band's 1991 LP that radically reworked their stadium rock bluster. He quoted Bono when he spoke about *Fuse* with *Rolling Stone*. 'Bono said [*Achtung Baby*] had to be the sound of [U2] chopping down *The Joshua Tree*, which I thought was great. That's where I found myself at.'

Keith, by his own admission, had developed a serious addiction to the musical app Shazam, which helped him search out new artists and sounds. He described himself as a 'mad Shazam-er'. 'Every time I would hear something on the radio, maybe just a rhythm that I loved, I would Shazam it,' he told *USA Today*.

Keith fell so hard for the Fall Out Boy track 'My Songs Know What You Did in the Dark (Light Em Up)' that he reached out to its co-producer Butch Walker; together they worked on three *Fuse* tracks. One of those, 'Heart Like Mine', was a song that had done some miles: Keith wrote the first verse in his New York apartment; the second came to him in LA as he was taking a shower; and he and Walker—an ordained minister in the state of Ohio, no less—thrashed out the chorus in the producer's Santa Monica studio. Keith's days of co-writing in the stuffy, windowless offices of music publishers were long gone.

Keith had also been rewatching the rockumentary classic *This is Spinal Tap*, which inspired him to name a track 'She's My 11'. No one had cited 'The Tap' on a country record before; nor had a scat/ganjo solo, which Keith improvised on the track, been heard much in Nashville.

Keith wasn't the only country act to dabble in cross-pollination. In 2004, his pal Kenny Chesney had teamed up with Uncle Kracker, former turntablist for rapper Kid Rock, on the number 1 country-chart hit 'When the Sun Goes Down'. The same year, Tim McGraw had featured on Nelly's smooth and sexy 'Over and Over', another big cross-over hit. Nelly had also worked with breakout Nashville duo Florida Georgia Line. Their 2012 jam 'Cruise'—described as 'bro-country', a feel-good mix of country, rock, partying and hip-hop—broke all kinds of records, spending 24 weeks at number 1 in the Hot Country chart and hitting the mainstream Top 10. Clearly, the Berlin Wall that once separated country from other genres was starting to crumble.

Then there was the musical makeover that Taylor Swift, Keith's former opening act, was undertaking. Her latest LP, 2012's *Red*, marked a sizeable shift away from Nashville—*Spin* magazine called it 'one of the best pop albums of our time'—with its traces of rock and folk and electronica, even dubstep. Three of the producers Swift worked with on *Red*—Dann Huff, Nathan Chapman and Butch Walker—also worked on *Fuse*. (Another *Red* contributor, Jeff Bhasker, best known for the records he'd made with Kanye West, would work with Keith in the near future.) *Red* went on to sell a handy seven million copies in the US alone and was seemingly nominated for just about every award known to the music biz. This, surely, was a sign to Keith that expanding your style didn't necessarily mean losing your audience.

Some Nashville purists may have accused Keith of trend-chasing, and the record did generate its fair share of head-scratching. *Rolling Stone*'s Will Hermes felt that the album sounded more 1980s than cutting edge, with its 'big, clipped drums and guitar-face soloing'. Lyrics still weren't his forte, and *Fuse* came with its share of clunkers, as Hermes—who gave the record three stars—made clear. 'Urban's lyrics remain pro forma: Dude drives around, thinks about hot girl ("Somewhere in My Car") or goes to bar/club, comes on to hot girl ("Good Thing").' Even *Entertainment Weekly*, hardly the bastion of incisive journalism, slammed Keith's sometimes clumsy wordplay. 'Urban's breezy, flirty lyrics are so dreadfully derivative that they undo his attempt at diversity,' their reviewer noted.

Fuse didn't perform nearly as well commercially as Keith's earlier records, selling only 98,000 copies in the week of its release. (*Get Closer* had sold 162,000 copies during its opening week, *Defying Gravity* 171,000.) Yet, given the huge impact that streaming was having on sales, *Fuse* still topped the *Billboard* 200 and the country album charts in its opening week. However, it wouldn't be until April 2017, almost four years after its release, that the album was certified platinum in the US, and even then it was based on a combined tally of sales and streams. Nonetheless, it was in parts a brave record, a clear sign that habitual 'Shazam-er' Keith was open to new sounds and sensations.

*

Change now seemed to be Keith's primary motivation for his every career move. When he returned to *American Idol* for Season 13 in 2013—the production, which was underway by July, intersected awkwardly with the completion of *Fuse*—he was part of a new judging panel, working alongside Harry Connick Jr, straight out of New Orleans, and Latin-pop superstar Jennifer Lopez, the former 'Jenny from the Block'. This was a more interesting (and less volatile) mix than the previous line-up of two divas, a lesser Jackson and 'that guy married to Nicole Kidman'. And the chemistry proved to be much more natural; it only took a few episodes, according to Keith, for them to find their groove. 'As personalities, I think we just clicked really quickly . . . it seems to be very, very good,' he told *USA Today*.

And Keith did quickly find his niche—once more he was the nice guy, the voice of positivity, but without building false hope for auditionees clearly out of their depth, or plain out of talent. 'Baby' became his buzzword; he threw it into most greetings—and the occasional awkward farewell. 'Thanks, baby,' 'That's great, baby,' and the rest of it. But he was never sleazy, always supportive.

Keith also displayed a wit that had been in short supply when he was stuck between the battling Carey and Minaj. During one *Idol* episode he asked a singer—contender number 40409, to be precise—to drop the pretence and sing 'like you were doing the dishes and there was no one around', which led to a panel rap about going off script. Keith then produced a page from beneath the desk, which he showed to the others.

'It says we're not scripted and then Jen says something after that,' Keith read, smirking like a cheeky teenager. It was a genuinely funny improv.

On camera, Keith would joke about the attention of the make-up team to his appearance—'hair 64B is out of place', he'd say, touching his head, pointing to a trouble spot—and he developed a steady, funny rapport with Harry Connick Jr, who laid on the Aussie jibes. ('He's from Australia', 'Don't worry, he's Australian', 'I'm from the South, Keith's from the Deep South', and so on.) They'd often laugh about being extras on the panel, as most hopefuls were fixated on Jennifer Lopez. ('It's all about Jen!' chuckled Connick Jr.) When one contestant began serenading J.Lo, crooning a little Marvin Gaye, Keith and Connick Jr shrugged and struck up a side conversation about lunch, eventually agreeing on burgers. As the audition dragged on they left the room, arm in arm, still talking food, leaving Lopez to deal with her starstruck fan. Another time, when the subject of doing the splits came up, Connick Jr and Keith compared their stretching abilities, each draping a leg over the judge's desk, flexing for the camera. (It was a draw.)

Some hopefuls admitted to not actually knowing who Connick Jr was, so he'd tell them he was Chris Isaak. 'You know "Wicked Game"?'

During a shoot, when left together alone on the set, Keith and Connick Jr improvised an audition—Keith was the hard-nosed judge, Connick Jr a very nervous contender. As he began to sing his song of choice, 'The Star-Spangled Banner', in a deep monotone, Connick Jr heard some chuckles. He stopped singing.

'Are they laughing at me?' he asked.

'No,' Keith assured him, 'they're laughing *near* you.'

Audition over, Keith gave Connick Jr a hard no, but did offer an autograph, so he signed Harry's leg. 'That's my phone number on the bottom,' Keith added, with a wink.

During another episode, when a hopeful admitted that she did a lot of work at funerals—'I sing for the dead'—Keith shot back, 'Harry does, too.' 'Most of my concerts,' Connick Jr agreed. The laughs that could be heard from the crew were loud and genuine. The rapport between them was obvious, very natural, and probably the best part of the show, which, unfortunately, slipped in the ratings, as viewers began to grow tired of TV talent shows.

*

In Keith's world, a tour would bookend with the release of a new record, but he messed it up with *Fuse*. Thinking that the album would be finished by July 2013, Keith had asked his management to set up a big tour. Then he decided to keep working on the record, so the Light the Fuse world tour, which kicked off on 18 July, actually preceded the release of the record by some six weeks. It also intersected with *Idol* auditions, which continued into the first week of September. It was a chaotic stretch: new record, new tour, second season of *Idol*—Keith was all over the place. He'd fly to the first gig of each week, ride the tour bus to the next few shows, and then fly back to Nashville at the end of the week to reconnect with his family, squeezing in *Idol* commitments as they arose.

'But I'd rather do that than be out for months at a time, away from home,' he explained to radio host Bobby Bones when he spoke on his show in August.

Keith and Nicole had an agreement—they did their utmost to not spend more than seven days apart at a time, despite the demands of their careers. 'Two weeks is still too long for us,' Nicole told *Vanity Fair*. 'We start to hurt after seven days.' Texting was second best for the Kurbans, too. If at all possible, they preferred to speak on the phone. 'Mainly we'll say, "I want to hear your voice",' Nicole said. They were quite the old-fashioned couple. Luckily for Keith, Nicole had a break between filming *Before I Go to Sleep*, which wrapped in February 2013, and *Strangerland*, which would be filmed in Australia, in Broken Hill and Alice Springs, during March and April 2014. Otherwise the au pair bills alone might have kept Keith on the road forever.

The *Fuse* tour would be broken down into three North American 'legs'—the first opened in Cincinnati, Ohio, on 18 July and closed at West Palm Beach in Florida on 5 October. Two weeks later, Keith and the band got back to work at Omaha's CenturyLink Center and rolled on until 8 December with a year-ending show at Louisville's wonderfully named KFC Yum! Center, playing to a nearly full house of 8500. A month later, the final leg opened in Grand Rapids, Michigan, and headed north to Canada—a very reliable market for Keith—before closing with a hometown gig for Keith at Nashville's 15,000-capacity Bridgestone Arena.

With more than two dozen country chart hits to his name, Keith's biggest challenge when it came to a 2013 set list was what to leave out. When he played to a crowd of 12,500 in Alpharetta, Georgia, on 27 July, he not only pumped out his own hits—'Sweet Thing', 'Kiss a Girl', 'Days Go By', 'Better Life', 'You Gonna Fly'—but playfully included a snippet of Bruno Mars' huge 'Locked Out of Heaven' and The Who classic 'Won't Get Fooled Again'.

'Hey Georgia!' cried Keith as he and the band wandered into the section of the crowd seated on the Verizon

Amphitheatre's grassy knoll. 'Who's got the good seats now?' Over the course of two hours, twenty-odd songs and four guitar changes, as *Billboard*'s Chuck Dauphin reported, Keith 'delivered one of the strongest performances of any country artists this year—or the past few years for that matter'.

On 6 September, during a break from *Idol*, Keith put in a Nashville music marathon, playing four gigs in the one night—outdoors at Cumberland Park, plus hit-and-run sets at intimate venues Legends Corner, The Stage and Tootsie's Orchid Lounge. These were the type of clubs Keith hadn't played since the days of The Ranch (though it was actually his first gig at Tootsie's). It may have been a lively night for Keith, but it was more so for his crew, who travelled ahead of him, setting up each room in advance. It was a guerrilla operation.

Opened in 1960, Tootsie's was a legendary honky-tonk, once the watering hole of choice for country's finest—Willie Nelson, Patsy Cline, Waylon Jennings and Kris Kristofferson had all been regulars. 'This is awesome,' Keith said as he squeezed onto the venue's tiny stage with bassist Flowers and drummer McHugh. The capacity audience—all 200 of them—were inches away, waving their phones madly. (Hundreds more were outside on the street, as word quickly spread.) 'We're grateful we've finally made the big time and made it to Tootsie's. So thanks for coming out tonight.'

Just before Keith started playing, one of his crew whispered in his ear, telling him that Aerosmith singer and former *Idol* judge Steven Tyler was in the house. One song into his set, Keith struck up a familiar riff. He had a plan.

'If you happen to be a bit of a bad-ass blues legend singer,' he told the crowd, 'this might be your cue.' The 65-year-old Tyler, after making his way through the crowd, slapped Keith a hearty high five and launched into ZZ Top's 'La Grange'.

'You're my favourite *Idol*, you know that,' Tyler told Keith, between songs. 'And give this to J.Lo for me.' With that, he planted a wet one on Keith's cheek. It was that kind of gig. Then they jammed, very loosely, Aerosmith's 'Walk this Way'.

'Steven Fucking Tyler!' yelled Keith as the song crashed to a finish. With that, the legend kissed him again and left the stage—and the crowd went crazy.

*

In June 2014, Keith returned to Australia for a run of capital city dates, playing his biggest venues yet, including Qudos Bank Arena in Sydney and Melbourne's Rod Laver Arena. He also played an open-air show on 27 June at Collins Park in Narrabri, New South Wales, a far-flung gig that was straight out of a Slim Dusty tour itinerary. Truth be told, the move was inspired more by French electro-pop duo Daft Punk, who a month earlier had chosen the annual Wee Waa Show near Narrabri as the launch site for their latest album, *Random Access Memories*, which many scribes rated as the weirdest launch in music history. (Millions of Daft Punk fans hit Google Maps to work out where the hell Wee Waa actually was.) Impressed by the numbers that Daft Punk drew, even though they didn't actually appear, the local council then lobbied to bring Keith to Narrabri, with Trent Bruinsma, a local venue manager, leading the push.

Keith, admittedly, was a little more familiar to regional

Australian audiences than boundary-busting twosome Daft Punk. Either way, mayor Conrad Bolton was understandably chuffed that Narrabri had become a new musical hotspot, telling *ABC News*, 'It was broadly viewed that there is an enormous fan base . . . that doesn't get a lot of opportunity to see big national and international artists.' And Keith, unlike Daft Punk, actually appeared in the flesh, playing to a crowd of 6000.

Keith played 79 gigs in total to promote *Fuse* and, as usual, the box office returns were very healthy. He drew more than 13,000 payers to a show in Calgary, which generated a touch over Can$1 million; in Edmonton, the full house of 12,379 at Rexall Place handed over another $1 million. The crowd at Toronto's Air Canada Centre, some 14,000 fans, contributed yet another $1 million to Keith's retirement plan. The Nashville show at the Bridgestone Arena generated a further US$769,000. This was big Keith Urban business, night after night.

19

'Ever since we've been married ... people make up the most insane crap'

In the northern summer of 2014, Keith was back on the road with the Raise 'Em Up Tour. 'Raise 'Em Up' was one of the more familiar-sounding songs on *Fuse*, a wholesome slice of country-pop acoustica that he cut with Eric Church, whose latest album, *The Outsiders*, would be the bestselling country record of 2014 in the US. Born in North Carolina, 37-year-old Church was from a generation of mostly hatless country acts that were more in tune with what Keith was doing than, say, the musical stylings of George Strait. And Church, like Keith, had started young, playing covers in local bars before he'd finished high school.

Keith had known Church for some time before they recorded the song; he was a big fan of Church's 2011 album *Chief*, citing it as one of his favourites of the previous ten years, 'from top to bottom'. Church was also the father of two young kids, and they'd go out for family dinners in Nashville. Whenever they caught up, they'd try to one-up each other by recommending obscure music. 'You've gotta listen to *Bankrupt* by Dr Hook,' Keith would tell Church, setting him a challenge for the next time they met.

'It's such a cinematic song,' Keith said of 'Raise 'Em Up', 'and I've always considered Eric a cinematic artist.' Like many others who Keith worked with, he'd later reconnect with Church. In 2019, when Keith had a hit with a Church co-write, 'We Were', he gave him a hell of a gift—a very rare 1933 Martin guitar, worth tens of thousands of dollars. 'I was floored,' said Church.

'Raise 'Em Up' was the fifth single released from *Fuse*, and yet another gold record for Keith. Curiously, he didn't actually play the song on the eponymous 25-date tour, which began on 12 July and took Keith and his band to some of the bigger summer outdoor events. Instead, Keith's set list stuck with the crowd-pleasers, the hits, with the odd surprise, such as the snippet of 'Another One Bites the Dust' that he squeezed into his usual closer, 'Somebody Like You'. Keith and his band played the Calgary Stampede, the Delaware State Fair and the Jamboree in the Hills, an annual country music bash in Morristown, Ohio.

As expected, the returns were good—more than US$1 million came through the box office at Calgary alone, and most nights generated around US$500,000. Keith drew almost 300,000 punters to the 25 shows, which closed disappointingly, at a half-full amphitheatre in Wheatland, California, on 7 September. But Keith was proving to be a major draw in other lesser-known locales; being a country star, a heartland act, meant that his biggest audiences weren't always in the hotspots of New York, Los Angeles, Chicago and so on. It wasn't that different to Australia, where you could be a huge drawcard in Tamworth and Gympie and all but unknown in the capital cities.

After Keith filled the Xfinity Center in Mansfield, Massachusetts, on 26 July, he learned that an eighteen-year-old man had been accused of raping a seventeen-year-old woman at the show. An onlooker had pulled the man away when she heard the woman say the act was not consensual. Keith was horrified. (The rape charge was later dropped.) It had been a particularly rowdy gig; some 50 fans required medical treatment, mainly because of excessive boozing. Many of them were under-age. Twenty-two people were hospitalised and there were a number of arrests.

Keith, by his own admission, had no issues with drinking at his shows, despite being on the wagon himself. 'I don't want people looking at the stage and thinking about sobriety,' he told a writer from *Rolling Stone*. 'That would be the death of a gig for me.' (He served alcohol to his guests at home but made sure they knew he was 'allergic' to booze.) However, the incident at Mansfield was inexcusable. 'This type of behaviour stands in stark contrast to the spirit of our shows,' he said in an online statement.

There was also a tragic coda to the Raise 'Em Up tour. Word reached Keith's family that Nicole Kidman's father, Antony Kidman, had died in Singapore on 12 September after suffering a heart attack. He'd been visiting Nicole's sister Antonia, along with her second husband, businessman Craig Marran—who identified Dr Kidman's body in the morgue—and her six children. Dr Kidman, who'd been made a Member of the Order of Australia in 2005 for his contribution to clinical psychology, was 75. It was a tough time for the Kidman family and for Keith, who had held his father-in-law in high regard.

Keith cancelled a show at the Washington State Fairgrounds and flew back to Nashville on a private plane. 'We are in a deep state of grief,' Keith posted on Facebook, as he and his family began making plans to return to Sydney for the funeral, which was to be held at the St Francis Xavier Church in Lavender Bay.

'I am one of the lucky ones,' Nicole said at the service, brushing away tears, while Keith, who was a pallbearer, sat nearby with their two daughters. 'I am a girl, a woman, raised by an extraordinary man.' She described her father as 'calm, wise, self-restrained and generous. What more could you wish for in a father?'

Keith then joined her; he strummed a guitar as the gathering sang 'Amazing Grace'.

Soon after, Nicole spoke about Keith during a chinwag with TV's Ellen DeGeneres. Keith had been especially strong in the wake of her father's death, which had hit her hard, she said. 'It's been a really tough time for me . . . to have my husband just step up in that way, it makes me cry . . . I was so devastated, it's just like, I'll do anything for that man.'

Unfortunately, Antony Kidman's death was just one of several family dramas. Antonia Kidman's first husband, Angus Hawley, would die in April 2015, aged just 46, in New York, from a suspected heart attack. And Keith's father Bob—'Poppy Bob' to his grandchildren—was in poor health, having been diagnosed with prostate cancer. It was a difficult period for both families.

★

January 2015 marked the tenth anniversary of Keith having met Nicole at G'Day LA. In the world of showbiz, staying together ten years was a lifetime, perhaps even two. Many celebrity marriages barely outlasted their vows—the Zellweger/ Chesney union of just four months was hardly unique, while Keith's *American Idol* co-host Jennifer Lopez had been married and divorced three times, and engaged at least one other time. (During the show, she laughed about her choice of partners.)

However, despite the obvious strength of the bond between Keith and Nicole, barely a week passed without yet another 'close friend' of the couple questioning their marriage in the tabloids. It seemed that the shock that had first greeted their romance—how could a Hollywood 'princess' date this Nashville 'coke-head'?—hadn't ever really faded.

Of late, completely unfounded rumours had linked Keith with Miranda Lambert, a country artist who sang on *Fuse*. And whenever Keith or Nicole turned up solo to an awards show or a premiere, headlines inevitably followed. On one occasion, Nicole missed the Grammys, which was blamed in print on a 'huge fight' between the couple, according to one anonymous source who knew the 'truth' (it was always an anonymous source, funnily enough). The truth, in fact, was far more mundane—she had the flu. Even then, the notion that a celebrity couple might actually fight sometimes seemed too much for the tabloids to digest. How could they be like normal people? It was unimaginable.

Typically, when either Keith or Nicole were no-shows, they were either working or having a night off with the kids. This, of course, didn't stop an endless flow of headlines— several forests were felled, and many servers crashed, in the service of the couple's alleged 'problems'. To their credit, the Kurbans learned to shrug off what were sometimes very hurtful rumours, but privately they were annoyed by the constant chatter. Keith made this very clear when he spoke with Channel 9's Richard Wilkins.

'It's total bullshit,' Keith replied when Wilkins asked how he responded to the rumours. 'Ever since we've been married . . . we get on with living our life and people make up the most insane crap.'

That meant, at least as far as their children were concerned, keeping them way out of the public eye. In family shots released online, Sunday Rose and her younger sister, Faith Margaret, were photographed only from the back—their faces were rarely, if ever, seen. The Kurbans were not the Kardashians, a family who seemed to live every moment of every day on social media. And while Keith could see that his family's commitment to privacy led to rumours—writers had to fill the void to fill their pages, after all—it didn't make him any less vexed.

'The fact that we're not documenting every single thing we do as a family, we're very private people, makes it possible for people to make that stuff up . . . then you get angry, [because you think], "Why do I have to defend this?"'

Certainly, if love could be measured in miles, their bond was unbreakable. During 2015, Nicole was in London, preparing to appear in a West End play called *Photograph 51*, while Keith was playing some shows in the US. Keith was hellbent on attending the play's premiere and made that clear to Nicole when they spoke on the phone.

'It's too much,' she told him. 'You'd have to fly here and then fly all the way back the next day. It's okay.'

'I'm coming,' Keith insisted, and did just that, flying ten

hours to watch her perform, and then catching the next flight back to the States.

'That,' Nicole told *DuJour* magazine, 'is love in action . . . I would do the same for him and that's what we've committed to as a couple.'

★

Keith and Nicole maintained a lively juggling act as parents and artists. Nicole alternated between smaller, independent films such as 2015's *Strangerland*, and mainstream flicks, including 2014's live-action *Paddington*, where she played villain Millicent Clyde. She also continued her work as a Goodwill Ambassador for the UN.

Keith, meanwhile, was either in the studio, on the road—he played 66 shows in 2014 and another 34 in 2015, and would do a further 78 in 2016—or, increasingly, on TV, as he prepared for his final hurrah with *American Idol* in 2016. Keith would shoot 150 episodes of *Idol* across his four seasons as judge. He'd also been landing his share of other gigs—at the 2015 Grammys he introduced his buddy Eric Church to the Staples Center stage, to perform 'Give Me Back My Hometown'. He was in huge demand.

In early July 2015, Keith was briefly back in Australia for an unlikely cameo: guest hosting Channel 7's *Sunrise* program. He may have been a small-screen regular, both in Oz and the US, but this was a new sensation—filling in for the man known simply as 'Kochie'. The *Sunrise* producers were shocked when he accepted their offer but, as Keith admitted on the set, he was up for it. 'I like to do stuff I've never done before.'

For what Channel 7 proclaimed 'Keith Urban Day', Keith dressed in very un-Kochie style, his chest tattoo visible underneath a loosely buttoned black shirt, matched with black jeans. Meanwhile, a group of his fans—the self-proclaimed 'Aussie monkeys'—were gathered outside the Channel 7 studio in Sydney's Martin Place, waving banners and placards, trying to catch his eye. Some of them had travelled from far-flung spots: Tamworth, Coonabarabran and beyond. Keith promised them he'd tour Australia next year. (Which he did, in December 2016.)

Looking far too good for a man suffering jet lag—he'd landed two days prior and was about to fly out for a gig in Boise, Idaho, the following night—Keith, within minutes, had slipped comfortably into morning TV mode. He flirted with co-host Samantha Armytage and joked about his *Idol* co-host J.Lo when he discovered that Armytage kept a heater under the desk. J.Lo did the same, apparently, 'but a much bigger heater, of course'. He rechristened the show's Cash Cow as 'CC'—Keith even made the call to the $10,000 Cash Cow winner, a hairdresser from rural Victoria named Gabrielle, who handled the shock pretty well—and read most of his cues with aplomb, ad-libbing constantly. He openly discussed his marriage (Keith and Nicole had just celebrated their ninth anniversary backstage at a gig in Michigan) and children, revealing that he'd nicknamed his daughters Fifi and Munchkin and that—shock, horror—they had to carry out chores for their pocket money, just like normal kids. ('They're earning their keep, which is good.') He even managed to squeeze a few words out of a mono-syllabic interviewee, a rough-diamond Australian bull rider named Ben Jones.

Clearly revelling in this one-off gig, Keith moderated a panel chat about gluten-free diets, talked sports and weather, guided Samantha Armytage through some guitar basics—and revisited an awkward concert moment when he was asked to sign a prosthetic leg thrown on stage, and had no idea how to return it to its owner. ('I gingerly passed it back.') Keith also rode a mechanical bull for the first time, having just sung the praises of 'mutton busting'—bull riding for juniors—which he was sure his eldest daughter Sunday Rose would be up for. 'Builds character,' he believed. Mechanical bull riding wasn't for Keith, however; he came a cropper after just a few seconds on board, freaking out his fellow panel members, who thought he might be injured. (He wasn't.)

Keith was more at ease on the couch; he was up for anything, enjoying himself immensely and staying upbeat and engaged for the entire three hours. 'I'm new here!' was his go-to phrase if he missed a cue. His co-hosts seemed genuinely surprised by how down to earth Keith was, how unpretentious. 'You're such an Aussie!' Armytage said more than once. If Keith ever chose to ditch music, morning TV was calling his name.

Within a day and a bit, Keith was back on the road—the Boise, Idaho, gig was the start of yet another hectic run of dates, which wound up with a show at the Washington State Fair on 19 September. In typical fashion, Keith was already at work on his next record, a period he would describe as 'a lot of searching, a lot of experimenting'. But a tragedy was about to jolt him back to reality.

20

A farewell, a guy named Pitbull and a bold new beginning

Throughout his career, Keith had always given his father Bob due credit. He was the man whose music collection had first inspired Keith to pick up the guitar and seek out this mysterious place called Nashville. But their relationship, like that of most fathers and sons, wasn't always smooth. According to Rob Potts, who knew the Urbans well, "Their relationship . . . was very tested and testy for a long time. Whereas Marienne was happy to go and live with them and experience the whole thing in America, Bob was always very reluctant. He felt that it was Keith's fame and success and was happy to stay in the background.'

Over the years, piece by piece, interview by interview, Keith had begun to reveal truths about his childhood life in Australia—his father's alcoholism, his reluctance to give praise. But Keith had written 'Song for Dad' in his honour, which seemed to lay to rest any conflict between them. And Keith had generously provided for his parents, setting them up on the Gold Coast, and funding Bob's love of American cars and Harleys. He'd become the proverbial good son. Becoming a father had also given Keith a better understanding of Bob, as he noted in a Facebook post earlier in 2015: 'Being a Dad gives me a WHOLE new love and appreciation for my Dad, and everything he's done for me.'

Bob had been battling cancer for almost a decade when the news broke that he'd died, on 5 December 2015, at home at Mooloolaba in Queensland. He was 73. Only days earlier, Keith had been honoured with an exhibit at Nashville's Country Music Hall of Fame Museum entitled 'Keith Urban So Far . . .'. It featured stage clothes, photos, instruments and other memorabilia from Keith's career. Among the many guests was Mary Martin, the woman who'd encouraged Keith to not give up after his first futile trips to Music City. 'I hope you come back to Nashville and find a home here,' she had written to Keith all those years ago. But tonight, Keith's mind was elsewhere. He was thinking about his father.

'He's probably only got a few weeks, if that,' Keith said when asked about Bob's condition. 'So [the exhibit] is bitter-sweet a little bit because [my dad] is the catalyst for all of this . . . for me living in America.'

When Bob died, Keith posted a statement on his website, which read, in part: 'His long battle with cancer is now over and he is finally at peace. My dad's love of country music and America set me on my life's journey and shaped so much of who I am today. Thank you to everyone who has kept us all in your thoughts and prayers.'

Keith travelled alone to attend his father's funeral. The cumulative effect of her own father's recent death, the loss of her former brother-in-law and now her father-in-law was too much for Nicole. She grieved for 'Poppy Bob' back in Nashville with their two daughters.

Bob Urban's funeral service was held on 17 December in Caloundra on the Sunshine Coast. Bob's prized Lincoln Continental, as well as some of his other vintage cars, formed part of the funeral cortege. Keith arrived on the morning of the service, understandably looking pale and drawn, clearly distraught, as he consoled family members and friends. Both Keith and his brother Shane delivered eulogies, speaking about Bob's passion for cars, motorbikes, country music and family—Bob and Marienne had been married for 52 years. Keith tried his best to find some hope amid his loss. 'I loved him so much.'

Marienne also spoke; she said that Bob was her 'soul-mate'. Shane's children then took the podium and gave Bob a musical farewell, Jessica singing and playing guitar, Blake on piano. Among the hundreds of mourners was country singer Troy Cassar-Daley, who had begun his own musical journey around the same time, and in many of the same places, as Keith.

As the mourners gathered outside, a huge roar sounded out. It was Bob's beloved Harley, being ridden out of the funeral home and onto the street by a family friend. It was a very fitting—and very loud—farewell.

★

Having endured the toughest Christmas of his life, Keith gradually returned to work on the record that he'd title *Ripcord*. One track in particular, 'Gone Tomorrow (Here Today)', would be an observation on the deaths of his father and his father-in-law, but not in an obvious way. 'When you lose people,' Keith told website Taste of Country, 'I think it shocks you into going, "Where did they go?" . . . We're never going to get time back.'

The work was liberating, but Keith also found that speaking with his sponsor helped him cope with this difficult time. If nothing else, it kept him very grounded.

As Keith related, his sponsor asked him, 'Keith, do you know how much people think of you? Rarely.' It may have been harsh, but Keith truly believed this kind of raw truth was the 'great leveller in all things'. It also kept him focused on what he felt was his mission as a muso: 'I'm just trying to put some good in the world, that's all. Thumbs up. Thumbs down. Whatever.'

There was something about the word 'ripcord' that Keith really liked. Nicole had mentioned a new play on Broadway with that title, and Keith was hooked. 'I love the energy in that word,' he told her. It also worked metaphorically, because as he admitted, 'Music is the ripcord I've reached for to save my life many times.'

Just like *Fuse*, *Ripcord*, which Keith worked on steadily until its release in early May 2016, was full of surprises and sonic left-turns. Again, he engaged enough producers—there were ten in all, including Keith—and players (among them, funk legend Nile Rodgers and rapper Pitbull) to fill several football teams.

Interestingly, what didn't make the record was almost as notable as what made the final cut. Keith spent a week working with 53-year-old American Rick Rubin, an acclaimed producer from a hip-hop and heavy rock background, the co-founder of Def Jam Recordings, who'd broken such acts as the Beastie Boys. Rubin had bridged the gap that once separated rock and rap with 1986's trailblazing 'Walk this Way', which Aerosmith recorded with Run-DMC. Rubin was hard to miss—he wore a beard that almost reached his nipples. (He hadn't shaved since 1986, allegedly.)

As a way of breaking the ice, Keith had compiled some of his favourite tracks on a laptop—after another bout of mad 'Shazam-ing'—and recorded himself singing and playing ganjo over the top of these songs. He played this to Rubin, who liked what he heard and assembled a group of players—'a phenomenal band', according to Keith—and booked some time in Rubin's Shangri-La studio in Malibu.

As Keith saw it, they weren't so much recording songs as 'building ideas'. Keith would yell out chords; the band would follow his lead and see where it led. The results—'a big mix of things', said Keith, drawing on everything from trance to pop and electronic dance music—didn't make the final record, although Keith fully intended to one day release the recordings. They were too good not to be heard. Keith described the week as 'exhilarating, incredibly liberating'—it didn't really matter to him that none of the music made it into *Ripcord*.

Working with funk great (and former Black Panther) Nile Rodgers on the track 'Sun Don't Let Me Down' was an equally big thrill. Keith was a lifelong fan of guitarist Rodgers, whose work was best heard on such era-defining records as Chic's 'Le Freak', David Bowie's 'Let's Dance' and, more recently, Daft Punk's huge hit (and dual Grammy winner) with Pharrell Williams, 'Get Lucky'. To Keith's mind, there was a symmetry between Rodgers' guitar playing—and he always played the same guitar, a seemingly ageless Fender

Stratocaster—and his own ganjo strumming, although Rodgers wasn't so sure when they first met in a New York studio. Rodgers, who at 62, with his dreads and shades and undeniable aura, radiated far more cool than players half his age, glanced at Keith's souped-up ganjo and asked him, 'Are you kidding? What did you bring that for?'

The pair spent several hours together, locking into a solid groove that formed the basis for the loose-limbed, deeply groovy 'Sun Don't Let Me Down', while Keith wrote a lyric that subtly referred to his wife's film work, as he sang, 'To die for, and it's killing me.' (Rodgers was so engaged that he whistled for the track, a first.) But there was a sixteen-bar passage in the track that Keith felt needed something, although he wasn't quite sure what. He had recently been tuning in to a SiriusXM radio show called Pitbull's Globalization. Pitbull was the tag of 35-year-old Miami-born Armando Christian Pérez, a bald-headed rapper who'd worked with Jennifer Lopez. Keith loved the sound of Pitbull's voice, as much as anything, and its distinctive Cuban/Latino influences.

Keith asked Rodgers, 'Do you know him?' Fortunately, Rodgers did, well enough to make a call, and Pitbull agreed to work on the track. Keith's direction was simple: 'It's a blank canvas. Just say what you want to say.' The result was perfect, even though Pitbull didn't do a whole lot more than shout two things several times—Keith's name, and 'Mr Worldwide', Pitbull's other pseudonym. (And what's a rapper without at least two nom de plumes?) What mattered more was the way he did it rather than the actual content. Talking with a writer from Rolling Stone, Keith described Pitbull's rap as having a 'mischievous, sexy swagger to it'. The track was also a ground-breaker—very few country records, even in 2016, featured a rapper; Keith was bridging musical divides. Yet while he was taking his music into hitherto unexplored places, Keith was contributing less as a writer. He co-wrote only five of the thirteen tracks that made the album. Production and playing, rather than writing, seemed to interest him more.

By April 2016, three hit singles—'John Cougar, John Deere, John 3:16', 'Break on Me' and 'Wasted Time'—had been released from *Ripcord*, even before the LP was released. Keith's label was growing increasingly impatient for the finished record. But there was one track Keith insisted on completing, called 'The Fighter'.

He was in London, working with producer busbee (aka Michael Busbee), who'd had huge success with pop acts Gwen Stefani and P!nk, and was the co-producer and co-writer of 'Sun Don't Let Me Down'. Keith was in an Uber, travelling to the studio, when the idea for a duet came to him—but not a traditional duet, more a conversation between a male and female singer, in the vein of Meatloaf's 'Paradise by the Dashboard Light' (although not quite as bombastic). Keith wrote a lyric that was inspired by a conversation he'd had with Kidman early on in their relationship when, as he put it, he felt 'this need for reassurance, [to know] that this is a good, safe place for me'.

Once in the studio, busbee recorded a demo of what would be the female vocal, while he and Keith discussed who'd be the perfect singer for the part. They agreed on country-pop star Carrie Underwood, the former *American Idol* winner who'd toured with Keith in 2007. When they reached out to her, Underwood said she was in—'thankfully she loved it', Keith reported—however, there was a hitch: she was currently in the midst of her own American tour. 'But I have one day off soon, in St Louis,' Underwood mentioned.

Keith checked his schedule and discovered that it was the same day he was committed to a video shoot, for the track 'Wasted Time'. So he recorded his vocal in advance, busbee flew to St Louis to book a studio for a day and work with Underwood, and Keith set off on his video shoot. Somehow, the end result was seamless, a near-perfect digital-era pop song, despite the vocalists never actually being together in the same room.

'It was very 2016,' Keith said of the process. 'It was fantastic.'

Keith also posted a Carpool Karaoke-style video of he and Nicole in their car, miming the lyrics of 'The Fighter'. 'Oh my god, I love this song,' Nicole shrieked as the track began. 'Thank goodness,' Keith deadpanned in reply. It was almost too cute for words.

The critical response to *Ripcord* was best summed up by a review on the Sounds Like Nashville website. 'Whether it's slick beats, guitar slinging or vivid storytelling,' noted writer Annie Reuter, 'Urban's eighth effort launches the singer into uncharted territory exemplifying exactly why he is one of the most highly regarded talents within the genre.' Less thrilled was *ABC News*'s Allan Raible in the US, though he couldn't help but admire Keith's vision. 'This album still reeks of formula,' he wrote, 'but at the same time, there's something enjoyingly adventurous about this record.'

Ripcord was Keith's fifth album to debut at number 1 on *Billboard*'s country album chart; it also reached number 4 on the *Billboard* 200 and debuted at number 1 in Australia. It took just under a year for *Ripcord* to reach one million sales in the US, making it his eighth platinum album on the trot.

And in the very 21st-century world of streaming, Keith racked up some serious numbers. Over time, the video of 'The Fighter', featuring 'street dancer' Lindsay Richardson (who Keith knew, and had recommended to director John Urbano), would clock up more than 100 million views and counting on YouTube. 'Blue Ain't Your Color', an atmospheric *Ripcord* track that sounded like a lost cut from some 1950s Sun Studio session, was streamed heavily *and* went on to be crowned Single of the Year at the 2017 CMAs.

The Ripcord World Tour, which began in Bonner Springs, Kansas, on 2 June 2016 and wrapped up six months later with two nights at the Brisbane Entertainment Centre, was equally successful. More than 612,000 fans attended the 61 shows, ample proof that Keith's rusted-on audience had few problems with his new musical adventures. And most fans knew the *Ripcord* songs inside out, as Keith bragged during a backstage chat: 'I could just walk away from the mic and let everybody sing.' However, Keith's policy of being joined by an audience member each night almost went haywire in Nashville. A very pregnant woman stepped up onto Bridgestone Arena stage and asked Keith to 'sing her into labour', as he later recalled. 'Thankfully that didn't work.'

★

In October 2017, *The New York Times* and Ronan Farrow from *The New Yorker* broke the sexual harassment scandal regarding Hollywood uber-producer Harvey Weinstein, and it hit close to home for Nicole. She'd acted in a number of films produced by the bear-like New Yorker, among them *Cold Mountain*, *The Others*, *Nine* and, in 2016, the acclaimed Australian-made biopic *Lion*. Nicole joined such actors as Meryl Streep, Cate Blanchett and Angelina Jolie in speaking out about Weinstein's monstrousness. 'We need to eradicate this behaviour,' Nicole said in an official release. She also made it known publicly that she kept her distance from Weinstein whenever he was on set because of his volatile temper.

As for Keith, as her husband and the father of two young girls, he decided to make his own statement and record a song about female empowerment. The song was simply called 'Female'. It was written by Shane McAnally, Nicolle Galyon and Ross Copperman, three of the more successful songwriters from the Nashville production line.

'It's about Harvey Weinstein,' Keith was told. He hadn't anticipated that, as he admitted in an interview with SBS's *The Feed*. 'It's not what I heard when I heard this song,' Keith said. 'It was not why I recorded it.' In another interview about 'Female', with a writer from *Billboard*, Keith explained his connection to the song. 'As a husband and father of two young girls, it affects me in a lot of ways.'

Keith cut 'Female' within weeks of it being written, with Nicole and co-writer Galyon singing background vocals. Admittedly, it wasn't the best song he'd ever recorded, despite the writers' very positive intentions. It was essentially a list of qualities—sister, lover, healer, mother, etc.—that, when combined, equalled 'female'. It seemed a little too simple, a bit too glib.

Keith premiered 'Female' at the 2017 CMAs on 8 November 2017, and while not a huge hit—although it did reach number 6 on *Billboard*'s Digital Songs Sales chart—the song made its point. However, *Late Show* host Stephen Colbert then kickstarted a 'Female' controversy that infuriated Keith.

Colbert had a long-standing relationship with the comedian Louis C.K., whose sexual misconduct came to light in early November 2017. Yet on the night after the CMAs, Colbert decided to ridicule Keith rather than call out his friend in any detail. He simply mentioned C.K. as part of a line-up of powerful men who'd been outed (among them Weinstein, Kevin Spacey and Bill O'Reilly) and tut-tutted a little, before really going to town on Keith and 'Female'.

Keith had been a guest on Colbert's show, and the host admitted that he was a fan, and that he admired the intention of the song, but as for its lyrics, 'not as much'. (Overlooking the fact, of course, that the lyrics weren't written by Keith.) Colbert didn't hold back, referring to 'Female' as Keith's 'new Harvey Weinstein–inspired female country empowerment anthem' and satirising it mercilessly with his own version, which Colbert called 'She-Person'. Given the events that had inspired 'Female', it was a serious misstep by the *Late Show* host. The original may not have been much of a song, but it was simply the wrong time to send it up. (If there actually was a right time.)

Keith was seriously pissed off, as he made very clear to *The Feed*'s Marc Fennell in a later interview. 'The issue I have with Steve Colbert is that Louis C.K. had issues that day that came out, and instead of reporting on that, which is one of his friends, he throws a guy like me under the bus . . . You attack a guy like me for that song, which I find just disgusting.' Almost three years would pass before Keith agreed to appear on *The Late Show* again.

★

'I love making records, being in that creative environment—the surprise, the discovery. I love it,' Keith admitted in an interview in 2017. He felt lost, he said, if he spent an extended period away from the studio. So it was no great surprise that 'Female' was part of a new collection of songs that he was working on through 2017 and into early 2018 for an album whose title—*Graffiti U*—could have been mistaken for something by Prince.

Bad news had filtered through to Keith during the recording: one of his key Australian allies, Rob Potts, had died in a motorbike accident in October 2017. Potts worked with Keith from his earliest days right through to his US breakthrough, until he was sidelined by Keith's manager, Gary Borman. But they remained close, and Keith was one of the first to offer up his sympathy, posting: 'Just heard of the passing of Rob Potts . . . stunned. Deepest condolences to Sally, Jeremy & Rob's family & friends. Peace be with you all.'

When *Graffiti U* emerged in late April 2018, it was clear that 'Female' wasn't a one-off. The hot button topic of female empowerment and the burgeoning #MeToo movement left its mark on Keith and on the record, even if the lyrics he sang sometimes seemed to be lifted straight from a greeting card or a self-help book. But it was the track 'Gemini' that got people talking. Nicole was a Gemini, so was she the woman in the song, who, as Keith sang, was 'a maniac in bed/But a brainiac in her head'?

Nicole certainly didn't deny it when she spoke about the song with celebrity-obsessed Sydney DJs Kyle Sandilands and Jackie O. She did admit, however, that the song had made her blush on first listen. 'I don't censor his art if I can be a muse for it,' Nicole figured. '[And] it's better than saying, "God, I'm so bored. Make an effort, Nicole."'

In keeping with his recent albums, *Graffiti U* was all over the place musically, a mash-up of faux reggae, EDM, break-beat, dance-rock, power ballads and more typical twangy fare. Keith's collaborators included British star Ed Sheeran, songwriter and up-and-coming solo star Julia Michaels and LA production team Captain Cuts, who'd worked with The Chainsmokers, Halsey and Grouplove. Keith tapped urban writer/rapper/producer/singer Shy Carter for the track 'My Wave', proof that his jam with Pitbull was no passing fad. And again Keith left much of the songwriting to the experts, contributing to just eight of the fifteen tracks. The record featured two vastly contrasting samples: on 'Coming Home' Keith used a favourite guitar lick from Merle Haggard's 'Mama Tried'—'which made me think of home', Keith told NPR's Eric Westervelt—while he used a snippet of Coldplay's 'Everglow' on 'Parallel Line'.

'You're showing a lot of colours on this record,' Westervelt said to Keith, who chuckled agreeably. 'The studio to me is like a blank canvas,' said Keith. 'I just go in and just start flicking paint around.'

Graffiti U topped the *Billboard* country album chart in the week of its release, selling 145,000 copies, but it didn't have the staying power of its predecessors. At the time of writing, it was Keith's first album not to go platinum; its sales sit at just over 500,000 copies. Critical response to the record was mixed. While *Rolling Stone*'s Jonathan Bernstein gave Keith due credit for continuing to take country music into hitherto unexplored territory, there was a caveat. 'On *Graffiti U* he ends up shining brightest in his well-worn comfort zones while struggling, perhaps for the first time, when he tries to break new sonic and lyrical ground.' Despite some strong songs—'Horses' and 'Texas Time' were stand-outs—and Keith's ongoing sonic broad-mindedness, *Graffiti U* was a first: a commercial failure, at least by Keith Urban standards, even though the world tour that followed, which ran from mid-June 2018 to March 2019—Keith's 12th head-lining tour—was a success.

Keith's gig at his second hometown of Nashville, at Bridgestone Arena on 24 August, which drew a full house of almost 16,000 punters, was an all-star event. First he welcomed Nicole, and then her *Big Little Lies* co-star Reese Witherspoon, a Nashville local, on stage. 'If I'd known I was coming out on stage,' Witherspoon laughed, 'I would have worn a different outfit.' Then a very pregnant Carrie Underwood joined Keith for a roaring version of their hit 'The Fighter'. As if that wasn't enough, Keith welcomed the Tennessee State University Marching Band on stage during the set closer, 'Wasted Time'. Confetti was shot out of cannons and rained down on the audience while the drum major did the splits, as the song built to a wild climax. It was a hell of a finale.

'We are home, finally,' Keith told the rapt audience. 'It feels very, very nice to be home.'

★

The US COVID-19 lockdown of March 2020 couldn't have come at a less opportune time for Keith, who was in the thick of recording yet another new record, bouncing between studios in the States and overseas and working with another big ensemble of collaborators. (Not 'The Fighter' producer Michael Busbee, tragically, who'd died of brain cancer in September 2019, aged 43.) Keith had just played the San Antonio Stock Show & Rodeo at the 20,000-capacity ATT Center in mid-February, as well as a run of Vegas dates at The Colosseum at Caesars Palace in January, shows that generated more than US$1 million at the box office each night. (Asking price for the best seats in the house was $224.) Not surprisingly, he had more Vegas shows on the books, gigs that were now indefinitely postponed.

Just weeks before lockdown, Keith had released 'God Whispered Your Name', a big-hearted song with unmistakable spiritual overtones, which contemporary Christian artist Chris August had co-written with, among others, rapper Shy Carter, who'd cameod on two *Graffiti U* tracks. In the video, Keith played his guitar in the basement of a claustrophobic Nashville warehouse, which proved to be a little too close to reality, certainly for the bulk of 2020.

Keith was a musician who thrived on momentum, who'd been in constant motion since he was fifteen years old, and who craved the routine of album-tour-album-tour and the energy generated by a live audience. When COVID hit and the world stopped, he felt as though he'd lost a limb. What does someone constantly in motion do in lockdown?

Keith's peers reacted in vastly different ways, as big tours were shut down and album releases delayed. Taylor Swift, who had intended to be on her Lover Fest roadshow, spent quality time with her cats, drank wine, watched vintage films and quietly sent money to unemployed fans. Brad Paisley, meanwhile, dyed the roots of his wife's hair and shared the results via Instagram. ('America needs this reality show,' commented one fan.) As for Keith, at first he felt paralysed, despite having a home studio at his disposal.

'I'd just sort of put my trackies on and sit on the couch with my family and watch TV and wait for the whole thing to blow over,' he told Australian *60 Minutes*, when asked about the three months he and his family spent in Nashville lockdown.

But a simple phone conversation with his sponsor snapped Keith out of his stupor. After talking for ten minutes, Keith's friend said, 'All I've heard is what you *can't* do. Tell me one thing you *can* do.'

'Well, I *could* get in my studio tomorrow,' Keith admitted. Then he called his engineer. It was time to get back to work.

'It really was a pivotal moment,' said Keith.

Besides getting back to work on his new record at home, Keith staged a one-man show, broadcast via Instagram on 17 March from the space in Nashville where he stored most of his gear. 'I'm supposed to be playing with my whole band tonight,' explained Keith, who was dressed in basic black, T-shirt, jeans and trainers, as he set up before an imposing rack of guitars. 'And that bums me out. So I'm basically playing karaoke in our little bunker.'

Keith wasn't quite alone—providing moral support was 'Nicole Mary', as he introduced his dearly beloved, just slightly off screen (and occasionally on screen, dancing and singing along when the mood struck her), while Jeff Linsenmaier, a collaborator, who Keith nicknamed 'InstaBand' for the occasion, was in charge of backing tracks. A cameraman named Andy documented the 30-minute set.

The show worked well enough, despite the lack of a band, Keith singing and playing guitar over the top of tapes, as thousands of fans logged in and looked on. 'Thank you,' Keith laughed, as a smattering of applause greeted his opener, 'Somebody Like You'. 'It's like my club days.'

'I'm fading this out now,' Keith spoke-sang as he wound down 'God Whispered Your Name', 'because there's not really a band behind me. So we'll fade it out right . . . now.' Keith laughed; he was enjoying the challenge. 'I love that song,' said Nicole, just off camera. (In his next post, at the end of the same track, Keith sang, 'This is how you fade on Instagram', having now mastered the art.)

Nicole joined Keith during 'The Fighter', mouthing Carrie Underwood's parts, eyes closed, swaying softly, before Keith ended his set with 'Wasted Time'. 'Stay safe, guys, we love you,' he said. 'See you soon.' This proved to be wishful thinking on his part; it was as close as Keith would get to a real gig for more than eighteen months.

Clearly inspired, within a week Keith was back online with another half-hour performance, this time broadcast from his home set-up, which he'd christened Skye Studio. He called this post Urban Underground, as he did subsequent 'gigs' that he continued to post throughout 2020. His support cast was much the same: Nicole was nearby, acting as his guitar roadie (standing in for Keith's long-time tech, Chris Miller) and occasional dancer, while 'InstaBand' was out of shot, providing the backing tracks for Keith to work with. Keith mainly played fan requests, also covering 'The Gambler', which he dedicated to 'the late great Kenny Rogers', who'd just died, aged 81, on 20 March. Keith hadn't played the song in some twenty years, but it came back to him in a flash, a black-clad Nicole joining in during the chorus.

'We love you, Kenny,' Keith said. 'What a great song.'

In between 'gigs', Keith was now chipping away at his new record. On 8 May, he shared a whimsical three-minute video trailer for his next album, in which he riffed on anything and everything: making coffee ('it can be really inspiring'), legal pads—'if I write something illegal . . .'—his despair that *Game of Thrones* was over, the voices in his head ('which one is the real me?'), driving as inspiration (which led to a reasonable 'Chicken Dance' gag) and, finally, the title of his new album, *The Speed of Now*, which had come to him pre-lockdown. 'I would never have imagined that in 2020 this album title would take on a whole new meaning and yet somehow still feel incredibly relevant.' Keith announced that 18 September was the go-date for his new record.

While still locked down in Nashville, Nicole asked Keith if he'd ever thought about staging a drive-in concert. He hadn't, but he loved the idea—a live audience and cars were two of his biggest obsessions. Among his ever-expanding auto collection was a 2011 V12 Pagani Huayra, a McLaren MP4, a Lamborghini Aventador, and a white Bugatti Veyron valued at US$2.7 million. He was a major petrolhead.

'That's fantastic,' Keith told Nicole, 'a great idea, playing to people in cars.'

The Stardust Drive-In, just outside Nashville, was the perfect location. Keith had no idea that drive-ins such as the Stardust still existed, as he told *ET Canada*. 'It was the greatest discovery,' he said. 'They've all got a great view, and there's this fricking killer video wall behind the stage.' The set-up was simple—Keith's crew would fix a camera on the stage (which was actually a flatbed truck) that would be linked up to the drive-in's screen. The audience, seated in their vehicles, would tune in to the show on their car stereos.

Keith asked that the 200-strong audience be composed strictly of frontline workers—doctors, nurses, emergency responders and so on—from the Vanderbilt University Medical Center. They'd be given tickets; it was a free show. With the help of his sidekick 'InstaBand', as well as Nathan Barlowe on keyboards and second guitar, Keith was ready to play on 14 May. He'd been sitting inside a makeshift dressing room as the cars gathered, so when he climbed up onto his truck-stage he got a shock.

'I thought I would see cars everywhere,' Keith told Downtown Country's Stuart Banford, 'but what I saw was people sitting on cars, sitting on the bonnet of cars, sitting near cars . . . It turned out more of a parking-lot party. It was so fun.'

Keith had a newie titled 'Polaroid' and in advance he'd asked people coming to the Stardust gig to submit selfies, which were projected on the big screen as he played the song. The sound of beeping horns almost drowned out Keith's playing, as people recognised their own snaps and reacted. It may have been a socially distanced concert, but there was a lot of love at the Stardust.

'Thanks so much,' Keith said at the end of the gig. 'And God bless the drive-ins.'

Keith was the first major star to rock the drive-in. Within months, everyone from the Beach Boys to rockers Bush and 311 would be hosting similar gigs. Heavyweight tour promoter Live Nation even staged a Live From The Drive-In series of shows. The concept, clearly, was a winner.

★

Whenever he had a new album set to drop, Keith would typically be holed up with his band and getting ready to hit the road. That was not the case with *The Speed of Now Part 1*. When it was finally released in September, Keith and family were emerging from quarantine and on their way to Byron Bay, New South Wales, where Nicole was shooting the mini-series *Nine Perfect Strangers*.

Just before leaving the States, Keith hosted the 55th Academy of Country Music Awards, his first time in the gig, on 16 September. It was a night of firsts for Keith: he'd never appeared at a virtual awards show before, and he also previewed a new song, which he'd recorded with pop star P!nk, called 'One Too Many'. Keith was a big fan; he admired the way in which Pink could get 'inside' a song and really bring it to life. 'I've always loved Pink's voice,' Keith said during a chat on Apple Music. 'She's a singer's singer.'

Things were changing, and quickly, as mainstream artists wised up to Music City circa 2020. Pink's performance on the ACM stage with Keith was her third appearance at the awards; she'd recorded a single with Kenny Chesney back in 2016. No Doubt's Gwen Stefani also performed at the 2020 ACMs, teaming up with Blake Shelton for a song called 'Happy Anywhere'. Beyoncé had performed at the CMAs, in 2016, singing 'Daddy Lessons' with the Dixie Chicks. Lady Gaga and Justin Timberlake had also undergone rootsy conversions on recent albums, while Justin Bieber had featured on '10,000 Hours', a 2019 Grammy winner for Nashville duo Dan + Shay. With Taylor Swift, whose music had 'crossed over' in a massive, mega-platinum way, leading the charge, and Keith releasing pure pop songs like 'The Fighter' and collaborating with Pitbull, Nile Rodgers and now Pink, lines had blurred so much between genres that Billboard must have been considering creating an entirely new chart for songs such as 'One Too Many'.

'Half of what I do I don't think lives in any category,' Keith said in an interview with Winnipeg's QX104 FM. He admitted that he'd sometimes have people disputing the authenticity of his music, telling him: 'That's not country.' Keith would reply, 'Absolutely. You're right, it's not country.' No argument. He cited the music that a lot of modern artists grew up with—'90s hip-hop, R&B, pop—as having a huge influence on the type of music now emerging from Nashville. 'It's just the way every artist filters those influences that makes it unique.'

When Keith and Pink performed 'One Too Many' at the ACMs, they were separated by a wall, which seemed fitting because they'd actually recorded their vocals in different parts of the country (Keith in Nashville, Pink on the west coast). The video, which quickly racked up tens of millions of views, was also shot under COVID conditions; it featured Pink stranded on an island while Keith was on a couch, bobbing on the ocean, searching for her. (This time Keith was in Australia, Pink still in California.) They'd not been in the same room during the entire process.

While hugely catchy, it was a curious track, another instance of the very-sober Keith recording a woozy drinking song, this one set in a bar, at the end of a long night, where he sat 'staring at my phone', trying to figure out what to do next. Keith had a well-rehearsed response to being asked how a teetotaller could 'sing' drunk. 'Dolly Parton didn't work nine to five either.' (Keith, admittedly, wasn't among the song's five co-writers.)

Keith put in an impressive performance as ACM host. 'We're still in the midst of trying to fight two pandemics: COVID-19 and social injustice,' he said during his intro, speaking from the stage at the Grand Ole Opry. And not only did he perform with Pink, but he accompanied breakout artist Mickey Guyton, who sang 'What Are You Gonna Tell Her?' with Keith accompanying her on piano. Remarkably, it was the first time a black female solo artist had performed her own song during the awards. Things really *were* changing.

Post-ACMs, as Keith and his family settled into life in Byron Bay, 'One Too Many' became his first single to reach the Australian Top 10. It had been a long time coming. The song was a global hit, also charting strongly in Canada, New Zealand, across Europe and in Iceland, and featuring in four different *Billboard* charts. (Keith had at this point cut 54 *Billboard*-charting hits, sixteen of them country number 1s in the US.)

As for *The Speed of Now Part 1*, Keith tapped into deep groove and electronic sounds and much more, with guests including rapper Breland (on the Prodigy/House-music–inspired banger 'Out the Cage'); Nile Rodgers, again (he now referred to Keith as 'my bro'); Benmont Tench from Tom Petty and the Heartbreakers; and Danish producer/writer/DJ Cutfather. It was also an Australian chart-topper and yet another *Billboard* country number 1, his seventh, even though it was a massive injustice to call it a country album. Writing about *The Speed of Now Part 1*, *Rolling Stone*'s Joseph Hudak perfectly summed up Keith circa 2020: 'With every album since 2013's *Fuse*,' he wrote, 'Keith Urban has had less and less creative fucks to give.'

★

Keith, Nicole and their children were in Bondi Junction mall doing some Christmas shopping in December 2020—just like normal people—when Keith's phone beeped. It was a text from Taylor Swift. She needed Keith's help.

Swift's battle over ownership of her first six albums was big news. Swift had been trying to buy the master recordings of those records for years, but in June 2019 they were acquired by Justin Bieber's manager Scooter Braun as part of his acquisition of Big Machine Records, which released Swift's music. (Braun on-sold the recordings to a company named Shamrock Holdings for, allegedly, more than US$300 million.) Swift had an immense dislike for Braun—who was also the former manager of her MTV Video Music Awards stage invader, Kanye West—and described his behaviour towards her as 'incessant, manipulative bullying'. She posted a letter that read, in part, 'I simply cannot in good conscience bring myself to be involved in benefitting Scooter Braun's interests directly or indirectly.'

In a gutsy move, Swift decided to re-record those six albums, thereby 'reclaiming' her songs, and gradually release them. In 2020, she set to work remaking *Fearless*, her 2008 debut, while also including some unreleased songs. This is when she texted Keith, who'd already featured on one of Swift's songs, 'Highway Don't Care', back in 2012. More recently, he'd made an impromptu decision to cover her hit 'Lover' during a 2019 show at the Washington State Fair, which left Swift gobsmacked. 'I am screaming . . . This is so beautiful,' she posted, fangirl-style. Keith's tweet of his take on 'Lover' was viewed more than 1.5 million times.

Keith sat in the shopping centre food court and read

Swift's text: 'I've got a couple of songs that I want you to sing on. Do you want to hear them?'

'Sure,' Keith replied.

Swift envisaged one of the two tracks a duet. She thought Keith's voice could be a good fit. What followed was surreal, even by Keith's standards, a guy who moved in elite musical circles.

'So I've got the AirPods in,' Keith told *Entertainment Tonight*, 'and I'm sitting in the food court with everybody walking around me, and I'm listening to these two Taylor Swift unreleased songs.' Keith took a quick look around, wondering if anyone had the faintest notion what he was doing—and if they'd believe him if he spilled. 'I'm like, *this is crazy*.'

Of course, Keith agreed to work with Swift; he was especially excited that he'd be collaborating on hitherto unreleased tracks. A creative collaboration that began in a Sydney shopping centre resulted in the melancholy slow-burner 'That's When', which formed part of an album that went straight to number 1 on the *Billboard* 200. Bizarrely, in what had to be a music industry first, the original version of Swift's album was also in the chart at the time as the 'new' *Fearless (Taylor's Version)*, as it was titled. Keith also contributed backing vocals to the track 'We Were Happy'.

Keith posted a new Urban Underground on 30 December, which he shot from the driveway of Bunyah, the Kurban estate in the NSW Southern Highlands. Nicole had been quarantining, again, after a quick trip to Ireland to shoot scenes for a new film called *The Northman*, a Viking epic, and was now holidaying with Keith and their daughters.

Christmas lights illuminated the greenery behind Keith as he settled in. 'Coming to you live/From the gravel drive,' he smiled, laughing at his accidental rhyme. Keith was more in the mood for singing than talking, so he ran through a few songs on an acoustic guitar, including 'God Whispered Your Name' and 'Blue Ain't Your Color'. While he still looked very much like a performer in need of an audience—it had been seven months since the Nashville drive-in show, and a full ten months since his last gig with a big crowd—Keith was clearly relieved that such a weird year was finally over. Just before wrapping up with 'Wasted Time', Keith paused to thank the frontline workers all over the world, who were still out there 'fighting the good fight'.

★

Keith made it very clear that he missed an audience—any audience—when he spoke to the *Switched on Pop* podcast in late 2020. 'For me, playing live is the thing I miss the most—people in front of a stage, the moshpit, the energy of the crowd—there's no substitute for that. Performing for a camera is like dating a mannequin.'

Keith did, however, get to front a decent-sized audience—albeit a television audience—when he joined forces with John Legend, Angélique Kidjo, Alejandro Sanz and the Suginami Children's Choir at the opening ceremony of the Tokyo Olympics on 23 July 2021. Together they sang John Lennon's 'Imagine'—'a spiritual classic', in Keith's estimation—as the athletes assembled in the main stadium and a fleet of drones formed the Olympic logo overhead. Almost 75 million viewers watched in Japan, some 17 million in the US and another 2.7 million back in Australia.

Keith signed on for his second Australian series of

The Voice in 2021, a full ten years on from his first stint. Two of his co-judges, Guy Sebastian and Jessica Mauboy, were talent-show alumni—Sebastian having won the first season of *Australian Idol* in 2003, Mauboy placing second to Irish expat Damien Leith on the show in 2006. Admittedly, the pair, unlike many of their *Idol* peers, had sustained stellar, post-*Idol* careers—Sebastian was a seven-time ARIA winner, while Mauboy had combined pop success with acting roles in such films as *The Sapphires* and *Bran Nue Dae*. Born in the former Yugoslavia but now UK based, singer/songwriter Rita Ora was the fourth judge for the 2021 series, which was filmed in Sydney during March and April 2021.

By the time *The Voice* finale screened on 12 September 2021, drawing 1.45 million viewers, Keith had finally returned to the stage. He kicked off The Speed of Now Tour, which had been derailed by COVID, on 28 August at the Soaring Eagle Casino in Mount Pleasant, Michigan. This was Keith's first large-scale show since 15 February 2020, which, for a performance junkie like Keith, must have seemed like several lifetimes ago. He'd also play in New York and undertake a four-night stand, starting 17 September, at Caesars Palace in Vegas. The Australian leg, originally set down for late 2021, was rescheduled to December 2022.

Keith's emotional desire to get back to playing live was very real, but in strictly commercial terms he had another reason to miss being on the road. Not only had it made him very wealthy, but it kept a lot of people—*his* people—in work. Since breaking out as a solo artist in 2000, he'd played more than 600 shows over the ensuing twenty years, generating a staggering US$327 million in ticket sales. And houses at Keith Urban shows were rarely less than full. He'd come a long way from playing to an empty Bayview Tavern in Gladesville. Keith was loyal to his live team, too—bassist Jerry Flowers had been with Keith for the better part of 25 years, while drummer Chris McHugh had started working with Keith back in 1999. Behind the scenes, Keith had been managed by Gary Borman since the time of his debut release in the US; he'd even used the same stylist for the past ten years. His guitar tech, Chris Miller, was another long-timer. Keith had surrounded himself with the right people and the returns had been huge.

In late 2020, when speaking with Scott Evans, a reporter for *Access Hollywood*, Keith mentioned how young he'd been when he started playing, and how he had dreamed of checking out this place called Nashville. Evans asked Keith what advice he'd have for his very young self: would he offer any warnings, or suggest he change something? After all, the road that led Keith to where he was now—an international superstar, one part of a very famous couple, a highly in-demand musician—had its fair share of potholes. Keith's reply was emphatic. Nothing. He wouldn't change one damned thing.

'All I wanted to do was to live in America and make records and tour, and maybe get my songs on the radio,' he explained. 'It's a life dream I've had since I was seven years old . . . To be able to have done that and still to be able to do it, I'm speechless about it, quite frankly. I'm grateful for it so deeply.

'All those detours, especially the really dark ones, got me to where I am now. I would not want to change one leaf on any tree on the whole journey.'

Keith Urban: selected awards

GOLDEN GUITAR AWARDS

1991 Best New Talent (aka Horizon Award)

1992 Male Vocalist of the Year

1992 Instrumental of the Year ('Clutterbilly')

1998 Instrumental of the Year ('Clutterbilly', re-recorded)

2001 Instrumental of the Year ('Rollercoaster')

2003 Video Clip of the Year ('Somebody Like You')

2004 Top Selling Album of the Year (*Golden Road*)

2007 Outstanding Achievement to Country Music (special award)

2010 Top Selling Album of the Year (*Defying Gravity*)

2012 Top Selling Album of the Year (*Get Closer*)

2012 Male Artist of the Year ('Long Hot Summer')

2017 Top Selling Album of the Year (*Ripcord*)

2019 Top Selling Album of the Year (*Graffiti U*)

2021 Top Selling Album of the Year (*The Speed of Now Part 1*)

AUSTRALIAN RECORDING INDUSTRY ASSOCIATION (ARIA) AWARDS

2001 Outstanding Achievement Award

2003 Best Country Album (*Golden Road*)

2004 Best Country Album (*Be Here*)

2007 Best Country Album (*Love, Pain & the Whole Crazy Thing*)
2014 Best Australian Live Act

GRAMMY AWARDS

2006 Best Male Country Vocal Performance ('You'll Think of Me')
2008 Best Male Country Vocal Performance ('Stupid Boy')
2010 Best Male Country Vocal Performance ('Sweet Thing')
2011 Best Male Country Vocal Performance (''Til Summer Comes Around')

SELECTED COUNTRY MUSIC ASSOCIATION AWARDS (CMAS)

2001 Horizon Award
2004 Male Vocalist of the Year
2005 Male Vocalist of the Year
2005 Entertainer of the Year
2005 International Touring Artist Award
2006 Male Vocalist of the Year
2009 Musical Event of the Year ('Start a Band' with Brad Paisley)
2014 Musical Event of the Year ('We Were Us' with Miranda Lambert)
2015 Musical Event of the Year ('Raise 'Em Up' with Eric Church)
2017 Single of the Year ('Blue Ain't Your Color')
2018 Entertainer of the Year

SELECTED ACADEMY OF COUNTRY MUSIC AWARDS (ACMS)

2001 Top New Male Vocalist

2005 Album of the Year (*Be Here*)

2005 Top Male Vocalist

2006 Top Male Vocalist

2009 Vocal Event of the Year ('Start a Band' with Brad Paisley)

2014 Vocal Event of the Year ('We Were Us')

2018 Vocal Event of the Year ('The Fighter' ft. Carrie Underwood)

2019 Entertainer of the Year

SELECTED CMT MUSIC AWARDS

2005 Video of the Year ('Days Go By')

2006 Video of the Year ('Better Life')

2009 Collaborative Video of the Year ('Start a Band' with Brad Paisley)

2017 Video of the Year ('Blue Ain't Your Color')

2017 Malc Vidco of the Year ('Blue Ain't Your Color')

2017 Collaborative Video of the Year ('The Fighter' ft. Carrie Underwood)

2017 Social Superstar of the Year

2018 Performance of the Year ('The Fighter' ft. Carrie Underwood)

2018 Performance of the Year ('I Won't Back Down' with various artists)

2019 Collaborative Video of the Year ('Coming Home' ft. Julia Michaels)

Ten essential Keith Urban performances

'Lights on the Hill' with Slim Dusty, Tamworth, 1993

'Desiree' with The Ranch, *Midday*, Sydney, September 1997

'Walkin' the Country' with John Fogerty, *CMT Crossroads*, Los Angeles, January 2005

'Gimme Shelter' with Alicia Keys, Live Earth, New York, July 2007

'Funky Tonight' with John Butler Trio, ARIA Awards, Sydney, October 2007

'Start a Band' with Brad Paisley, CMA Awards, Nashville, November 2008

'With a Little Help from My Friends', CMA Music Festival, Nashville, May 2010

'Tumbling Dice', *The Tonight Show Starring Jimmy Fallon*, New York, May 2010

'Sweet Thing' with John Mayer, *CMT Crossroads*, June 2010

'To Love Somebody', *Stayin' Alive: A Grammy Salute to the Music of the Bee Gees*, Los Angeles, February 2017

Acknowledgements

A huge thanks to my Allen & Unwin team: Jane Palfreyman, Samantha Kent, Emma Driver and Luke Causby, without whom this book would not exist.

My heartfelt thanks go out to the following people who, over the course of the past dozen years, also played their part in helping me tell Keith Urban's story: Bob Allen, James Blundell, Peter Blyton, Cheryl Brown, Leisa Bye, Cheryl Byrnes, Chrissie Camp, Michael Caulfield, Jeff Chandler, Barry Coburn, Jewel Coburn, Drew Cuthbertson, Cameron Daddo, Dan Daley, John Elliott, Tommy Emmanuel, Nick Erby, Fiona Ferguson, Rob Fisher, Melinda Gill, Brian Harris, Kevin Harris, Todd Hunter, Wade Jessen, Kris Katsanis, Fiona Kernaghan, Anne Kirkpatrick, Narelle Lightfoot, Kirk Lorange, Ged Malone, Angie Marquis, Joy McKean, Gina Mendello, Mark Moffatt, Tony Mott, Glen Muirhead, Mark O'Shea, Joanne Petersen, Rick Price, Sherry Rich Plant, Neil Richards, Ricky Rogers, Anthony Sasso, Mike Smith, Rhianne Smith, Cat Swinton, June Underwood, Jeff Walker, Rob Walker, Tom Wall, Biff Watson, Tim Wedde, Frank White, Neil Wickham, Jon Wolfe and Zac @ KeithUrban Superfan.

And, as always, love and sympathy to my people: Diana, Elizabeth and Christian, as well as the support team of Neela, Rani, Poe and the fish with no name.

Selected bibliography

Aly, Chuck: *Music Row*, 1 October 2002

Anon: 'Sweet Thing by Keith Urban', Songfacts, 2008, www.songfacts.com

Anon: 'Keith Urban readies "Escape Together World Tour"', Sounds Like Nashville, 1 May 2009, www.soundslikenashville.com

Anon: 'Keith Urban: We're All for the Hall 2009', Country Music Hall of Fame, 13 October 2009, http://countrymusichalloffame.org

Anon: 'Keith Urban saved my life', *The Tennessean*, 22 January 2017

Anon: 'Nicole Kidman to paparazzi: Cheers', *China Daily*, 21 June 2006

Anon: 'Keith Urban's tattoos: Here are the meanings behind all 7', The Boot, 26 October 2020, https://theboot.com

Anon: 'Keith Urban reveals newfound peace on "Defying Gravity"', *VOA News*, 2 November 2009, www.voanews.com

Anon: 'Keith Urban shows off newborn Faith Margaret', *People*, 1 December 2020 (updated)

Anon: 'How Nicole Kidman's new husband cheated on her with a party girl', *Daily Mail Australia*, 24 December 2006

Anon: 'Womack, Paisley top CMA nominees tonight', Associated Press, 16 November 2005

Anon: 'Sex symbol new images of the 90s', *Sun-Herald*, 28 January 1990

Anon: 'Star rises above an early failure', *Caboolture Shire Herald*, 14 February 2006

Anon: 'Keith Urban', *Playgirl*, April 2001

Anon: 'Remember when Taylor Swift pranked Keith Urban on tour?', *Music Mayhem*, 7 September 2020

Anon: 'Kidman in plea to media over baby', BBC News, 7 August 2008, http://news.bbc.co.uk

Anon: 'Nicole Kidman's IVF journey', Infertility Aide, n.d., www.infertilityaide.com

Anon: 'Keith Urban plays surprise show in Penn Station', *New York Post*, 16 November 2010

Anon: 'Urban's guitars ruined in Nashville floods', ABC News, 7 May 2010, www.abc.net.au

Anon: 'Keith Urban opens up to "Get Closer"', NPR, 19 November 2010, www.npr.org

Anon: 'Nicole Kidman's dad died from a heart attack', SBS News, 13 September 2014, www.sbs.com.au

Anon: 'Urban family bids a fond farewell to beloved Bob on the Sunshine Coast', *Daily Telegraph*, 18 December 2015

Anon: 'Stephen Colbert addresses Louis CK allegations, rips Keith Urban's "Female"', *Hollywood Reporter*, 10 November 2017

Anon: 'Go into the studio and "start flicking paint around": Keith Urban on making *Graffiti U*', WBUR, 25 April 2018, www.wbur.org

Anon: 'Keith Urban crashes motorcycle', ABC News, 2 October 2007, www.abc.net.au

Apter, Jeff: Keith Urban album review, *Rolling Stone* (Australia), December 1999

Apter, Jeff: *Fortunate Son: The Unlikely Rise of Keith Urban*, William Heinemann Australia, 2009

B., Lisa: 'Keith's $320k drug binge exposed', *New Idea*, 23 August 2017

Bernstein, Jonathan: 'Review: Keith Urban's Graffiti U is the work of an eclectic, enlightened man', *Rolling Stone*, 26 April 2018

Best, Sophie: 'Urbane cowboy', *Sunday Age*, 19 October 2003

Bierly, Mandi: 'On the scene: Keith Urban at Madison Square Garden', *Entertainment Weekly*, 14 February 2008

Birrell, Oliver: 'Nicole Kidman and Keith Urban's second daughter Faith Margaret was born via gestational surrogacy, and it differs from traditional one', Fabiosa, 22 October 2019, https://fabiosa.com

Boldt, Blake: 'Album review: Keith Urban—Get Closer', Engine 145, 24 November 2010 (accessed via www.archive.org)

Braun, Kelly: 'Nicole Kidman remembers the intense moment when she knew Keith Urban was the love of her life', *Closer Weekly*, 9 January 2019

Burch, Cathalena: 'Urban renewal yields a hot country career in US', *Arizona Daily Star*, 28 April 2000

Capozzoli, Michael A., Jr: 'Keith Urban on Chris Gaines', *Entertainment News Wire*, 29 October 1999

Capitol Records, press release, August 1999

Capitol Records, *Keith Urban* press release, 1999

Capitol Records, press release, December 2001

Capitol Records, *Be Here* press release, 2004

Carlton, William: 'Down Under wonder', *Columbus Republic*, 19 September 2002

Conniff, Tamara and Ray Waddell: 'Urban developments', *Billboard*, 11 November 2006

Cook, Tim: 'Keith Urban fans get real close for free show at one of world's largest malls', The Canadian Press, 1 December 2010

Cooper, Peter: 'The resurrection of Keith Urban', *The Tennessean*, 15 May 2005

Cooper, Peter: 'Rosanne Cash shares her pain', *The Tennessean*, 16 April 2006

Couric, Katie: 'Country star Keith Urban discusses his career and performs', *NBC News Today*, 14 April 2005 (transcript)

Daley, Dan: *Nashville's Unwritten Rules: Inside the Business of Country Music*, New York: The Overlook Press, 1998

Darden, Beville: 'Glen Campbell remembers Keith Urban as a kid', The Boot, 11 August 2008, https://theboot.com

Dawson, David: 'Our Urban success story', *Sunday Advertiser*, 7 January 2001

Dumas, Daisy: 'Nicole Kidman and Keith Urban farewell Antony Kidman', *Sydney Morning Herald*, 19 September 2014

Dunkerley, Beville: 'Keith Urban joins Australia's "The Voice"', The Boot, 30 November 2011, https://theboot.com

Dupre, Elyse: 'Nicole Kidman recalls the romantic motorcycle date that caused her to fall in love with Keith Urban', E!, 29 April 2020, http://eonline.com

D'Zurilla, Christie: 'Keith Urban "horrified" by Boston woes; rape suspect pleads not guilty', *Los Angeles Times*, 1 August 2014

Elder, Bruce: 'Just the twang', *Sydney Morning Herald*, 27 May 1993

Elder, Bruce: 'Urban tops the country in Nashville', *Sydney Morning Herald*, 2 October 2000

Eliscu, Jenny: 'Keith Urban on "Ripcord" album's sonic curve-balls', *Rolling Stone*, 28 March 2016

Feiler, Bruce: *Dreaming Out Loud: Garth Brooks, Wynonna Judd, Wade Hayes, and the Changing Face of Nashville*, New York: Avon Books, 1998

Flippo, Chet: 'Keith Urban goes into rehab', CMT, 20 October 2006, http://www.cmt.com

Gawley, Paige: 'Keith Urban recalls knowing Taylor Swift would be a huge star when she was his opening act', E!, 16 April 2021, http://eonline.com

Goldman, David: 'Music's lost decade: Sales cut in half', CNN Money, 3 February 2010, https://money.cnn.com

Goos, Aileen: 'Keith Urban discovers there is no escape from suffering', *Winnipeg Free Press*, 15 April 2000

Graff, Gary: 'With awards and success, Urban's having the time of his life', *Plain Dealer*, 28 October 2005

Graff, Gary: 'Keith Urban's "Defying Gravity" set to soar', *Billboard*, 30 March 2009

Graff, Gary: 'Keith Urban sets date for "Fuse," talks "diversity" of new album', *Billboard*, 8 May 2013

Grant, Sarah and Larissa Cummings: 'Tragic Nicole pledges to stand by her man', *Hobart Mercury*, 23 October 2006

Grigsby, Karen: '20 things to know about the 2010 Nashville flood', *The Tennessean*, 30 April 2015

Hackett, Vernell: 'Keith Urban recovering from throat surgery', Reuters, 26 November 2011

Harding, Charlie (host), 'Keith Urban on The Speed of Now Part 1' (podcast episode), *Switched on Pop*, 2 October 2020, https://switchedonpop.com

Heaton, Dave: 'Keith Urban: Defying Gravity', PopMatters, 23 April 2009, www.popmatters.com

Hedegaard, Erik: 'Keith Urban's hard road', *Rolling Stone*, 16 June 2016

Heller, Corinne: 'Keith Urban mourns dad Bob Urban at funeral', E!, 18 December 2015, http://eonline.com

Henderson, Erica: 'Keith Urban returns to the Sunshine Coast to farewell dad', *Sunshine Coast Daily*, 17 December 2015

Hitts, Roger: 'Angry rocker: I'm the real Chris Gaines', *The Star*, 16 November 1999

Holmes, Randy: 'Keith Urban recalls how Kenny Chesney helped him after his second stint in rehab', ABC News Radio, 4 November 2016, http://abcnewsradioonline.com

Hornery, Andrew: 'PS Private Sydney', *Sydney Morning Herald*, 17 June 2006

Ingall, Jennifer: 'Keith Urban includes Narrabri on tour list', ABC News, 29 November 2013, www.abc.net.au

Jacobs, Matthew: 'Keith Urban's Grammy performance of "Ain't No Sunshine" includes appearance from Miguel', *Huffington Post*, 6 December 2013

Jameson, Julietta: 'Urban living', *Daily Telegraph*, 23 October 2003

Jansen, Ara: 'Australian Urban legend', *West Australian*, 7 January 2000

Jarvis, Susan: 'Keith's far from your average urban artist', *Sun-Herald*, 8 October 1995

Keefe, Jonathan: 'Review: Keith Urban, Get Closer', *Slant*, 15 November 2010

Kemp, Mark: 'Album review: Defying Gravity', *Rolling Stone*, 17 March 2009

Kent, Simon: 'Going country', *Sun-Herald*, 20 January 1991

Koha, Nui Te: 'Love, pain and the whole crazy thing', perthnow.com.au, 13 May 2007

Laffer, Lauren: 'Keith Urban talks about his collaboration with

Eric Church', Sounds Like Nashville, 14 October 2013, www.soundslikenashville.com

Laffer, Lauren: 'Nicole Kidman on Keith Urban: "I'll do anything for that man"', Sounds Like Nashville, 1 November 2014, www.soundslikenashville.com

Laffer, Lauren: 'Nicole Kidman praises Keith Urban for keeping strong family unit', Sounds Like Nashville, 23 September 2015, www.soundslikenashville.com

Lalor, Peter: 'Creating the Urban legend', *Daily Telegraph*, 29 August 1999

Lester, Libby: 'The young country', *Sunday Age*, 16 January 1994

Lewis, Randy: 'Keith Urban reveals a piece of himself on "Get Closer"', *Los Angeles Times*, 16 November 2010

Linton, David: 'Charges dropped against teenager accused of rape at Mansfield Xfinity Center', *Sun Chronicle*, 25 September 2014

Lomax, John: 'Another country', *The Australian*, 11 January 1997

Maloney, Katie: '"Raise 'Em Up" by Keith Urban: Story behind no. 1 hit with Eric Church', Outsider, 27 December 2020, https://outsider.com

Mansfield, Brian: '10 things you should know about Keith Urban's "Fuse"', *USA Today*, 23 August 2013

Mansfield, Brian: 'Keith Urban finds right chemistry for new "Fuse"', *USA Today*, 10 September 2013

Mansfield, Stephanie: 'Up from Down Under', *USA Weekend*, 4 November 2001

Marx, Richard: *Stories to Tell: A Memoir*, New York: Simon & Schuster, 2021

McCabe, Kathy: 'Aussie set to wow Nashville', *Sunday Telegraph*, 22 August 1999

McCabe, Kathy: 'Success in US charts country music career', *Sunday Telegraph*, 22 October 2000

McCabe, Kathy: 'Country's new king is no urban myth', *Daily Telegraph*, 12 November 2004

McCabe, Kathy: 'Singing praises of a true Mr Nice Guy', *Daily Telegraph*, 22 June 2006

McLean, Sandra: 'Caboolture remembers its young musician', *Courier-Mail*, 17 June 2006

McMahon, Bruce: 'Lone star', *Courier-Mail*, 15 October 2005

McWhirter, Erin & Jonathon Moran: 'Once wild Keith Urban sets sights on quieter life', Australian Associated Press, 22 June 2006

Morris, Edward: 'Kenny Chesney and friends rock Nashville with eight hour homecoming show', CMT, 7 July 2008, www.cmt.com

Nankervis, David: 'Country's perfect match', *Sunday Mail*, 24 August 2003

Netherland, Tom: 'Urban development', *The Richmond Times-Despatch*, 17 November 2005

Nicholson, Sarah: 'Urbane country', *Courier-Mail*, 11 September 2004

Overington, Caroline: 'Country battler who won the girl', *The Australian*, 24 June 2006

Parton, Chris: 'Keith Urban says he thought he "peaked" in 2005', Sounds Like Nashville, 6 January 2021, www.soundslikenashville.com

Pastorek, Whitney: 'Defying Gravity review', *Entertainment Weekly*, 25 March 2009

Perry, Michael: 'Nicole Kidman confirmed pregnant', Reuters, 8 January 2008

Price, Deborah Evans: 'Aussie Keith Urban debuts on Capitol', *Billboard*, 25 September 1999

Quan, Denise: 'Keith Urban loses guitars, gains perspective', CNN, 1 December 2010

Quill, Greg: 'A bit of outback country', *Toronto Star*, 27 September 2004

Quinn, Karl: 'Darren Percival has the voice, now he's finding an audience', *Sydney Morning Herald*, 5 October 2012

Reid, Poppy: 'The Curious Case of Keith Urban', *Rolling Stone* (Australian edition), 26 October 2021

Reuter, Annie: 'Keith Urban reveals why he was fired from his first radio job', Sounds Like Nashville, 28 February 2017, www.soundslikenashville.com

Rocca, Jane: 'An urban charm', *Townsville Bulletin*, 24 September 2004

Rockingham, Graham: 'Keith's about more than Nicole', *Hamilton Spectator*, 7 November 2005

Rodley, Aidan: 'I won't get an invite to Kidman wedding', *Waikato Times*, 5 May 2006

Rodman, Sarah: 'Urban update: Life is good', *Boston Herald*, 18 July 2003

Rodriguez, Brenda and Stephen M. Silverman: 'Nicole Kidman and Keith Urban welcome a baby girl', *People*, 7 July 2008

Rollings, Grant: 'Don't marry Keith . . . It will not last long', *Sun*, 27 December 2005

Rutland, Joe: 'Country throwback: Keith Urban, John Mayer perform "Til Summer Comes Around" in 2010', Outsider, 22 January 2021, https://outsider.com

Sams, Christine: 'ARIA Award will add to Urban myth', *Sun-Herald*, 23 September 2001

Saurine, Angela: 'Urban affairs', *Daily Telegraph*, 20 May 2006

Scott, Paul: 'Nicole and the crack addict cowboy', *Daily Mail*, 26 November 2005

Seay, Nikki: 'Keith Urban says Nicole Kidman saved his sobriety', American Addiction Centers, 18 December 2019, https://www.recovery.org

Shedden, Iain: 'Demons bottled up', *The Australian*, 22 March 2007

Shelburne, Craig: 'Keith Urban plays it cool at the Ryman', CMT, 2 March 2004, www.cmt.com

Shelburne, Craig: 'Keith Urban surrounds himself with famous friends at We're All for the Hall concert', CMT, 14 October 2009, www.cmt.com

Skates, Sarah: 'We're All for the Hall nets $500,000 and counting', *Music Row*, 22 October 2009

Smith, Michael: 'Fresh out of The Ranch', *Drum Media*, 24 August 1999

Sprankles, Julie: '8 things to know about Nicole Kidman & Keith Urban's 12-year-old daughter Sunday Rose', SheKnows, 7 July 2020, www.sheknows.com

Standifer, Stacie: 'The Women's Edit: Director and screen-writer, Trey Fanjoy', The Nashville Edit, May 2019, https://nashvilleedit.com

Stewart, Paul and Erin McWhirter: 'Urban myth: Ex-girlfriend doubts Urban will settle', *Sunday Times*, 25 June 2006

Stooksbury Guier, Cindy: 'Meet country's new talent', *Amusement Business*, 29 September 1997

Sung, Ellen: 'Crossover crooner', *News & Observer*, 17 February 2006

Taraborrelli, J. Randy: 'Keith Urban's fall from grace', *Australian Women's Weekly*, 18 December 2006

Tauber, Michelle: 'The secret behind baby Sunday Rose's name revealed!', *People*, 8 July 2008

Taylor, Andrew: 'Country's troubadour', *Sun-Herald*, 27 January 2008

Thomas, Sarah: 'Exploding another Urban myth', *Adelaide Advertiser*, 30 December 1999

Thompson, Gayle: 'Keith Urban, Vince Gill: "We're All for the Hall" concert inspires country music pride', The Boot, 16 April 2013, https://theboot.com

Tolle, Eckhart: *The Power of Now: A Guide to Spiritual Enlightenment*, Novato, CA: New World Library, 2004

Toombs, Mikel: 'Manchild in The Promised Land', *San Diego Union-Tribune*, 8 December 2005

Torpy, Kathryn: 'Learning guitar never child's play for Urban', *Courier-Mail*, 26 October 2002

Tucker, Ken: 'Keith Urban keeps it real at radio', *Billboard Radio Monitor*, 10 February 2006

Vaughn, Grace Lenehan: '10 things you may not know about Keith Urban', Sounds Like Nashville, 25 May 2021, www.soundslikenashville.com

Waddell, Ray: 'Country touring rebuilds in 2002', *Billboard*, 6 April 2002

Watson, Chad: 'Urban sprawl', *Newcastle Herald*, 28 October 2000

Watts, Cindy: 'Keith Urban exhibit "bittersweet" as father fights for life', *USA Today*, 1 December 2015

Watts, Cindy: 'Keith Urban show recap', *The Tennessean*, 25 August 2018

WEA, press release, 8 May 1998

WEA, press release, 17 November 1998

Whitaker, Sterling: 'Remember when Keith Urban played with

John Fogerty?', Taste of Country, 19 February 2021, http://tasteofcountry.com

Willman, Chris: 'Living gay in Nashville', *Variety*, 5 April 2018

Woods, Erika: 'When I was 10', *Sunday Life*, 9 September 2007

Yorke, Ritchie: 'Creating the Urban legend', *Sunday Mail*, 10 December 2000

SELECTED INTERVIEWS/APPEARANCES

Midday with Kerri-Anne, September 1997

'Extraordinary alien', *Music Country: True Stories*, 2000

Sudzin Country, 2000

A Current Affair, 2001

Family Feud, 8 November 2001

'Urban cowboy', *60 Minutes* (Australia), 2002

'Keith Urban and John Fogerty', *CMT Crossroads*, January 2005

'Keith Urban and John Mayer', *CMT Crossroads*, June 2010

The Oprah Winfrey Show, 1 December 2010

Country Music Hall of Fame All Access, 15 September 2012

The Voice Australia (various), Season 1, 2012; Season 10, 2021

A Current Affair, March 2013

60 Minutes (Australia), August 2013

Bobby Bones Show, August 2013

American Idol (various), Seasons 12–15, 2013–2016

Sunrise, 15 July 2015

Today (Australia), November 2016

The Tonight Show Starring Jimmy Fallon, 18 November 2016

A Conversation with Keith Urban, SXSW Festival, March 2018

The Feed, May 2018

The Late Show with Stephen Colbert, 6 March 2020
QX104 Country, 8 May 2021

WEBSITES

AllMusic: www.allmusic.com
CMT: www.cmt.com
Discogs: www.discogs.com
Billboard.com
Pollstar.com
Setlist.fm